18TH-CENTURY WEDGWOOD

18TH-CENTURY WEDGWOOD

A Guide for Collectors & Connoisseurs

by David Buten

with Jane Perkins Claney
and contributions by Patricia Pelehach

A Main Street Press Book
Methuen, Inc.
New York

Library of Congress Catalog Card Number 79-55758
ISBN 0-416-00561-6

Published by Methuen, Inc.
733 3rd Avenue
New York, N.Y. 10017

Produced by The Main Street Press, Inc.
William Case House
Pittstown, New Jersey 08867

Designed by Carl Berkowitz

Printed in the United States of America

Contents

Preface

The year 1980 is the 250th anniversary of Josiah Wedgwood's birth. As anniversaries are an occasion for taking stock as well as for celebration, the Buten Museum of Wedgwood has chosen with this volume to illustrate and describe the breadth and scope of Wedgwood's contribution to the world of ceramics. The ways in which the objects were used and enjoyed at the time they were made are discussed, and the part that Wedgwood's manufacturing innovations, his character, and personality played in ceramic development and 18th-century industrial history are assessed.

The book is published in conjunction with a major international loan exhibition of 18th-century Wedgwood, organized by the Buten Museum and held at Independence National Historical Park, Philadelphia, during the summer of 1980. From the objects selected for the exhibition, the authors have illustrated in the book not only aesthetically exceptional early Wedgwood objects, but also objects that would help to evaluate the range and variety of Josiah Wedgwood's *oeuvre*. Wedgwood, himself, may have had something similar in mind when he wrote in 1774: "I have often wish'd I had saved a single specimen of all the new articles I have made to be left as a sacred deposit for the use of our Children & Children's Children which with some acc.t of what *has* been done & what *may* be done, some *hints* & *seeds* for future discoveries, might perhaps be the most valuable treasure we could leave them" (Farrer, II, 193-94). Impossible as it is today to gather together "all the new articles," this book is an attempt to fulfill Wedgwood's wish to render "some acc.t of what *has* been done."

There are many ways of classifying ceramic bodies, and nomenclature varies as well. The authors have used contemporary terms to name seven major varieties of ware produced during the 18th century and have divided them into chapters accordingly. In some instances, the names are trade names that Wedgwood used, and, in other cases, they are not; terminology is described in the introductory material to each chapter.

It was decided not to limit the choice of objects to those known to have been made during Josiah Sr.'s lifetime, but to extend the limits of the book to the end of the 18th century. All of the kinds of objects illustrated, however, were introduced during his lifetime. The cut-off date of 1800 is, of course, somewhat arbitrary. While techniques used in identifying objects made during the 18th century are described in the text, production methods did not alter radically at the very moment the century turned; objects have been chosen, therefore, on the premise that they could have been, and probably were, made by 1800. Also, a conservative method of dating has been employed. Instead of centering production around an approximate date with an indeterminate number of years' leeway implied on either side, date approximations have been bracketed by the earliest possible date that the object could have been made and the latest. End dates for objects marked "Wedgwood & Bentley," for example, are the year of Bentley's death, 1780. End dates for some objects have been assigned through the authors' interpretation of documentary material.

Unless otherwise noted, marks are impressed in the clay by stamps. If they are incised or painted, it has been noted in the text. Owing to limitations of space, collateral marks such as individual potters' signs have not been described except for those whose significance is discussed.

There would have been no book and no exhibition, for that matter, without the kind cooperation of the institutions and private owners who lent objects and allowed them to be photographed. Many of them gave generously of their time and knowledge, and some lent their resource materials to the Buten Museum for the duration of the project.

L. Cathryne Foedisch, of the Buten Museum, has been of invaluable help in the research. Also, for their gracious assistance in research, the authors wish to thank Lucy J. Batchelder, Registrar, Peabody Museum, Salem, Massachusetts; Fred Gaffer, Canadian War Museum, Ottawa, Ontario; Elinor and Horace W. Gordon; Mrs. S. K. Hopkins, National Army Museum, London; Kathryn B. Hiesinger, Curator, Department of European Decorative Arts, Andrew Lins, Conservator, Decorative Arts, and Marjorie K. Sieger, Division of Education, Philadelphia Museum of Art; Andrew Kaplan, Buten Museum; Shirley B. Little, Assistant Curator, Delhom Gallery, Mint Museum of Art; A. Mackay-Smith, Chairman, National Sporting Library; Michael J. McAfee, Curator, West Point Museum; Elizabeth M. Moyer, Curator, The Mütter Museum of The College of Physicians of Philadelphia; Susan H. Myers, Museum Specialist, Division of Ceramics and Glass, Smithsonian Institution; Christina H. Nelson, Curator, Glass and Ceramics, Department of Decorative Arts, Henry Ford Museum; Professor David D. Perkins, Chairman, and Michele Lawton, Department of English, Harvard University; Gaye Blake Roberts, Curator, Wedgwood Museum, Barlaston, England; Betsy Shuman, The Pennsylvania Horticultural Society; and Diana and J. Garrison Stradling.

For bringing to their attention the Wedgwood reference in the Jefferson papers, the authors are indebted to Arlene M. Palmer, Associate Curator, Ceramics and Glass, The Henry Francis DuPont Winterthur Museum.

The following archivists and librarians have given generously of their time: Merle Chamberlain, Philadelphia Museum of Art; Ian Fraser, University of Keele, England; John Kupersmith, University of Pennsylvania; Gretchen Lagana, University of Wisconsin Rare Book Library; Mary S. Leahy, Bryn Mawr College Rare Book Library; Miriam Lesley, Free Library of Philadelphia; Richard McKinstry, Henry Francis DuPont Winterthur Museum; and the research staffs of The Library Company of Philadelphia and The Ludington Library.

For aid in translation and for assistance with the manuscript, the authors wish to thank Seline H. Dreifus, Eda Diskant and Carol I. Biba. Martin Greif and Lawrence Grow, of The Main Street Press, have given greatly appreciated editorial direction and invaluable suggestions; Jonathan H. Claney has provided much needed, and much appreciated, support; and John Flood, Thomas Walsh, and Byron Born have aided and advised on the preparation of the photographs.

The following members of the firm of Josiah Wedgwood & Sons have been instrumental in funding the exhibition upon which this book is based, and unfailing in their support: Sir Arthur Bryan, Peter Williams, Raymond Smyth, and Derek Halfpenny.

It is not possible to cite the many ways in which Mrs. Harry M. Buten, founder of the Buten Museum of Wedgwood, and the members of the Museum have been of assistance, but it would have been equally impossible to produce this volume without their help.

Introduction

Josiah Wedgwood was the twelfth child born to Thomas and Mary Stringer Wedgwood of the "Churchyard" pot works, Burslem, Staffordshire. Not only was his father a potter, but a majority of his relatives and associates were also potters. Most of the firms were small operations, selling their wares in local market towns or at fairs, and the income derived from them was moderate at best. Josiah's financial legacy was to have been £20 (it was never paid to him)—a modest beginning for a man who would accumulate an estate valued at £500,000 at his death (McKendrick, *Wedgwood: Entrepreneur*, 408), a figure roughly equivalent in today's currency to £7.5 million to £10.5 million or $17 million to $24 million.

When Josiah started his own business, the richest potters in the area were his cousins John and Thomas Wedgwood, makers of salt-glazed stoneware. Their house, known as "The Big House," was made of brick, a showy building material by Staffordshire standards. Josiah rented a small house and pottery from them, but within a decade, he was to buy the 350-acre Ridge House estate between Hanley and Newcastle-under-Lyme and convert it into Etruria Hall and the Etruria pottery.

Although Josiah was taught well, being fortunate enough to have a schoolmaster versed in the classics as well as in basic studies, the duration of his schooling was lamentably brief. His father died when Josiah was nine years old, and he had to leave school and enter into pottery apprenticeship with his older brother Thomas.

Probably the most significant factor contributing to Wedgwood's success—and to the popularity of his wares today—was that he viewed the relatively limited state of the Staffordshire pottery industry when he entered it as a young man as an opportunity rather than an impediment. As he noted in his first experiment book: "I saw the field was spacious, and the soil so good, as to promise an ample recompense to any one who should labour diligently in its cultivation."

His labors were diligent indeed. He vastly expanded the variety of objects produced in ceramics, and he not only invented new ceramic bodies, but transformed those already in existence into highly sophisticated materials for ceramic expression. Wedgwood did not confine his innovations to technical advances. In an extraordinary departure from the generations-old Staffordshire tradition of repeating familiar forms, Wedgwood sought to lead the fashion in household utensils and ornaments by studying and working in the neoclassical taste that was captivating Europe at the time.

Another factor that distinguishes both Wedgwood and his product was the care that he lavished on even the most humble object to make it both serviceable and beautiful. He would redesign an entire room so that light would fall on the workmen's lathes at just the proper angle to allow them to shape objects as true to form and as smoothly as possible, and he oversaw and demanded perfection in the design of even the tiny punches used in perforated decoration.

A third contribution to the popularity of 18th-century Wedgwood ware is that it is identifiable. Although it is safe to say that he was the only potter of his time to manufacture consistently superior goods in great quantity and variety, still it is fair to say that other Staffordshire potters produced wares that were in some instances equally as good as Wedgwood's. Until late in the 18th century, most of these wares were not marked, while, except for the early years of production, Wedgwood ware *was* marked. In addition to the mark, Wedgwood used another sales technique far in advance of his colleagues to make his work identifiable. He issued descriptive catalogues, occasionally illustrated, that help to classify, as well as to identify, even his unmarked products.

After serving his apprenticeship, Wedgwood entered into a short-lived partnership with John Harrison and Thomas Alders of Stoke. Following that, he was taken on as a partner by Thomas Whieldon, a prosperous potter who made high-quality solid agate and mottled- or tortoise shell-glazed earthenwares and salt-glazed stoneware. An arrangement of great importance to Wedgwood's career was made at Whieldon's.

Wedgwood was to experiment with new bodies and glazes to improve the partners' wares, but was not required to divulge the methods by which he arrived at the improvements—an ideal situation for one who might be planning to start his own business. While at Whieldon's, an accident befell Wedgwood that might have had an even more significant effect upon his future. He was confined to bed with inflammation in his knee (the leg was amputated when he was thirty-eight). During his enforced rest he read avidly, particularly in chemistry and other sciences. His studies trained him in scientific method invaluable in his future experiments, but, perhaps most important of all, they prepared him to join in social intercourse with a group of intellectuals concerned with scientific progress. Another accident to his knee forced him back to bed again, and, as an antidote to the restlessness of confinement, his doctor introduced Wedgwood to Thomas Bentley. Bentley, a merchant dealing in textiles, was the same age as Wedgwood, but he had had the benefits of an extensive classical education as well as practical training in business. He was sophisticated, proficient in several languages, and moved with ease in the company of gentlemen and ladies. Wedgwood became friends with Bentley and his circle, including such eminent thinkers of the day as Joseph Priestley and, later, Sir Joseph Banks.

Wedgwood and Bentley's interests and opinions coalesced and complemented each other so that they became firm friends, mutual consultants, and confidants. Their business relationship grew from Bentley's serving as Wedgwood's Liverpool export agent to their eventual partnership and inauguration of a factory to produce ornamental ceramics—a specialization that had not taken place in the Staffordshire potteries before.

The commencement of the partnership coincided with the revival of interest in the aesthetics of classical Greece and Rome, and it was Bentley who introduced Wedgwood to the attitudes and language of neoclassicism, and who interpreted for him fashionable taste. Wedgwood, with his innately discriminating vision, was able, in turn, to materialize decorative forms to satisfy the new taste. He employed the legends and symbols of antiquity in his designs, and the meaning of each figure and attribute on the tiniest cameo would have been familiar to his patrons. While it was the architect/interior designers, such as Robert and James Adam and William Chambers, who were the arbiters of taste, Wedgwood and Bentley's collaborative efforts led the way in fulfilling the demand for ornament created by the trend setters.

Working on new products was what excited Wedgwood most, as Sir John Leslie, tutor to the Wedgwood family in the 1790s recorded: "He knew by want of attention to accounts he lost very large sums annually, but he believed that if he had suffered his mind to be Deviated from attending the progress of his works of innovation he should have lost a great deal more" (A. Burton, 28). Wedgwood, however, applied equally well his genius for factory organization, management, and selling to meet and overcome competition.

In addition to training his own artists and craftsmen, Wedgwood relied throughout his career on the talents of established artists. Included among those he hired or whose work he commissioned were sculptors John Flaxman and John Bacon, the painter George Stubbs, Lady Elizabeth Templeton, Lady Diana Beauclerk, and James Tassie. Additional designs were commissioned from artists working in Rome, a city that Wedgwood considered "the fountain head of taste" (Finer, 323). Using Flaxman as liaison, Wedgwood employed Angelo Dalmazzoni, Camillo Pacetti, and other lesser-known artists. He rarely, however, allowed the artists to sign their work.

Although Wedgwood kept the progress of the works under his own supervision as much as possible, he had to rely on the help of others, and depended thoroughly on his partners. Chief among these, aside from Bentley, was his cousin Thomas Wedgwood, who managed the "useful" works. In 1790, Josiah started gradually to withdraw from the business, having established Wedgwood, Sons & Byerley. Only one of the sons, Josiah, Jr., remained with the firm, however, and Thomas Byerley managed it after the elder Wedgwood's death. Byerley was Wedgwood's nephew, who had worked for the firm at its beginning, and, after pursuing other careers, returned in the late 1770s to become an able and responsible member of the firm. Wedgwood's wife, Sarah, helped throughout his career, first in transcribing his coded experiments, and by passing aesthetic judgment on many of the designs.

Wedgwood relied on promotional techniques to spread the popularity of his ware in a way that was heretofore completely foreign to the Potteries. He earned royal patronage by boldly accepting a difficult commission that other potters had evidently feared to undertake. It was to make a tea set that reversed the familiar gilded green-glazed pattern of decoration to a far more difficult-to-achieve gilt ground with applied green decoration. Some years later, Wedgwood produced a prodigious Queen's Ware service for Empress Catherine the Great of Russia, extracting the utmost in publicity from the commission by displaying the service in his London showrooms before it was delivered. Another sales technique that Wedgwood used was that of courting the patronage of the aristocracy, knowing that the "Middling people" would follow its lead. He sought the advice of leaders of society on matters of design and set high prices, knowing that those who were accustomed to setting their tables with imported porcelain would not accept cheap Staffordshire earthenware, but perhaps could be attracted to expensive and novel Queen's Ware.

At first the useful wares (including table, tea, and toilet articles and sickroom, druggists' and laboratory equipment) were produced at Burslem, while the ornamental wares (which included household and personal ornaments, objects for collectors' cabinets, snuff and patch boxes, desk fittings, and medallions or plaques for installation in everything from sewing tables to sword handles) were made at Etruria. The two operations were kept separate because Wedgwood shared the profits of the useful-ware works with Thomas Wedgwood, and the ornamental-ware profits with Bentley. In 1773, however, the Brick House works were closed, and the production of all the wares continued at Etruria, but with separate account books.

While the majority of the useful wares were made in the glazed earthenware bodies trade-named Queen's Ware and Pearl White, exquisite tea and breakfast sets, flower and bulb pots, tankards and countless other items still classed as "useful" ware were produced in the stoneware bodies of Black Basalt, Jasper, Cane Ware, and Rosso Antico. Conversely, many ornamental items were produced in the earthenware bodies—especially the Variegated Queen's Ware, which was colored to imitate polished semi-precious stones. Pearl Ware seems to have been the most strictly utilitarian body—with exceptions, of course, such as jelly core molds (*see* figs. 63 and 64).

The cream-colored earthenware bodies were made both from local clays and from clays brought in from Devonshire, Dorsetshire, and, later, Cornwall, and were made whiter with the addition of ground flint. The Pearl Ware, which was a whiter-bodied product than Queen's Ware, was introduced by Wedgwood. Ground flint and lead were the main ingredients of the clear glaze used on Queen's Ware; mineral oxide colorants were added for colored lead glazes.

The stoneware bodies are referred to as "dry bodies" because they were unglazed—stoneware being dense and nonporous, and capable of containing liquids without a protective glaze. Three of the stoneware bodies —Black Basalt, Cane Ware, and Rosso Antico—were improvements on existing bodies and used clays from the same areas as the earthenwares, but Jasper was entirely new.

The marks found on 18th-century Wedgwood are illustrated here. Not all Wedgwood wares of the period, however, were marked. Some plaques meant for installation, the original editions of the Portland Vase and

---

18th-Century Trade Marks

Wedgwood   WEDGWOOD   W & B
& Bentley   & BENTLEY

Used from approximately 1769-80

wedgwood   Wedgwood   WEDGWOOD

Used from approximately 1769 to 1800

Found around a bolt in a plinth or as a separate applied wafer approximately 1769-80

the Slave medallion, early cream-color or Queen's Ware and Black Basalt made before marking was begun—the "First Day Vase" itself (*see* fig. 71)—are examples of unmarked Wedgwood. Also, even after marking became common practice, workmen would sometimes forget to impress the mark in the unfired clay.

It is not known precisely when Wedgwood began to mark his ware, although it seems doubtful that any was marked before he entered into partnership with Thomas Bentley in 1769. Absence of the trademark on *any* pieces that can be definitely dated by inscription or documentation before the partnership bears out this assumption. Soon after the partnership began, however, it is clear that they had started to mark. In July of 1771, Wedgwood wrote to Bentley mentioning the making of a middle size of letters for a trademark—implying that large and small sizes were already in use. By November of 1772, Wedgwood was determined to mark all of his products, as he wrote to Bentley: ". . .we are going upon a plan to mark the whole if practicable . . ." (Finer, 150).

Evidence that some ware left the factory unmarked, or that Wedgwood was subcontracting to fill orders, but above all that trademarking was a boon to his business, is contained in a 1787 order for Queen's Ware and black tea and milk pots: "I wou'd be much obliged to you if you would cause Wedgwood to be stamped upon every article you send me be it ever so small. I am sure you'll excuse this liberty if you know what consequence it was to this Warehouse" (MS 9244-11).

The attribution to Wedgwood of unmarked and undocumented wares, particularly the cream-colored and Black Basalt of the 1760s, is tenuous, although transfer-printed wares of that period can be attributed to Wedgwood with reasonable certainty because, with few exceptions, John Sadler and Guy Green printed only Wedgwood creamware, and Wedgwood only employed Sadler and Green to print his wares. Beyond that, careful comparison of shapes and color with documented or otherwise stongly attributed examples is necessary. Becoming familiar with the potting techniques employed by Wedgwood is essential—remembering that habits of workmanship tend to be consistent and characteristic of an individual or factory. For example, round-bottomed objects like the mug (fig. 7) or the teapot and cream jugs in plate II (p. 66) were finished on the lathe so that when the piece is turned upside down, a projecting ring can be seen at the circumference of the bottom. Pieces that are not finished on the lathe are perfectly flat on the bottom. Since, in at least one instance, Wedgwood was known to have sold his old molds to another potter (cauliflower ware molds to John Baddeley in 1766), the same designs would be produced by different potters, and the only way to tell them apart would be by quality and color of glaze or by potting techniques. Although it cannot, of course, be seen in the photograph, the foot of the cauliflower jug is not lathe-finished, so that while the jug may be from a Wedgwood mold, it was probably not produced in the Wedgwood pottery.

Just as there are elements of workmanship that are characteristic of Wedgwood, so there are features that distinguish 18th-century pieces from ware of later periods:

Eighteenth-century Black Basalt and Jasper *plinths* show signs of hand finishing. While the exteriors are smooth, the interiors appear rough, and marks made by potters' tools are visible. The edges are sharp, although the actual shape of the plinth may not be truly square. There is no flange at the bottom of the plinths.

Eighteenth-century Wedgwood busts are normally bolted into a waisted base, known as a *foot* or *socle*, that differs from later socles in that it is lathe-finished at the base to form a short cylinder. Later socles flare to the base.

In order to assure that a piece would fire evenly, clay surfaces had to be relatively uniform in thickness. When pieces were much thicker in some areas than others, such as the Jasper plaque (plate I, p. 65), holes were drilled in the thick portions allowing the heat to pass through and fire the piece evenly. *Firing holes* also appear on busts in the 18th century, but their use in the 19th century was mostly limited to plaques. Earlier firing holes are rough at the edges, showing that they were made by hand rather than machine drilled.

Molds must be wider at the top than toward the middle so that the molded piece can be successfully removed. For that reason, some applied relief designs such as parts of the human figure look flabby when applied just as they come from the mold, and the potter must cut away material behind them to achieve a three-dimensional effect. This extra care given relief decoration, known as *undercutting*, was used less and less after the 18th century when labor costs became more significant. Another example of the extra work done in the earlier period was the care taken with the finger- and toenails of the relief figures. Each one was distinctly outlined by the potter.

The edges of Jasper plaques, cameos, and medallions were sometimes *polished* by a lapidary, as were the interiors of some of the useful Jasper pieces. Because of the change in formulation of the Jasper body in the early 19th century, polishing could no longer be done. Some Basalt pieces were also mechanically polished (*see* fig. 87). This was done only on a limited number of pieces in the 18th century and very rarely in the early 19th century.

Eighteenth-century Queen's Ware and Pearl Ware pieces are extremely light in *weight*, while Basalt and Jasper objects are heavy. Post 18th-century earthenwares tend to be heavier, being no longer thinned on the lathe, while the stonewares are lighter, as less clay was used in them.

A pronounced stippled effect, frequently called "*orange peel*," was purposely put on some Jasper pieces (*see* fig. 172) as a decorative element. It is not known to have been used after the 18th century.

The surface of 18th-century Jasper is very smooth to the *touch* and can be best described as "silken." A slightly different Jasper formula than that which produced the silken surface resulted in "waxen" Jasper, in which the surface has the feeling of candlewax. These surfaces are found only on 18th-century Jasper; the later wares were of a different composition that is more grainy or rougher to the touch.

In spite of changes from firing to firing, or even among pieces in the same firing, certain *colors* are rarely found after the 18th century. Although a brownish Black Basalt did appear in the 18th century, most of the pieces were a deep black, almost a blue-black, that has not been duplicated. The deepest red of Rosso Antico is seen in the earlier period, while the palest of lilac Jasper is almost always an 18th-century color. Many colors of blue Jasper were made, but a grey-blue of the Wedgwood & Bentley period has only rarely been produced in later times.

Although many potters made pieces somewhat similar to Wedgwood's, their wares were either marked with their factory name—Turner, for example—or they were dissimilar enough to have been made at another factory, such as that of William Adams. Wedgwood did complain, however, of fakes during his lifetime. Especially noteworthy is his correspondence with Bentley about seals made by John Voyez and marked "Wedgwood & Bentley." If there were such Voyez-forged seals, they either no longer exist or are not recognizable. That is not to say that fakes do not exist. The most common example is an attempt to upgrade a 19th- or 20th-century piece by attaching an 18th-century plinth to it. This type of manipulation is called making a "marriage." It is amusing to note that unknowledgeable dealers have occasionally taken a piece from the highly sought-after Wedgwood & Bentley period and ground down the "& Bentley" leaving only the "Wedgwood," since they thought the "Bentley" indicated that the piece was from some other less desirable manufacturer. The removal can be easily spotted.

Wedgwood attempted in many ways to prevent other potters from stealing his secrets, the most notable being the building of a separate set of outside stairs to each workroom so that laborers could not mingle freely and thereby learn all of the processes. Wedgwood, however, took out only one patent, which was for the "bronzing" and "encaustic" painting process on Black Basalt. The patent was infringed upon by Humphrey Palmer. It was not possible to prevent anything from being copied for very long, and although this discomfited Wedgwood, he was an inventive person and never lost confidence in his ability to produce something new. His philosophy was expressed in a letter about "encaustic" painting written to Bentley early in their partnership: ". . . confine yourselves to the red shaded with black, 'till that is mimick'd, & then strike out into other colours. When this is pretty well imitated then we may begin with ____ after this too has had its day, surprised the World, & got into other hands then we have ____ ready to keep the public attention awake . . ." (Farrer, I, 289). Wedgwood's inventive genius, of course, enabled him to fill in the blanks as the need arose.

Chronology

1730	Josiah Wedgwood baptized, July 12. ☐ Thomas Bentley born.
1739	Thomas Wedgwood, Josiah's father, dies. ☐ Josiah leaves school and is apprenticed to his older brother Thomas (formal papers dated November 11, 1744).
1742	Josiah suffers smallpox attack.
1749	End of apprenticeship.
c. 1752	Partnership with John Harrison and Thomas Alders of Stoke.
c. 1754	Partnership with Thomas Whieldon of Fenton.
1756	William Cookworthy discovers china clay in Cornwall. ☐ John Sadler and Guy Green demonstrate transfer-printing on earthenware tiles.
1759	Green lead glaze developed. ☐ Wedgwood enters business on own account in May. ☐ Ivy House Works, Burslem, rented from distant relatives John and Thomas Wedgwood who ran the biggest salt-glazed stoneware pottery in the area. ☐ Hires another cousin, Thomas Wedgwood, as journeyman.
1760	Yellow glaze perfected.
1761	Working arrangement with John Sadler begins.
1762	Moves to Brick House (Bellworks), Burslem. ☐ Meets Thomas Bentley, Liverpool merchant. Bentley & Boardman appointed export agent. ☐ Petitions for Turnpike through Burslem to join with one from London to Liverpool.
1763	Transactions with David Rhodes begin. ☐ Succeeds in lightening creamware body. ☐ Begins experiments with engine turning.
1764	Marries his third cousin Sarah Wedgwood (b. 1734–d. 1815).
1765	Daughter Susannah (Sukey) born. ☐ Establishes London office. His brother John is agent. ☐ Order from Queen Charlotte for green and gold tea service. ☐ Presents cream-colored ware, including engine-turned vase, to the Queen.
1766	Eldest son, John, born. ☐ Partnership with Bentley proposed. ☐ Cousin Thomas Wedgwood becomes manager of Brick House works and partner of Josiah Wedgwood. By 1770 he is getting one-eighth share of the profits of the "useful" ware production.
1767	Second son, Richard, born; dies the following year. ☐ Brother John Wedgwood (London agent) dies. ☐ London showrooms open. William Cox, former clerk at Burslem, sent to manage them. ☐ "The Demand for this said cream-colour, alias Queen's Ware, alias Ivory" establishes that royal patronage has been conferred.
1768	Josiah Wedgwood sends Thomas Griffiths to America to buy kaolin from the Cherokees in North Carolina. ☐ Leg amputated. ☐ Showrooms moved to St. Martins Lane and then to Newport Street. ☐ Black Basalt ornamental ware perfected. ☐ Cookworthy takes out patent to manufacture Cornwall ingredients into porcelain.
c. 1768	Variegated ornamental ware introduced.
By 1768	David Rhodes starts enameling for Wedgwood in London.
1769	Partnership with Bentley begins. Bentley takes charge of London warehouse. ☐ Etruria factory opens for the purpose of producing ornamental ware (useful wares continue to be pro-

duced at Brick House works until 1773). ☐ Wedgwood family moves to Etruria Hall. ☐ Six "First Day" vases produced in Black Basalt, with Wedgwood throwing and Bentley turning the wheel, June 13. ☐ Building to house enameling works purchased in Chelsea. ☐ Son, Josiah II, born. ☐ First full-time modeler, William Hackwood, hired. ☐ Tassie's first bill to Wedgwood. ☐ Wedgwood takes out a patent for his Black Basalt "Bronzing" and "Encaustic" painting process.

1770	Empress Catherine the Great of Russia orders Queen's Ware dinner service with maroon flowers for about twenty-four people.
From 1770	Cane Ware produced.
c. 1770	John Bacon, sculptor, designs for Wedgwood.
1771	Son, Thomas, born.
1773	Brick House works closed. ☐ Empress Catherine of Russia orders Queen's Ware dinner and dessert service ("frog service") for fifty people. ☐ Cookworthy sells porcelain patent right to Richard Champion of Bristol. Champion attempts to extend sole right for seven years. ☐ First ornamental ware catalogue produced. Subsequent ones appear in 1774, 1775, 1777, 1779, and 1787.
1774	New showrooms in Greek Street open with exhibition of the Russian dinner service, June. ☐ Jasper introduced. ☐ First Queen's Ware catalogue. ☐ Daughter, Catherine, born.
1775	Solid Jasper introduced. ☐ Josiah Wedgwood opposes extending Champion's monopoly on using Cornish ingredients to make porcelain.
1776	Transfer-printed outlining combined with hand-enameling perfected. ☐ Daughter, Sarah, born.
c. 1776	Applied bas-relief to Black Basalt vases perfected. ☐ John Flaxman, sculptor, starts to design for Josiah Wedgwood.
1777	Trent & Mersey Canal completed.
1778	Last child, Mary Ann, born.
1779	Pearl Ware introduced.
1780	Bentley dies.
1783	Josiah Wedgwood named Fellow of Royal Society for invention of pyrometer.
c. 1783	Cane Ware body improved.
c. 1784	Wedgwood starts to do some of the transfer-printing at Etruria.
1787	Flaxman goes to Rome; stays seven years. ☐ Cousin Thomas Wedgwood, manager of the useful works, dies.
1788	Wedgwood uses clay again from overseas (New South Wales).
1790	Partnership established with sons John, Josiah, Thomas, and nephew Thomas Byerley (Wedgwood, Sons & Byerley). ☐ First replica of Portland Vase.
c. 1790-95	Second Queen's Ware catalogue produced.
1793	Sons John and Thomas Wedgwood discontinue active interest in the firm.
1795	Josiah Wedgwood dies, January 3. ☐ Josiah II leaves management of the firm to Byerley.
1796	Susannah Wedgwood marries Robert Waring Darwin, son of Dr. Erasmus Darwin. They become the parents of evolutionist Charles Darwin.

1. Queen's Ware

The demand for this s^d *Creamcolour, Alias, Queen's Ware, Alias, Ivory,* still increases. It is really amazing how rapidly the use of it has spread almost over the whole Globe, & how universally it is liked.

Josiah Wedgwood
March 12, 1767

After winning royal patronage for his cream-colored earthenware in the mid-1760s, Wedgwood adopted the trade name "Queen's Ware." Soon the name was freely used by his competitors; but it was Wedgwood's high-quality product and the innovative methods he developed for promoting and marketing it that made Queen's Ware the world-wide generic term for cream-colored earthenware. In fact, Queen's Ware may be one of the most long-lived brand names in manufacturing history. The name was so common and readily accepted that even 100 years later, as America was celebrating the centennial year of the War of Independence, the American press was exhorting crockery manufacturers to substitute the term "cream-color" for the ubiquitous "Queen's Ware." The change made sense, argued the editors of *Crockery Journal*, "as we Americans do not propose to do homage to foreign potentates."

Made from a mixture of ground flint and a variety of clays, Wedgwood's Queen's Ware was a hard lead-glazed earthenware that could range in color from tan to straw-color to ivory. Similar cream-colored earthenwares had been produced to some extent in Staffordshire even before 1740. The ceramic composition that was used then was actually the same as that used for common white stoneware, but it was fired to a lower temperature and glazed with lead instead of salt.

When Josiah first went into business for himself in 1759, he continued to produce ware similar to the ceramics he had made in partnership with Thomas Whieldon, such as the mottled or tortoise-shell patterned tea canisters in plate II, p. 66. He continued to make white salt-glazed stoneware, and he experimented with new green and yellow lead glazes, realizing that there was need for a new style of pottery as the agate and tortoise-shell were no longer selling in the quantities that they had been. The new green glaze was applied as a solid color, which was occasionally embellished with gilding. At first Wedgwood applied it to tea and tableware shapes that were already being produced in Staffordshire, but new designs soon followed that fully exploited the rich glaze. One example was teaware, designed with the cauliflower in mind, in which the green glaze was discreetly applied to the "leaves," and colorless glaze to the "head" (*see* plate II, p. 66). Designs that relied for their effect on the green and the equally rich yellow glaze, that followed in 1760, were "pineapple" and striped "melon" wares. These designs took their place beside the fruit-shaped teaware, such as apples, quinces, and pears already in fashion, the important difference being that these wares were previously colored with mottled glazes; the all-over green and yellow was a striking innovation.

Although there is no proof that Wedgwood introduced the new fruit and vegetable forms, several factors—even beyond the assumption that he would have sought new ways to show off his glazes—suggest that he did. Within a few months after entering into business on his own,

---

1. *Opposite page:* Portrait of Josiah Wedgwood, enamel on biscuit earthenware, 20″ long (50.8 cm.), inscribed: "Geo. Stubbs pinxit 1780," 1780.

Wedgwood probably was employing a designer. Correspondence reveals that he was doing business with William Greatbatch, a talented modeler, who had been apprenticed to Whieldon. In 1762, Greatbatch set up his own pottery in Lower Lane, and by then (and probably before) he was designing for Wedgwood and supplying him with block molds as well as ware fired to the biscuit state to be finished with Wedgwood's beautiful and dependable glazes.

Block molds of many designs, including pineapple shapes, that had remained unopened at Etruria, probably from the time they had been retired from use until they were discovered in 1905, link Wedgwood to the designs. In addition, documentary evidence strongly suggests that Wedgwood had proprietary rights to the cauliflower design. Jos. Astbury of Lane Delph, a potter with whom Wedgwood had a trading relationship, asked Wedgwood to provide him with cauliflower ware, writing on April 4, 1764: "I have an order for a Crate of Colly flower ware . . . if it's agreeable to you to let me have them . . . . [As long] as I am alive I will not offer to make any, but hope You'l alow me some little Proffitt . . ." (MS 4903-6).

Biographers writing in the Victorian period and writers ever since have been speculating not only on what Wedgwood was producing during the early years of his new company, but when it was produced. According to Wedgwood factory records, Wedgwood did not produce the green and yellow glazed fruit and vegetable ware at the Ivy House factory before 1762 (melon) and 1763 (cauliflower and pineapple). This information comes from an unpublished letter written in 1934 by John Cook, Curator of the Wedgwood Museum, Etruria, and now in the Buten Museum archives. This does not preclude the possibility that before these dates the ware was being molded and fired by Greatbatch at Lower Lane for Wedgwood to glaze at Burslem. It does not imply either that all the early colored-glazed wares were of Wedgwood's manufacture. On the contrary, positive attribution to Wedgwood of these wares is difficult because the Staffordshire potters copied each other promptly and freely — letters such as Astbury's, quoted above, were the exception rather than the rule.

The taste for colored wares seems to have peaked in the mid-1760s, and, while Wedgwood continued to receive orders well into the 1770s, the demand for these items fell off, probably owing to the preference for pale colors that was the prevailing taste in costume as well as in household decoration, and which was admirably gratified by Wedgwood's cream-colored clear-glazed Queen's Ware. As Wedgwood wrote to Bentley on March 5, 1774: "The Agate, the Green, and other colour'd Glazes, have had their day, and done pretty well, and are certain of a resurrection soon, for there are, and ever will be, a numerous Class of People to purchase shewy and cheap things. The Creamcolor is of a superior Class, and I trust has not yet run its race by many degrees" (Finer, 159).

After the introduction of the solid-colored glazes, Wedgwood's primary goal became the improvement of cream-colored earthenware. In about 1763, he achieved his first major breakthrough, changing the color of the creamware body from a brownish tint to a significantly lighter shade. This was, he said, "a species of earthenware . . . quite new in its appearance, covered with a rich and brilliant glaze, bearing sudden alterations of heat and cold, manufactured with ease and expedition, and consequently cheap . . . ." The color of Queen's Ware was difficult to control; however, the improvements were generally in the direction of whiter ware. Still, throughout the century, customers occasionally referred to Queen's Ware as "yellow ware." Evidence of Wedgwood's exasperation with the problem of color variation is contained in a postscript to an invoice dated January 27, 1768: " . . . it is impossible that any one colour even though it were to come down from Heaven, sho^d please every taste; & I cannot regularly make two creamcolours, a deep and light shade, without having two works for that purpose. Nor have I any clay to make with certainty a very light colour for Teaware" (Meteyard, *Life*, II, 58).

The movement toward a still lighter color continued throughout the next decade. In February, 1774, Wedgwood wrote, "I am endeavoring to make the tea-ware a little white; we must have a new glaze to make it much so . . ." (Finer, 178). After 1775, he began to experiment with Cornish clays and stone, which made further whitening of the body possible.

Although Wedgwood did not invent cream-colored earthenware, his improvements in body, color, and glaze set new standards of quality. Wedgwood created a consistently clean, fine-textured body that looked well either decorated over the glaze with enamels or simply left plain. His glaze, which was smooth and brilliant, lay neatly on the body and was usually free from crazing. Wedgwood's cream-colored ware was more durable than both tin-glazed earthenware, which was prone to chip, and salt-glazed stoneware, which was more brittle.

These successful improvements did not come easily; they were the result of a great deal of time-consuming experimentation and analysis. As early as July of 1765, however, Josiah was able to write to his brother, John, saying: "Dr. Swan dined with Lord Gower this week; after dinner your Brother Josiah's Pottworks were the subject of conversation for some time, the Cream colour Table services in particular. I believe it was his Lordship said that nothing of the sort could exceed them for a fine glaze etc." (Finer, 36).

As soon as he was sure of his product, Wedgwood aimed straight for the top. On July 6, 1765, he wrote to his brother that he was sending a box of patterns to the Queen (Farrer, I, 47). Precisely what was sent has not been recorded, but the samples evidently met with great approval; Queen Charlotte honored Wedgwood by naming him "Potter to Her Majesty," a title that carried considerable prestige and influence. Although it is not known exactly when royal patronage was conferred or when Wedgwood officially adopted the term "Queen's Ware," the name certainly was beginning to be used by 1767 when Josiah wrote: "The demand for this s^d *Creamcolour*, Alias, *Queen's Ware*, Alias, *Ivory*, still increases" (Farrer, I, 127).

Wedgwood was a shrewd businessman. He recognized the great advantages that could be gained from royal and aristocratic patronage, and he actively courted the higher echelons of English and Continental society. He also recognized the value of well-placed advertisements and puffs, which would inform the public of his latest improvements and innovations. Many of Wedgwood's marketing techniques were far in advance of his time; for example, he developed the concept of salesmen's sample pattern boxes which could be shown, together with an illustrated catalogue, to retail merchants and, occasionally, to private customers. Wedgwood's first Queen's Ware catalogue was published in 1774, and a revised edition was issued sometime during 1790-95, when the firm was known as Wedgwood, Sons & Byerley. It is interesting to note that another catalogue, intended for factory use only, also exists. This catalogue is a compilation of Queen's Ware shapes redrawn in about 1802 from earlier factory records. The date is based on the watermarks found on the paper.

Wedgwood's pricing policy shows further evidence of his ability to move beyond the conventional business ideas held by other Staffordshire potters. Rather than trying to undercut the prices set by his competitors, Wedgwood arbitrarily set his prices well above current rates. One merchant complained that Wedgwood's *wholesale* prices were twice as high as the *retail* prices of other potters (MS 4899-6). Although the high prices may be explained in part by the higher cost of producing top-quality goods, that is not the significant factor; rather, Wedgwood realized that higher prices would enhance the perceived value of his Queen's Ware. In order to appeal to those who were accustomed to setting their tables with expensive, imported porcelain, Wedgwood knew he had to keep his prices high. Only after his ware had met with aristocratic approval was Wedgwood willing to consider lowering the price. Referring to vases in particular, though he routinely used the same strategy with his other wares, Wedgwood commented: "The Great People have had their Vases in their Palaces long enough for them to be seen & admir'd by the Middling Class of People . . . & though a great price was I believe, at first necessary to make the Vases esteemed Ornaments for Palaces that reason no longer exists. Their character is established, & the middling People would probably buy quantitys of them at a reduced price" (Farrer II, 91).

Wedgwood was unusual among his contemporaries in the extent and vitality of his foreign trade. According to Alan Smith, Wedgwood's export trade began modestly in 1763 with a few requests from John Wyke, a Liverpool watchmaker, for some Wedgwood ceramics to be sent to friends in Lisbon. By early 1764, Wedgwood's reputation for leadership in the pottery industry had reached the Continent, as a letter from an Amsterdam merchant illustrates: "I am informed you make the most new patterned things and Rarieties in the Country so took the Liberty to give you a Small order . . . ." The "small" order was for two crates of tea sets in cauliflower ware, and twenty sets of teaware in "copper plates," by which he meant transfer-printed earthenware. Finally, he concluded with a request for twenty additional sets "if you make Enamelled ware" (MS 4987-6).

To encourage foreign trade Wedgwood had ware designed specifically to suit certain markets. Some countries that he considered to be behind the times in matters of taste—such as Russia and America—were useful outlets for styles that were no longer fashionable in England. In 1766 Wedgwood wrote to Bentley: "I am quite clearing my Wareho. of Colour'd ware." He added that he was "heartily sick of the commodity" and had been so for a long time (Farrer, I, 97). Later, upon hearing that the ware had been disposed of, Wedgwood wrote playfully to Bentley saying: "I am rejoyced to know you have shipped off the Green and Gold—May the winds and seas be propitious and the *invaluable* Cargo be wafted in safety to their destined Market, for the emolument of our American Brethren and friends . . . " (Finer, 58).

With his high-quality ware and innovative sales strategy, Wedgwood developed a loyal international clientele that depended upon him as a purveyor of desirable goods and as an arbiter of taste. So successful was Wedgwood in his efforts that during times of depression in the pottery industry he could, according to Neil McKendrick, "sell at a higher price what his rivals could not sell at all . . . ."

One member of this "clientele" who was in many ways typical of Wedgwood's customers was Mrs. Eliza Mainwaring. Her correspondence with the company spans over twenty years and provides significant insight into Wedgwood's daily business activities. Mrs. Mainwaring's first contact with Josiah was evidently in person at her residence in London, for she refers to the occasion in a 1784 letter saying, "Perhaps Sir if you look back 20 years you will recollect seeing me at my own house Chancery Lane London" (MS 9708-11). At that time she apparently placed an order for some Wedgood ware, since a letter dated April 7, 1769, requests more of the same "Burslem Ware you sent before" (MS 9707-11). A number of years after these first two orders, Mrs. Mainwaring wrote to order "a neat sett" of Wedgwood ware, adding, "I think the green Edge pretiest" (MS 9708-11). Later, in 1789, she evidently decided to completely equip her home with new pottery and porcelain. She wrote to Wedgwood asking for descriptions of "ware lately come out" and, if possible, patterns to examine. "I shall want a complete service for the Table," she said, adding that she also wanted "a Desert set to match each other," and some recommendations for suitable breakfast sets. Two weeks later, having failed to get a response from the company, she wrote again repeating her request for "any breakfast ones that was Elegant . . . " (MS 9711-11).

Wedgwood finally sent the pattern samples that Mrs. Mainwaring requested, and on April 7 she wrote to say that she had decided upon the "Blue broad & fine line edge." Her order was extensive. She wanted two dishes each of the 21-, 19-, and 17-inch sizes, and four each of the 13-, 11-, and 9-inch sizes. In addition, she ordered a fish drainer to fit the 17-inch dishes, one soup tureen, two large and four small sauce tureens, one oval root dish (divided), one oval salad bowl, two pickle saucers, two 10-inch round twiffle dishes, two pie dishes in the 9-inch size, and the same in a smaller size "if you have any," four dozen flat plates, and one dozen soup plates. For her dessert service, Mrs. Mainwaring needed one "middle" piece and eight compotiers for the "sides, corners & flanks" of the table. She also wanted two cream and sugar bowls and two dozen dessert plates.

The choice of a pattern for the dessert service she left to Wedgwood's discretion, but, she said, "it is designed to be used after China, therefore I^d wish to have it elegant." She added, "I have seen some of your ware with a plain gilt edge that I have admired, & if you have nothing much ready or that you w.^d more particularly recommend I w.^d like something of that sort." Finally, she closed by saying, "I would also be obliged to you to send 5 small pieces for to bring in fruit of the same pattern as the Dinner Service & 1 dozen of small plates—the Breakfast set need not be sent, as I upon consideration prefer China—Also two jugs to match the Dinner Service one for small beer, & the other for ale & two tea pots of a dark color 1 large & the other small—likewise 4 wash hand basons & 4 jugs to hold water for Lodging Rooms" (MS 9712-11). Mrs. Mainwaring's order, while admittedly more extensive than most of the orders that Wedgwood received, does give a good idea of what was considered *de rigueur* in table and dessert ware at the time.

As noted in the discussion of trademarks found in the Introduction to this volume, Josiah began to mark his products with the name "Wedgwood" in order to take full advantage of his growing reputation for high-quality ceramics. The lack of such marks earlier makes it difficult to achieve an accurate assessment of creamware production at least in the 1760s. Complicating the matter is evidence that Wedgwood consistently bought great quantities of ceramics from other Staffordshire potters. A letter written to Bentley when he was Wedgwood's agent in Liverpool (June 26, 1766) makes this explicit: " . . . as you are to be a Pot merch.^t you may rest assured that in everything I can make *or purchace* [emphasis added] you shall be enabled to serve your friends to the utmost of their wishes, so take in orders for anything this country produces . . . " (Farrer, I, 89-90).

Ceramic items from other potters were sometimes purchased to fill an order for a type or style of ware that Wedgwood did not ordinarily produce. Such may have been the case with the red China teapots, "sprig'd & cannon spouts," that Wedgwood purchased from Jos. Astbury to help complete an order from Ben Whitey of Kingston. (MS 4935-6). On other occasions, Wedgwood purchased ware that he customarily did produce, but which he simply did not have on hand at the time. The system worked in reverse as well, for other potters are known to have purchased wares from Wedgwood. In 1764 Wedgwood had numerous business dealings with Phillips & Greaves of Stoke, from whom he bought blue and white enameled ware (probably salt-glazed stoneware) and to whom he sold quantities of creamware. Presumably, in this instance, Wedgwood creamware was being sold to the public as "Phillips & Greaves" ware. It is not known whether Wedgwood had other potters stamp the Wedgwood mark upon ware made specifically for him, but, except for the marks found on a few Staffordshire figures, there is no evidence that he did.

Throughout his lifetime, Wedgwood feared that the demand for Queen's Ware might diminish, and he was constantly planning ahead to introduce new wares to take its place; however, its popularity continued unabated throughout the 18th century, as the following letter from a merchant illustrates. After ordering some Black Basalt teapots, the shopkeeper commented: "I thought to have got out of this yellow ware but I am now got into a large shop in the Market place that I am asked for it every day" (MS 9740-11). Thus, Wedgwood's smooth, lustrous Queen's Ware became the basis for his manufacturing success and laid the foundation for future innovations.

Among the designs for unmarked ware that are linked to Wedgwood and Greatbatch by documentary evidence are several different teapots with molded chinoiserie decoration, and an elaborately modeled teapot on which a pastoral scene is depicted. All are known in creamware decorated in colored glazes, but the pastoral or landscape teapots exist also in redware and in salt-glazed stoneware. Both unpainted and painted versions of the salt-glazed stoneware examples exist. The decorated ones are painted over the glaze in bright enamel colors. There are two sizes of block molds for the "Landskip" teapots at the Wedgwood Museum, Barlaston.

Overglazed-decorated examples of one of the chinoiserie teapots are also known, but they are made of lead-glazed cream-colored earthenware rather than salt-glazed white stoneware. They are painted in the same bright enamel colors as the salt-glazed ware attributed to Wedgwood/Greatbatch. A note from Greatbatch to Wedgwood, dated July 12, 1763, suggests that a Mr. Courzen did the enameling: "I shall send Mr. Courzen's ware to his painting shop to night" (Towner, Creamware, 36).

2. Teapot with molded relief and overglaze enamel decoration in black, pink, yellow, green, and rust red, 5⅞" high (14.9 cm.), unmarked, design attributed to William Greatbatch and probably made for Wedgwood, c. 1763-70. The taste for chinoiserie that prevailed throughout the 18th century, even surviving the restraining influence of neoclassicism, was in full flower in the 1760s, and, as early as the summer of 1760, Greatbatch was consigning "Chinese" teapots to Wedgwood. They were itemized one or two at a time, a fact which suggests that the bills were for block molds rather than fired ware. Indeed, there are in the Wedgwood Museum, Barlaston, several different teapot block molds in the chinoiserie style that are attributed to Greatbatch. The seated-figure finial, variations of which appeared on silver as well as ceramic objects in the rococo style, remained in Wedgwood's inventory of ornaments long after the rococo taste had passed, appearing on fluted and festooned pistol-handled vases, and Cupid-bedecked Basalt teapots. Wedgwood, in discussing these figures, referred to them first as "old women" and, in later references, as sibyls.

3, 4. Teapots, white stoneware, molded relief decoration, salt glazed, unmarked, design attributed to William Greatbatch, c. 1764. *Top*, 5¼″ high (13.3 cm.). *Above*, painted over the glaze with green, pink, brown, and yellow enamels, 4⅞″ high (12.4 cm.). Wedgwood purchased salt-glazed stoneware for resale from, among others, Aaron Wedgwood (MS 5030-6), who was in business with William Littler, and from his cousins John and Thomas Wedgwood, who billed him for many thousands of pieces between 1763 and 1775 (MS 5012-6 to 5027-6). Whether or not Wedgwood actually glazed salt-glazed ware in the kilns at Burslem or Etruria isn't known, and no marked examples are known to exist, but it is almost certain that these wares were included in Greatbatch's production for Wedgwood; the block molds themselves were salt-glazed. The mold for this teapot was among those found at Etruria, and on January 11, 1764, Greatbatch billed Wedgwood for it, charging £1 4s. for "1 Landskip Tpt."

Whether self-employed or working for one of the pottery manufacturers, the designer-modelers, or block cutters as they were called, were of utmost importance in the Staffordshire pottery industry. Ultimately, their interpretation of styles determined the shape of most of the output of the district, for the majority of the ware was produced by the molding process rather than by throwing on the wheel. In addition to William Greatbatch, whose work has already been discussed, Ralph Wood, whose work in Staffordshire figures is well known, and his younger brother Aaron were important block cutters whose designs appeared in Wedgwood ware.

Block cutters would often supply working molds from the same master mold to more than one potter, so it is not surprising to find the same shape produced in different bodies. Another explanation for a shape appearing in both creamware and salt-glazed stoneware is that it is technically possible to produce both types of ware from the same mixture of clays. After molding, the ware may be fired to the high temperature necessary for salt glazing, or it may be fired at a lower temperature and glazed with lead. The former produces white salt-glazed stoneware; the latter produces cream-colored earthenware.

Salt-glazed stoneware manufacturers John and Thomas Wedgwood were Josiah's landlords during his tenure at the Brick House in Burslem. They provided him with large quantities of unfired ware, suggesting that he produced creamware from their unfired or "green" ware.

5. Sauceboat, cream-colored earthenware of a slightly grey tone, molded relief decoration, lead glazed, 8″ long (20.3 cm.), mark: "WEDGWOOD," design attributed to Aaron Wood, c. 1770-72. In 1772 Wedgwood wrote to Bentley that, having found that the granite they had been using to grind flint was imparting a grayish cast to the cream-color body, he had "recommended the Derbyshire Chert, which has since been tryed, and answers very well in preventing, or rather Anihilateing, those myriads of black specks in our body, which altogether gave it a coarse and grayish complexion, or sometimes a brownish one . . ." (Finer, 120). Examples of sauceboats in precisely the same scalloped edge, trellis-and-scroll design are known in salt-glazed stoneware and in porcelain made both at Longton Hall and at Bow. This sauceboat may be tentatively identified as the design of Aaron Wood, in that it relates to objects known to have been modeled by him. The pattern is similar to the rim of a plate that Aaron's son, Enoch Wood, identified as having been modeled by his father in 1759 or 1760.

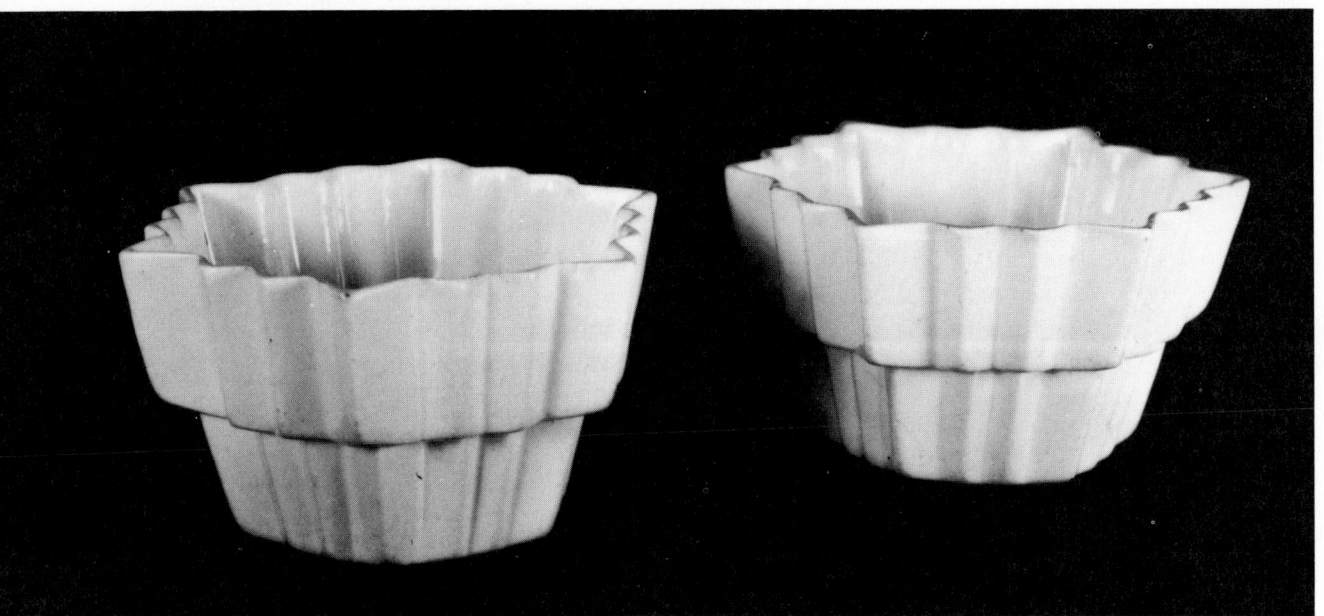

6. Molds, molded and lead glazed, marked: "Wedgwood," design by Ralph Wood, 3⅛″ wide (7.9 cm.), c. 1770-1800. Queen's Ware molds of this type, for jelly, blancmange, or flummery, were made in a great variety of shapes according to the Queen's Ware catalogues. The fluted two-tiered star shape was described as "double-star petty" in the account books of John and Thomas Wedgwood, who manufactured them in salt-glazed stoneware, and they were among the most numerous forms listed in the invoices the brothers sent to Josiah. John and Thomas employed Ralph Wood from time to time as a block cutter and perhaps as factory manager, according to Arnold Mountford. The block mold from which these blancmange molds were probably formed is signed "Ralph Wood 1768" and is in the collection of the City Museum, Stoke-on-Trent, Staffordshire.

One of the most felicitous and mutually beneficial business arrangements in English ceramic history was that of Josiah Wedgwood and John Sadler of Liverpool. Sadler is said to have introduced the transfer-printing process on earthenware in 1752, employing it at first in the decoration of tiles, until Wedgwood's timely introduction of improved cream-colored earthenware vastly broadened the possibilities for the decorative technique. Wedgwood and Sadler began their collaboration in September of 1761. After trying several different methods of operation, including Sadler's buying the creamware, decorating it, and then selling it back to Wedgwood, they finally settled upon Wedgwood's owning the creamware and paying Sadler to decorate it.

As well as being a novelty at the time and an economical decorating process, an additional advantage was that pictures could be duplicated exactly, without the variations that would occur in hand painting. Tea, table, and dessert services, as well as ware for public houses, were all decorated with transfer-printed subjects, which included depictions of tea parties, exotic or idyllic landscapes, flowers, fruits, birds, insects, and other natural subjects, famous persons, coats of arms for guilds and societies, and topical subjects. Tableware might have been introduced somewhat later than the other forms.

The transfer-printing process was employed by Wedgwood throughout his lifetime. He would send undecorated ware to Liverpool to be printed by Sadler and his partner Guy Green. It would then be returned to Wedgwood unless it was for export, in which case Sadler and Green would fire it and it would be shipped from that port. Vast quantities were decorated for shipment to the Continent, Ireland, and America. Although Wedgwood started to do some of his own transfer printing at Etruria by about 1784, he continued to work with the Liverpool firm until his death in 1795. After this time it is thought that the company no longer called on Green's services.

7. Mug, tan earthenware, transfer-printed over the glaze in black, 6⅝″ high (16.8 cm.), unmarked, c. 1761-64. The mug is quart-sized, cylindrical, and "cross handled," as printer John Sadler called it in notes that he kept during his business relationship with Wedgwood. The handles terminate in molded leafage decoration. The color is a deep cream or tan that suggests it was made before October of 1764, when Sadler is quoted by his biographer E. Stanley Price as having said that the new lighter color was "liked better by everybody than the deep 'yellow." The print is signed "I. Sadler Liverp!" and depicts the coat of arms of the society of Free and Accepted Masons. The arms display instruments and symbols associated with stonemasonry. Sadler's records first list the Mason's Arms design on April 29, 1763. In that listing they were printed on quart- and pint-sized mugs. Requests for the design appear in numerous orders, including one which states: "6 setts of Mason's arms printed teapots, coffeepots, milks, sugrˢ & bowls—write to Sadler about them & red setts" (MS 4935-6).

8. Bowl, transfer-printed decoration over the glaze in red, 7" in diameter (17.8 cm.), mark: "Wedgwood," c. 1770-1800. The slop bowl, which was part of a complete tea service, was used to empty the remaining tea and dregs from the teacup before it was refilled. If the cup was rinsed with hot water before refilling, the water could also be discarded into the bowl. This object is decorated with four groups of peacocks in natural settings and was probably printed by Sadler and Green at Liverpool, for Wedgwood mentions the bird pattern in 1771 (Finer, 117), and Goeffrey Godden quotes a letter written in April of 1772 in which Wedgwood stated that he was sending tableware to Liverpool to be printed with the bird pattern in black. The bird pattern was probably still in use after Wedgwood started printing at Etruria, for William Burton states that in the inventory of the useful ware works that was taken at the time of Thomas Wedgwood's death in 1787 were listed engraved plates including "Printed bird pattern" and "Red birds."

9. Plates, transfer-printed decoration in black, 9⅞" in diameter (25.1 cm.), marks: "WEDGWOOD," c. 1772-1800. The plates illustrate the continuous printed border which had not been mastered by Sadler and Green before November of 1771 (Finer, 117) and which replaced six different sprays of flowers, one in each compartment. The shape of the plate—with serpentine-curved and molded edge, and with the rim divided into six compartments by molded bands—was called the Queen's pattern, so named, according to the story told by Simeon Shaw, because Queen Charlotte, having commissioned Wedgwood to make a table service in cream color for her, rejected the proposed plate pattern, which was the traditional barley corn pattern, produced by Wedgwood in green glazed ware, in which the compartment rims were molded in kernel-like relief. Taking away the "kernel" relief pattern left a smooth-surfaced compartmented rim. There is strong evidence, however, that Wedgwood produced this shape before the Queen's commission could have taken place—at least by the spring of 1765—for on February 13, 1765, Wedgwood wrote to his brother: "I wish he [Sir William Meredith] wo^d give me a copper plate with his Arms suitable of Tableplates, & a Crest (if he wo^d like it) to fill up one of the compartm^{ts} in the dish rims . . ." (Meteyard, *Life* I, 358). It is probable that this table-plate shape, already in production, was among the patterns submitted to the Queen in 1765 and that her acceptance of it gave a new name to an old shape.

10. Teapot, transfer-printed decoration over the glaze in black, 7½″ high (19 cm.), mark: "WEDGWOOD," c. 1779. Wedgwood seized the opportunity whenever possible to represent topical subjects or persons in the news on his ware. Delays in getting topical items into production frustrated him, as his letters show. Augustus Keppel (1725-86) was a British admiral who had been accused by his second in command of neglect of duty and misconduct. He was courtmartialed in January of 1779, acquitted February 11, and thereafter he received the thanks of both Houses of Parliament. On the 25th of February, Wedgwood wrote to Bentley: "But why do you not send me his [Keppel's] head when it is advertised every day in shade —etching & wax, by Mrs. Harrington" (Farrer, II, 480). Four days later, he followed with: "Mr. Byerley . . . says he could sell thousands of Keppels at any price. Oh Keppel Keppel—Why will not you send me a Keppel. I am perswaded if we had had our wits about us as we ought to have had 2 or 3 months since we might have sold 1000 £ worth of this gentlemans head in various ways" (Farrer, II, 482).

11. Teapot, transfer-printed decoration over the glaze in black, 5⅜″ high (13.7 cm.), mark: "wedgwood," c. 1770-1800. A portrait of John Wesley (1703-91) is printed on the front of the teapot, while on the reverse an inscription enclosed within a cartouche reads: "Let your Conversation be as becometh the Gospel of CHRIST." Wedgwood was not among Wesley's Methodist following; in fact, quite the reverse was true. Wesley, as it happened, had only charitable words for Wedgwood. While preaching in the Potteries in 1760, he commented in his journal upon the rude manners of the inhabitants, but he noted an exception: "I met a young man by the name of J. Wedgwood, who had planted a flower garden adjacent to his pottery. He also has his men wash their hands and faces and change their clothes after working in the clay. He is small and lame, but his soul is near to God" (Kelly, *Story*, 13).

12. Jug, transfer-printed decoration over the glaze in black, 8¾″ high (22.2 cm.), mark: "WEDGWOOD," c. 1776-1800. Benjamin West's painting *The Death of Wolfe*, executed in 1771, was so well received that West made four replicas of it, and the engraving made in 1776, from which the print on this jug was copied, was widely sold. The print on the reverse depicts a British gunboat firing upon another ship. The king's monogram, "GR," is in a cartouche which is part of a trophy at the bottom of the print. The monogram of the reigning sovereign was used customarily on military uniforms and equipment, and it also appears on the reverse side of the Keppel teapot (fig. 10).

13. Tea canister, transfer-printed decoration over the glaze in black, 4¼″ high (10.8 cm.), mark: "WEDG-WOOD," c. 1790. Wedgwood sought the patronage of Americans by producing ware with such patriotic decorations as a portrait of George Washington. A picture of a soldier in the uniform of the Continental Army is on the reverse. The scroll that surrounds the portrait reads "HIS EXCELLENCY GENERAL WASHINGTON," and the partially obliterated inscription which once extended in an arc under the scrolls and portrait read, according to Robert H. Mc-Cauley, "Commander in Chief of the Forces of the United States of America and President of the Congress." While the inscription that remains, however, retains parts of the phrase "Commander in Chief," and the phrase "of America" can be inferred from the position of the inscription, there does not appear to have been room for "and President of the Congress." The portrait is from an engraving by "B.B.E." after Pierre Eugene Du Simitière from the painting by Joseph Wright (1756-93), suggesting that McCauley had seen the print which contains the entire inscription.

Although elaborate and effective results could be achieved with the relatively inexpensive transfer-printing technique, it was nevertheless limited to one color. Overglaze enameling could employ a great range of color, but it was expensive. A combination of the two, perfected in 1776, achieved multicolor decoration at a modest price. Outlines were printed and filled in with enamel colors applied by hand—a task which required relatively unskilled labor. Guy Green employed children for the job at 1s. 6d. per week—a meager weekly wage, which was equivalent at the time to the cost of four pounds of turkey or about two ounces of tea. By comparison, a field laborer was paid the same salary per day.

Ten days after Green showed Wedgwood the first successful result of the printing and painting combination, Wedgwood wrote enthusiastically to Bentley: "Yes, I make no doubt but Painting & Printing may exist together. I hope we shall do both in quantities both in Table and Teaware. Many patterns cannot be Printed & these will employ the pencils [fine brushes]" (Farrer, II, 336). Two weeks later, December 28, 1776, he added: "Some shell plates I have just rec'd from Liverpool, convince me of a revolution being at hand, but our Painters may nevertheless be continued, if it is not their own fault. The tawdry appearance is all vanish'd & I am fully convinc'd that the Ivy and Grape bord.ʳˢ may be done at one third of what I now pay" (Meteyard, Life, II, 349).

14. Plate, transfer-printed decoration over the glaze in black, enriched with green enamel, 7½" diameter (19.1 cm.), mark: "wedgwood," c. 1776-1800. Wedgwood introduced the subject of shell and seaweed decoration to Bentley with such faint enthusiasm that it is somewhat surprising that he actually put the pattern into production at all. In November, 1771, he wrote: "Our next proposed subject is shells and Seaweed in groups &c. These may be placed on the ware just as our flowers are at present. They will be very pretty, but uninteresting. . . . Shells and weeds have been somewhat hackneyed in prints (Ladys Amusement) and printed Linnens . . ." (Finer, 117). Production was underway by 1776 or early 1777. On December 15, 1776, Wedgwood wrote to Bentley: "I had wrote to Mr. Green upon the first sight of the Shell patterns that they were coloured too high, & must be kept down, especially the green—Shells and weeds may be colour'd as chaste as any subjects whatever, & I hope we shall get into the way of it in time. But this pattern was intended chiefly for abroad, & foreigners in general will bear higher colouring & more forcible contrasts than the English" (Farrer, II, 336).

The Ladies Amusement; or Whole Art of Japanning Made Easy (a page of which may be seen behind the plate) was a manual and book of design patterns, which despite its title was frequently consulted by cabinetmakers and other craftsmen. It first appeared in about 1760, with subsequent editions in 1762 and possibly 1771. Although the shell and seaweed groups on the plate are not copied precisely from any prints in the book, the style of the drawings, and the format of shells superimposed on sprays of seaweed are so similar that they bespeak at least a common pool of design sources.

15, 16. Jugs, transfer-printed over the glaze in black, and enriched with hand-painted enamels, marks: "Wedgwood," c. 1779-84. *Above*, green, yellow, and red enamels, 7⅛" high (18.1 cm.); *Left*, green, yellow, blue, and brown enamels, 8⁷/₁₆" high (21.4 cm.). Both jugs show the same transfer-printed picture of three foot soldiers on one side and a mounted cavalry officer on the other. The soldiers are wearing the uniforms of the Irish Volunteers, a militia group formed after England withdrew her troops from Ireland in 1779 to send them to America and the Continent. The Volunteers, who were predominantly but not exclusively Protestant, were the toast of Ireland during the opening years of the 1780s. The jug (*above*) was made for the Volunteers from County Wexford and is inscribed under the lip: "May they and their Commanders, Live happy many Years; Their king and their Country's best Support, the Wexford Volunteers." The word "Unanimity" is enclosed within a cartouche under the quatrain. The jug (*left*) was made for the regiment from County Wicklow. The inscription is in a cartouche under the lip of the object and reads: "Success to Colonel Hayes & the INDEPENDENT WICKLOW FORRESTERS." The footed shape of the Wexford jug is illustrated as number 605 in the 1802 Wedgwood shape book. The Wicklow jug is not illustrated in either the Wedgwood Queen's Ware catalogues or the shape book. This swelling baluster-shaped jug with angular spout is the shape often called Liverpool jug.

17. Coffeepot with cover, decorated with relief molding, transfer printing, and enamel painted over the printing, 13½" high (34.3 cm.), mark: "WEDG-WOOD," c. 1785. The large coffeepot displays the tilted flower finial and crossed handles that were one of the combinations of shapes that Wedgwood used for coffee and teapots most frequently after about 1775. On the front is depicted a sailing ship. The inscription is in Dutch. On the reverse side is transfer-printed in black a picture of a gentleman leading a lady down steps into a formal garden. This object was probably one of a number decorated with these prints. The inscription would have been added later (perhaps in the country where it was sold). Here the inscription can be seen to extend partly over the painted ship scene.

18. Jug, transfer-printed decoration enriched with hand-applied polychrome enamels, 9½" high (24.1 cm.), mark: "WEDGWOOD," c. 1786-1800. A more ambitious transfer-printed undertaking than merely filling in outlined pictures with color is illustrated in this jug. The picture is printed in monochrome, but painted with a wide range of colors. Another jug with the same picture of a dancer and musicians, but painted in different colors, is in the collection of the Wedgwood Museum, Barlaston. The printed jugs were probably stock items that were then custom-decorated, in this instance probably for a Colonel Leigh who is listed in the Wedgwood factory crest book with a line drawing of a mounted soldier beside his name. Such a figure from a unit of Light Dragoons is shown on the reverse side of the jug, and jugs of the same design have descended in the Leigh family. The lobed jug, number 591 in the 1802 shape book, was more difficult to work with in transfer printing than many others, and a spot where the print did not stick to the surface can be seen in the groove at the center of the picture. It is a blank spot in the drawing of leaves to the left of the seated figure's leg.

A letter, dated August 31, 1768, from Wedgwood to William Cox, manager of the London showrooms, might be taken to indicate that a shift in emphasis from transfer-printed to painted decoration of creamware was taking place at that time. It reads: "I have wrote to Sadler about the desert service of Pea Green, and he does not choose to undertake it . . . so that I would not have you shew that printed pattern at present, Messrs Rhodes and Company are to do us the coloured patterns, for which reason I have not lately urged Sadler to do them" (Finer, 67).

Enameling had been done previously, however, and Wedgwood seems to have subcontracted the work to independent decorators, as did all the Staffordshire potters. It was later that potters employed their own enamelers. Wedgwood evidently used Courzen, and, according to Simeon Shaw, he also sent ware to be painted to Mrs. Astbury of Hot Lane (not Mrs. Warburton, as has been stated in other works). It may be that Wedgwood's arrangement with D. Rhodes & Co., beginning in 1768, initiated the transition to in-house decorating. A building to house the enameling works was purchased in Chelsea in late 1769; David Rhodes and his assistants were moved there from Charing Cross, and Rhodes became chief enameler, although some ware was enameled at Burslem and later at Etruria.

Many of the names of enamelers who worked for Wedgwood are known, such as James Bakewell, William Hopkins Craft, Nathaniel Cooper, Thomas Green, Thomas Simpcock, Robert and Catherine Willcox, and Ralph Unwin, but for the most part their work cannot be definitely identified.

19. Jug, decorated over the glaze with brown, orange, yellow, black, and beige enamel colors, 9⁵⁄₁₆" high (23.7 cm.), mark: "WEDGWOOD," c. 1770-1800. The words on the ribbon at the top of the coat of arms read "The Hatters Arms," and on the bottom is the legend, "We Assist Each Other in Time of Need." A transfer-printed version of the same design is known. It appears on an unmarked jug that has a portrait of President John Adams on the other side and would probably date, therefore, from about 1796 to 1800. On the reverse side of the jug illustrated is a church and graveyard painted in a rosy beige and charcoal grey. Under the spout is inscribed "T M Twist". It is not known whether the more costly hand-enameled version of the hatters' arms was done before the transfer print was made or after the plate for the print was no longer in use, or whether it was enameled rather than printed simply to suit the customer's preference. This jug shape is illustrated in the 1802 shape book with specifications indicating that it was also available with a cover.

20. Covered dish, decorated over the glaze with red and brown enamel, 14″ long
(35.6 cm.), mark: "WEDGWOOD," c. 1770-1800. The dish would have fitted with
three other identical pieces around a central bowl to form a supper set, as illustrated
in the 1802 shape book. The decoration is of tiny red flowers or berries, each with a
fine pale-brown stem. A leaf design runs through the middle of the border, which is
repeated on the inside of the dish. Overlapping circles surround the handle. They
are shaded to give a three-dimensional effect and are colored with thin brown lines.
Extraordinary patience was required to perform the time-consuming task of painting this design, but the work of applying the line borders that edged many of the
plates and dishes was expedited and improved in 1771 by the use of a device that was
introduced to Wedgwood by an engraver named P. P. Burdett. Wedgwood, saying
that it was "a little machine by which they do 6 or 8 [plates] for one, and ten times as
well," described it to Bentley in a letter of November 23, 1771: "It is little more than a
steel pen such as we buy with cases of instruments. . . . There is another part which I
call the shoulder. This serves to guide the pen by being kept steady to the outer edge
of the plate . . ." (Finer, 116).

Although correspondence reveals that Wedgwood was engaged in business transactions with the enameling firm of Robinson and Rhodes of Leeds (later called D. Rhodes & Co.) as early as 1763, there is no evidence that David Rhodes enameled creamware for Wedgwood before 1768. If he did decorate Wedgwood ware, it was probably for sale in his own shop at Leeds, as Rhodes and Robinson were pottery and porcelain merchants as well as enamelers.

Rhodes sold copper scales and copper dust to Wedgwood for his green glaze, and he purchased from Wedgwood both colored-glazed and cream-colored ware, probably for resale. One letter from Rhodes, dated November 21, 1764, suggests that he was consulted by Wedgwood about gilding earthenware and glazing it with white glaze: "I received your Favour and shall be glad to serve you in anything I can do. I have burnt Gold on China often and am certain I can do it on your ware. As to a white glaze I have not tried it on Cream Colourd ware, but if you chuse to send a piece or 2 I'll try it. I think it would do best unglazed or extraordinary thin glazed as the Lead is rather apt to strake most Colours that are laid very strong on it. To glaze with white and gild your ware well wd. require it twice fired. My partner has turned over the business to me since March last and works for me at it" (Towner, "David Rhodes," 7).

Rhodes remained an independent decorator for at least a year, billing Wedgwood for his services, but by 1770 letters from Wedgwood to Bentley indicate that Rhodes was Wedgwood's head enameler. Rhodes had died by January 27, 1777.

21. Teapot, decorated over the glaze in red, purple, black, green, and yellow enamel colors, 4½" high (11.4 cm.), mark: "Wedgwood," decoration attributed to David Rhodes, c. 1770-77. David Rhodes's landscapes were characteristically rendered with animation that must have pleased Wedgwood, for he wrote to Bentley in April of 1773, "I think Mr. Rhodes cannot be better employ'd than in painting Landskips" (Towner, "David Rhodes," 11). On the reverse of the teapot is inscribed "Long may we Live/Happy may we be/Blest with content/ & from misfortunes free."

22. Mug, decorated over the glaze in red, purple, black, green, and yellow enamel colors, 5⅛″ high (13 cm.), unmarked: decoration attributed to David Rhodes, c. 1768-77. The jaunty figures in Rhodes's designs are freely drawn, the parts of the body where skin is exposed, the facial features, and hair characteristically outlined in thin red lines. Other parts are sometimes outlined in black and filled in with broad washes of color.

James Bakewell was an enameler in Wedgwood's
employ from at least 1769 until the middle or late
1770s. He worked first at Burslem and then in
London. Wedgwood first mentions him in a letter
concerning a prospective employee dated June 25,
1769: "Could you inquire his character from better
authority than Bakewell" (Finer, 75). The following spring Wedgwood sent Bakewell to Liverpool
to hire painters from the factories that produced
tin-glazed (delft) ware. He wrote confidently to
Bentley (May 19, 1770): "J. Bakewell sets out by
tomorrows coach & promises to be a very des-
patchfull hand" (Farrer, I, 347).

From this time on, Wedgwood's opinion of
Bakewell seems to have shifted from resigned acceptance — "With him all I can think of undertaking will be Bronzeing and the black and
yellow, and purple enamelling and this not to any
extent" (Towner, "David Rhodes") — to evident
respect, for Bakewell was, according to Eliza
Meteyard, one of the chief landscape painters on
Wedgwood's table service for Catherine the Great;
and ultimately by 1777 to contempt — "Bakewell
always was a fool & being now become a very
troublesome one a good drubbing was well be-
stowed upon him" (Farrer, II, 385).

Enamel-decorated pieces are attributed to Bakewell on the basis of a number of initialed pieces inscribed either "JB" or "B" in overglaze colors. They
are characteristically monochrome or black-and-
yellow floral paintings, realistically rendered, and
achieving a three-dimensional effect.

23. Plate, decorated over the glaze in purple enamel, 8½″ in diameter
(21.6 cm.), unmarked, c. 1769-77. The plate, which is decorated with
purple flowers, is attributed to James Bakewell on the basis of the initial "B" painted in overglaze purple on the bottom and the similarity in
style to other floral decoration credited to Bakewell. The painting on
the molded shell edge is feathered carefully into the grooves, in contrast to the striping illustrated on the plate decorated with shells and
seaweed shown in fig. 14.

The design sources for enameled decoration on creamware range from the elegant pursuits of pleasure depicted by Antoine Watteau—whose work would have been interpreted for Wedgwood by printmakers and through the porcelains of Worcester, Chelsea, and the Continental porcelain factories—through the pretty rococo delicacies of François Boucher, to contemporary painters and printmakers whose names are unknown to us. Books illustrated the architecture, frescoes, and pottery of the ancient world, some of which were in Wedgwood's own library, and collections of antiquities lent to him for copying by patrons provided Wedgwood with decorative motifs with which to meet and lead the new taste for classical design. The rococo and classical tastes are typically combined in the covered sauce tureen (See plate VIII) which is illustrated in the 1779 Queen's Ware catalogue (without ladle). The form, especially that of the handles, is rococo; the decorative border is classically derived.

24. Pair of custard cups, decorated over the glaze with polychrome enamel, 2½" high (6.4 cm.), mark: "WEDGWOOD," c. 1770-1800. The neoclassical taste was overtaking the rococo by the time Wedgwood had started to produce his more elaborate enameled decorations, making the Watteau-style design somewhat rare in Wedgwood ware. On one of the cups illustrated a gentleman is extending his hand to a lady, and on the other a musician is playing a mandolin for the lady seated next to him. The cups, with domed covers with round knobs, are shown placed on a salver in the Queen's Ware catalogue of 1790-95.

25. Plate, pierced decoration and painted over the glaze in red, yellow, green, and blue enamel, 7^{15}/$_{16}$" in diameter (20.2 cm.), marked: "WEDG-WOOD," c. 1770-1800. Combining delicacy and airiness in the painted and pierced decoration, Wedgwood produced a dessert plate providing splendid visual relief from the weighty excesses of the first two courses customarily served at 18th-century English dinners. The couple in the painting, surrounded by a floral cartouche that somehow seems like a trellised bower, are rendered in the manner of François Boucher, whose work epitomized the light, agreeable, and pretty aspects of the rococo style in painting.

The pierced border design was made by punching each hole separately with metal tools. Wedgwood outlined the shapes desired and had the tools fabricated by, among others, a Mr. Finney; John Wyke, a Liverpool watchmaker; and Mr. Stamford of Derby, the father of Bentley's second wife.

26. Chamber candlestick, decorated over the glaze with brick-red and black enamel, 2½" high (6.4 cm.), mark: "WEDGWOOD," c. 1770-1800. Both table and toilet candlesticks are listed in the first Queen's Ware catalogue. The toilet or chamber candlestick had a handle so that it could be carried to light the way when walking, and it had a short shaft in order to keep the center of gravity low so that the candle was less likely to topple when being carried. Eight varieties of the stick with attached saucer and handle are illustrated in the 1802 shape book. The two with ring handles are the footed version with bobeche illustrated here, and a cylinder without bobeche. The background of the border is painted in a rich brick red, and the Greek fret and leaf designs and line border are in black. Meteyard states that this border appeared in various colors, but it was generally a rich brown red.

27. Plates and dish, decorated over the glaze with brick red and black mat enamel, c. 1789-1800. *Left,* 9¾" in diameter (24.8 cm.), mark: "WEDGWOOD"; *center,* 9½" long (24.1 cm.), mark: "WEDGWOOD"; *right,* 7¹⁵/₁₆" in diameter (20.2 cm.), mark: "WEDGWOOD." Whole table and dessert services were made in these designs with borders in the egg and tongue and Greek fret motifs, and with figures or vases in the center. The designs for some of the series were copied from plates in Sir William Hamilton's *Collection of Etruscan, Greek, and Roman Antiquities* and were kept in a book of stock designs for factory use. The vase with figures that appears on the dish is taken exactly, including the shape of the vase, from vol. II, plate 61.

The "vase" series seems to have been marked with black printed or painted numbers followed by a "T." The plate and dish are marked "57T" and "10T" respectively, while an oblong dessert dish and a plate from the series in the Falcke Collection at the British Museum are marked "17T" and "50T" respectively.

While maintaining a fresh supply of print sources from which to copy was a perennial problem, the greatest strain of all was placed upon Wedgwood's resources by a commission received in 1773 from Catherine the Great to provide table and dessert services for 50 people – the services to be decorated with views of English country estates. The service was to be used at her palace of La Grenouillère, named for its proximity to frog-filled marshes, and had, therefore, a green frog placed within a shield on each piece. Statements about the number of pieces vary, but Bentley catalogued the service for its exhibition in June of 1774 prior to delivery to the Empress, and he listed 952 pieces decorated with 1,244 views.

It was a prodigious task for Wedgwood to obtain the views. For some he relied on published materials; for others he had artists draw sketches. His staff of artists at the Chelsea enameling works, plus those he was able to employ outside, proved equal to the task, and, although the views were painted by many different artists with differing styles, they were all executed in monochrome (in a sepia tone) which proved to be a unifying factor.

It was difficult for Wedgwood to evaluate the expense incurred in producing the service, but the return in good publicity must have been enormous. The continued and expanded patronage of the pleased and flattered owners of the country houses was an intangible benefit that Wedgwood took into account early in the project. In a letter to Bentley on August, 14, 1773, he wrote: "I wish you would send me a good camera obscura, not to cumbersome that I could take to the Neighbouring Gent.^{ns} seats here, as I find it will be in my power to pay some acceptable comp.^{ts} [compliments] in that way to some Gent.^{n} in our Neighbourhood" (MS 18487-25).

28. Plate, decorated over the glaze in sepia enamel, 9⅞" in diameter (25.1 cm.), unmarked: "30" painted in sepia, c. 1773-74. In Bentley's catalogue of the Russian service, which is reprinted in translation from the French version and annotated by George Williamson in his book *The Imperial Russian Dinner Service* (1909), number "30, View of Brivals Castle, Gloucestershire, the property of the Crown" is preceded by an asterisk which was Williamson's way of indicating that the plate was no longer in existence. He based his finding on a list of pieces still to be found, and exhibited in 1909, at the Peterhof Palace. Eight pieces, one of them being number 30, appeared subsequently and are said to have been discovered in England by antiques dealers. These were either never included in the original shipment to Russia or were somehow removed from the country subsequently.

The plate here illustrated was part of the dinner service rather than the dessert service as is indicated not only by the larger size, but by the oak leaf and acorn decoration on the rim. The dessert service was decorated with an ivy vine border. The frog is green, the rest of the decoration being in a sepia monochrome.

29. Plate, decorated over the glaze in polychrome enamels, 8⅞″ in diameter (22.5 cm.), unmarked, c. 1773. Although the scenes on the Russian service were executed in a monochrome, the illustration of Bothall Castle, Northumberland, is realistically rendered in a broad range of colors. Probably after trying polychrome, Wedgwood discarded the idea in favor of the more unifying monochrome, indicating, as M. Mellanay Delhom has suggested, that this plate is an experiment in the development of the service. "Bothol Castle, Northumberland, the property of the Earl of Oxford" is listed as number 431 in the dessert service in the Bentley catalogue. Williamson stated in 1909 that this view was "no longer in existence," indicating that the monochrome version was destroyed or then unknown. The plate was designed for the dessert service, being smaller than the dinner size, and having the ivy vine border.

Wedgwood was always of two minds about filling custom orders, or "uniques" as he called them, because, while he realized their value in attracting and holding customers, he found them time consuming—as he told Bentley in a letter of January 10, 1770: "Defend me from particular orders, & I can make you allmost double the qu.^{ty} . . . " (Farrer, I, 330). He also feared the danger of being left with custom-decorated orders that had been refused. Nevertheless, he sought custom orders from potentially influential patrons as early as 1765.

The following year, however, he told Bentley (September 25): "Crests are very bad things for us [potters] to meddle with & I never take any orders for services so ornamented. Plain ware if it sho.^d not happen to be firsts, you will take off my hands as seconds, which if Crested wo.^d be as useless as most other Crests, & Crest wearers are, for this & other reasons, the additional expence is more than the buyer can be perswaded to believe it ought to be" (Farrer, I, 103).

Ten years later the demand for ware decorated with coats of arms caused Wedgwood to reverse his decision, telling Bentley (September 12, 1776): "I have many reasons to believe there will be a great demand for services with Arms if they can be done at a moderate expence, and I am losing my best customers, one after another, as well for plain ware as painted, because I have either refused such orders, or been obliged to ask such prices as has driven them to other Potters . . . " (Finer, 197).

Not all custom pieces required arms. Plate V (p. 67) illustrates a jug with special polychrome enamel decoration. Under the spout is a square clock face framed in bellflowers, "T. SHAW" is inscribed on the clock face, and the hands point to 2:53. "Another. jug. 1790" is inscribed enigmatically within a wreath.

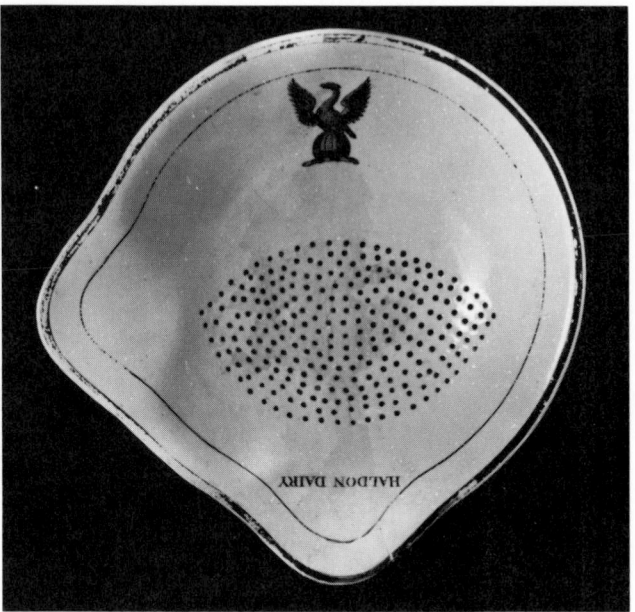

30. Cream strainer, decorated over the glaze in brown enamel, 7¾" wide (19.7 cm.), mark: "WEDGWOOD," c. 1776-1800. By Wedgwood's time, dairying, an essential rural function, became, as well, a fashionable pleasure of the rich, and fancy-tiled dairies, furnished with matched sets of utensils such as milk settling pans, cream vases, and cream strainers, sometimes marked with the family crest, had become status symbols. The crest on this strainer is that of the Palk family of Haldon House, Devonshire. Creamware, being easy to keep clean, was considered an ideal material for dairy ware, and Wedgwood was called upon to produce sets of it in Queen's Ware for his fashionable clientele. According to Alison Kelly in *Decorative Wedgwood*, Wedgwood first started taking orders for dairy ware in 1769. A full page of the 1802 shape book was devoted to such ware, the cream strainer being one of the items illustrated.

31. Plates and soup plate, polychrome enamel decoration over the glaze. *Left*, 10″ (25.4 cm.), mark: "WEDGWOOD," with "Blagrove Esqʳ" painted in overglaze brown, c. 1777; *center*, 9¾″ (24.8 cm.), mark: "WEDGWOOD," c. 1778; *right*, 9¾″ (24.8 cm.), mark: "WEDGWOOD," c. 1776-1800. According to Jessie McNab, armorial ware was more usually produced in porcelain than in earthenware. As Queen's Ware was increasingly accepted by the well-to-do, Wedgwood was forced to fill orders for armorial table services. The plate on the right was probably made for a cardinal, as a cardinal's tasseled hat dominates the arms, which are more elaborate and dramatic than those found in British heraldry. The soup plate in the center is decorated with the arms of Sir John Honywood and his wife, The Honorable Frances Courtenay, who were married in 1778. The Honywood family crest, a wolf's head, is centered above the arms on the rim. The family crest on such ware was sometimes placed directly over the arms instead of on the rim, as shown on the plate at left. The palm tree was the crest of the Blagrove family, which owned property in Jamaica. The arms are those of John Blagrove and Anne Shakespeare.

"And with regard to Elegance of form, that was an object very little attended to. . . ." So Wedgwood described, in the preface to his early experiment book, the state of the pottery industry in Staffordshire when he entered business on his own in 1759. Wedgwood improved the body and glaze of creamware and introduced "elegance of form" to the point where Queen's Ware took its place beside porcelain and silver on the tables of the affluent and became a fashionable replacement even for pieces that had heretofore been manufactured only in those more glamorous materials.

32. Epergne, molded relief decoration painted with overglaze green and brown enamel, 17¾" high (45.1 cm.), mark: "WEDGWOOD," c. 1770-1800. The epergne was primarily made in silver before Wedgwood ventured into its production, although some had previously been manufactured in porcelain. It was a centerpiece for the dining table and also a space-saver since small dishes were placed in it on two or three levels. The word *epergne* comes from the French *épargne*, meaning saving or thrift. This epergne, described as "Eagle Epargne" in the 1802 shape book, is shown there with sweetmeat baskets hanging from the hooks and with covered, footed bowls in the sockets of the lower level. The baskets and bowls are dessert fittings, but the epergne was also sometimes used during the preceding dinner courses to hold condiments and pickles.

33. *Above*: Basket and stand, decorated in transfer-printing and enamel over the glaze, basket: 9$^{1}/_{16}$" long (23 cm.), stand: 10¼" long (26 cm.), mark: "WEDGWOOD" on stand only, c. 1770-1800. Table baskets of silver fashioned in reeded trellis-work designs were made throughout most of the 18th century. The porcelain factories, too, produced trellis-work baskets, sometimes with reeding on the lattice, and often with applied flowers at the intersections of the straps, that were echoed in Wedgwood's painted floral designs on the lattice work of this fruit basket and stand. The print in the center of the basket and stand is a virtual catalogue of the exotica that were displayed also on textiles and furniture, and installed in gardens—perhaps to distract from the correct rectangularity of Georgian houses. On the left of the scene, replete with classical ruins, a dead tree frames the landscape, a romantic cliché introduced earlier in the century by William Kent, who planted a dead tree in Kensington Gardens for the sake of picturesqueness. At least four different states of the print are known. Two are in public collections; one in the British Museum and one in the Victoria and Albert Museum.

34. Ice-cream cooler, decorated over the glaze with red enamel and gilding, 7" high (17.8 cm.), mark: "WEDGWOOD," c. 1775-1800. Ice-cream coolers, or "glacières" as Wedgwood called them, were made to keep ice cream cold at the table by surrounding it with crushed ice. This cooler was made in three parts: the bottom, which would have held ice; the galleried top, into which ice would also have been placed; and a bowl (missing in the photograph), which would have fit into the bottom section and held the ice cream. If the bowl were in place, the edge of the flange would be visible between the top and bottom of the cooler. Although these coolers are sometimes referred to as fruit coolers, their use for ice cream in the 18th century is confirmed by at least one of Wedgwood's customers who ordered in 1784 "Two Large Sized Ice Cream Vases" (MS 9655-11). The shape of this cooler is illustrated along with nine others in the 1802 shape book. It is decorated on all sides and on the cover with trophies—decorative groups of musical instruments, or implements of battle, or a combination of both, usually bound with ribbons.

35. Monteith, decorated over the glaze in polychrome enamel, 12¾" long (32.4 cm.), mark: "WEDGWOOD," c. 1770-1800. The 1774 Queen's Ware catalogue illustrates this lobed and footed monteith shape, describing its use as follows: "Monteiths, for keeping Glasses cool in water, two sizes." Various purposes have been ascribed to the form. According to Williamson, it was called a flower stand in the 1909 listing of pieces from the Russian service at the Peterhof Palace, and it is sometimes referred to as a punch bowl. In fact, silver bowls with detachable notched rims were made in the 18th century which could be used as monteiths with the notched rims in place and as punch bowls with the rims removed. Its use as a wine glass cooler was described as early as 1683, however, by historian Anthony à Wood of Oxford: "This yeare in the summer time came up a vessel or bason notched at the brims to let drinking glasses hang there by the foot so that the body or drinking place might hang in the water to cool them. Such a bason was called a 'monteigh' from a fantastical Scot called 'Monsieur Monteigh' who, at that time, or a little before, wore the bottome of his cloake or coate so notched." The monteith illustrated is decorated in sepia and pastel tones with a "Sacrifice to Priapus" on one side and an altar on the other.

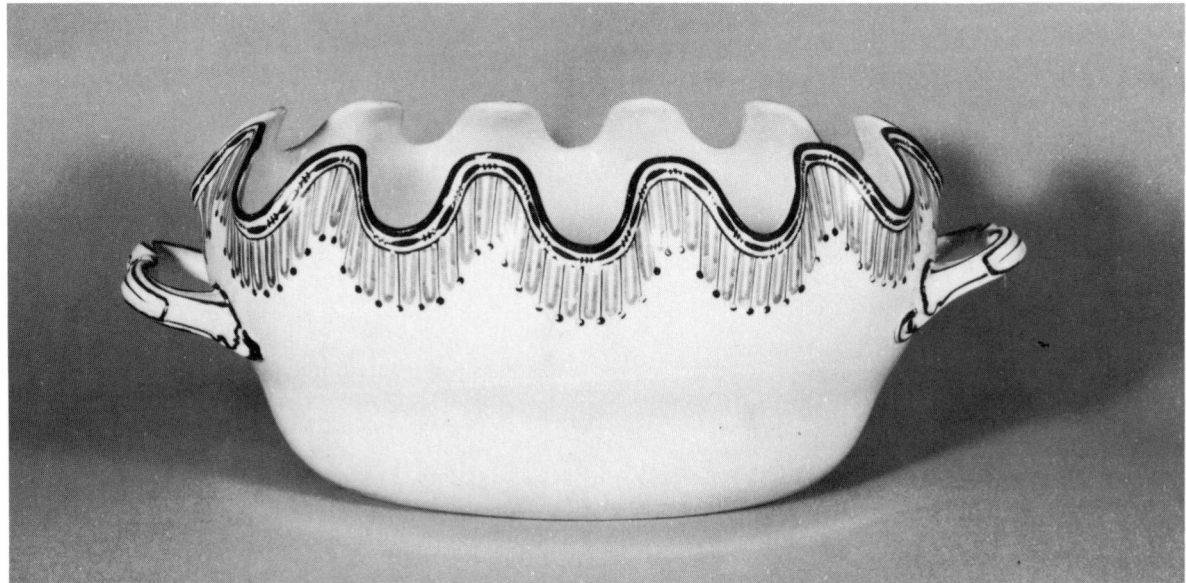

36. Monteith, decorated over the glaze in green and black enamel, 12¾" long (32.4 cm.), mark: "WEDGWOOD," c. 1775-1800. The Queen's Ware catalogue produced between 1790 and 1795 introduced this monteith shape. Both it and the preceding one appear in the 1802 shape book. Meteyard states that the pattern, a combination of the reel bead and egg and tongue border, was "copied from the original coloured slips appended to an order of M. Rost, a German merchant" (*Life*, II, 344).

Although classical motifs dominated Wedgwood's wares after the 1760s, some natural forms, particularly leaves and shells, continued to provide design inspiration throughout his career. His interest in conchology, about which he wrote frequently to Bentley during the 1770s, might have contributed to some of the elaborate creations in which shell forms were employed.

37. Dish, decorated with yellow glaze and green and brown overglaze enamels, 9″ long (22.9 cm.), mark: "WEDGWOOD," c. 1770-1800. The 1774 Queen's Ware catalogue lists "Leaves and Shells of different kinds," and this shape, illustrated in the 1802 shape book, was called a pickle [dish]. It is an unusual variation of the color combination found in Wedgwood's colored glazed wares of the early 1760s. The same rich yellow glaze is employed, but the green is an opaque enamel, applied over the glaze replacing the transparent green glaze with which Wedgwood inaugurated his many departures from the Staffordshire pottery traditions.

38. Tureen, molded relief decoration enriched with yellow overglaze enamel, 9″ high (22.9 cm.), mark: "WEDGWOOD," c. 1770-1800. The tureen, oval in shape, is decorated with molded cockleshells. It is said to have originally belonged to Dr. Erasmus Darwin, a long-time friend of Wedgwood, whose son married Wedgwood's eldest daughter Susannah. Their son was the 19th-century scientist Charles Darwin. The tureen is said to have been acquired by Frederick Rathbone, an English dealer in Wedgwood, from William Erasmus Darwin (1839-1914), eldest son of Charles Darwin.

Not all Wedgwood Queen's Ware was embellished with colored glazes or with transfer-printed or painted decoration. Some objects such as kitchenware, items for the sickroom or for hygienic purposes, or ware made for commercial use such as barbers' or apothecaries' equipment were often unadorned, and some customers preferred their Queen's Ware table services plain, as the following order of 1769 indicates: "I should be glad to know the Price of a Compleat Service of the best yellow Ware and Likewise the Number of Dishes, Plates, etc. that a Service consists of. I choose Oblong Dishes and plain as can be . . . " (MS 4926-6).

39. Mold, intaglio relief molding, 7¼" high (18.4 cm.), mark: "WEDGWOOD," c. 1770-1800. Visual pleasures were stressed at least as much as gustatory ones at the dinner tables of 18th-century Englishmen in comfortable circumstances, and cookbooks of the period counseled on "dressing out" the table and fashioning molded fantasies of flummery and blancmange that could be turned out of such elaborately pinnacled molds as this. Four cones surround the central obelisk, and between each cone are crisply intaglioed nuts and strawberries with leaves. Flummery and blancmange were similar in substance, both being stiff, opaque white, gelatin-based sweet puddings that were flavored with almonds. The relief-molded strawberries, leaves, and nuts would have been colored with food dyes: cochineal, bruised and steeped in brandy for red; spinach juice for green; and chocolate dissolved in coffee for brown.

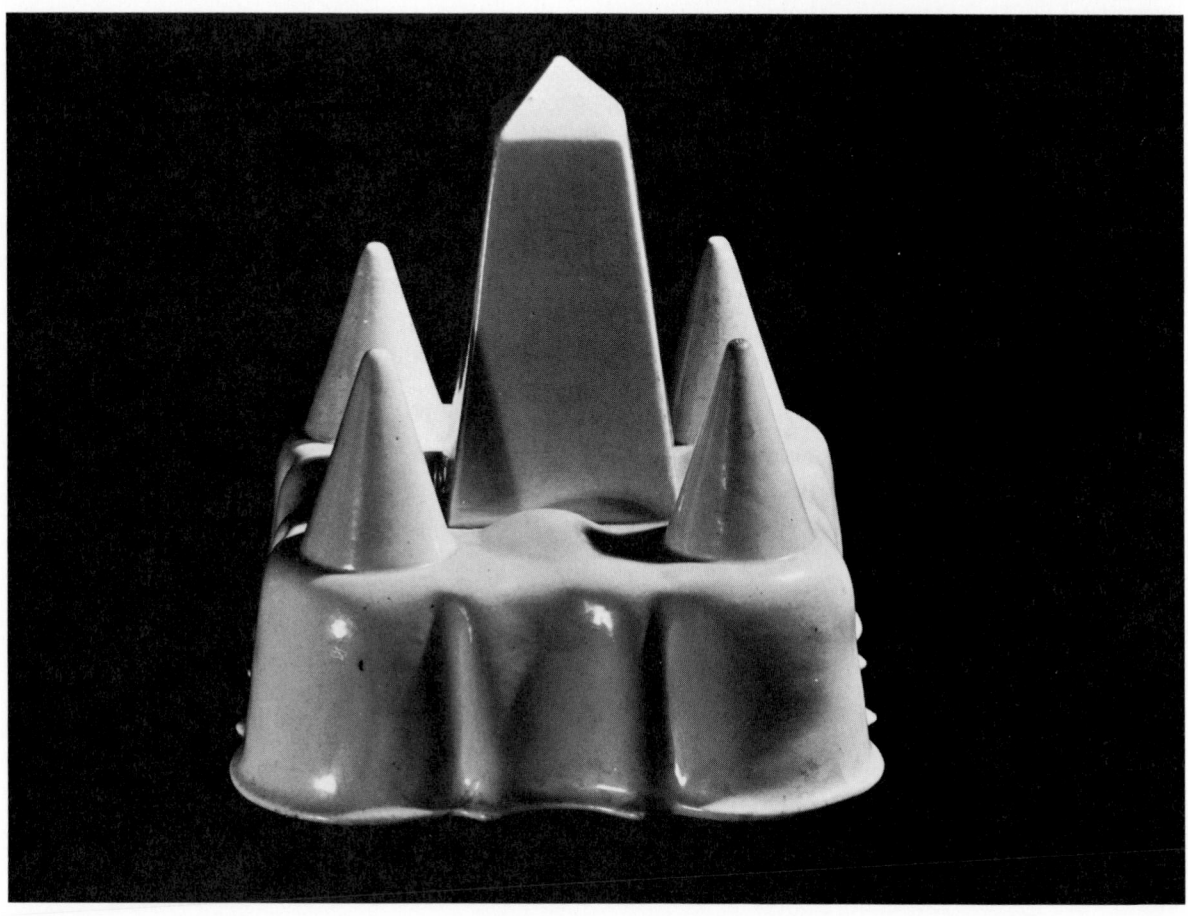

40. Veilleuse, molded and pierced decoration, 10⁵/₁₆″ high (26.2 cm.), mark: "wedgwood," c. 1770-1800. Although this lamp, a combination night lamp and food warmer for the nursery or sickroom, is unpainted, thus making it a less costly item to produce, care was taken in the appearance of the object. Double-twisted handles were applied instead of plain ones, the knob on the cover is a visually appealing artichoke shape, and five different punches were used to form the pierced floral design. An oil lamp would have been inserted into the large aperture; the pan with food in it was set over the opening of the cylinder. The lamp flame would be the proper height to show through the V-shaped top of the cutout, and the light coming through the air holes would give the appearance of a cheerful yellow flower on the nightstand. Wedgwood listed "Night Lamps, to keep any liquid warm all night" in the first Queen's Ware catalogue, suggesting that perhaps only a teapot and not a pan was offered at that time. The teapot, only, was illustrated in the 1790 catalogue, but in the 1802 shape book the teapot, pan, and a similar pan, but with pouring lip and acorn finial, are illustrated.

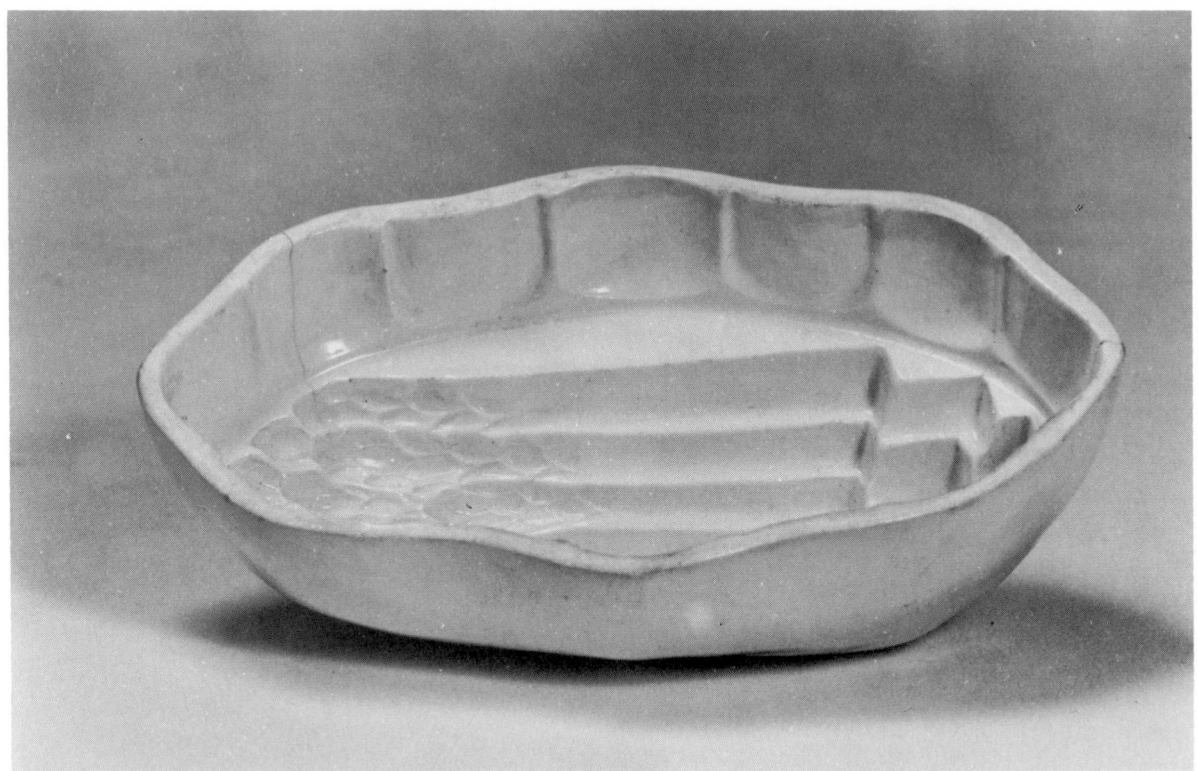

41. *Above:* Mold, intaglio relief molding, 7" long (17.8 cm.), mark: "WEDGWOOD," c. 1770-1800. As it was customary in Wedgwood's time to serve sweets during the second course with meats and vegetables, a molded "asparagus" blancmange might have been a pleasant reminder of spring during the rest of the year when asparagus was out of season. To make "Green Blanc-Mange of Isinglass," advised Elizabeth Raffald in *The Experienced Housekeeper* (1769): "Dissolve your isinglass, and put to it two ounces of sweet and two ounces of bitter almonds, with as much juice of spinage as will make it green, and a spoonful of French brandy; set it over a stove fire till it is almost ready to boil, then strain it through a gauze sieve; when it grows thick, put it into a . . . mould, and the next day turn it out."

42. Eggbeater, 3⅞" high (9.8 cm.), mark: "WEDG-WOOD," c. 1770-1800. Egg-beating or cream-whipping was accomplished with this ingenious device by shaking the box. The spikes inside both the top and bottom sections of the box would aerate the contents. Eggbeaters were first introduced in the 1802 shape book, although they were probably manufactured long before that. They would not have appeared in the Queen's Ware catalogues because only objects with particular visual appeal were illustrated in them, while the 1802 shape book was a record book for factory use.

43. Syrup pot, 8¾" high (22.2 cm.), mark: "WEDGWOOD," c. 1770-1800. The syrup pot was one of numerous forms Wedgwood manufactured for apothecaries and surgeons. Used for mixing and storing liquids, syrup pots were sometimes made with handles, but the long, waisted foot served that purpose in two out of the three such pots Wedgwood displayed in the 1802 shape book. The rim was notched so that a parchment could be tied over the top to form a cover; the spout would have been closed with a cork. Tin-glazed earthenware pots in the same footed globe shape were made in the 17th century and throughout the 18th. James Lucas, writing in 1800 in *A Candid Inquiry into the Education, Qualifications, and Offices of a Surgeon-Apothecary*, indirectly credits Wedgwood with the disappearance of the earlier type of ware at the end of the 18th century: "pots of Wedgwood's manufacture, are preferable for conserves, confections, cerates, extracts, gums, liniments and other articles."

44. Spittoon, 6¾″ wide (17.1 cm.), mark: "WEDGWOOD," c. 1770-1800. Wedgwood illustrated five spittoons or cuspidors (he called them "spitting pots") in the 1802 shape book, several of which were of decorative shapes that would have been suitable for the public rooms of the house. This pot, more clinical in appearance, was of a size suitable for the nightstand in a sick room.

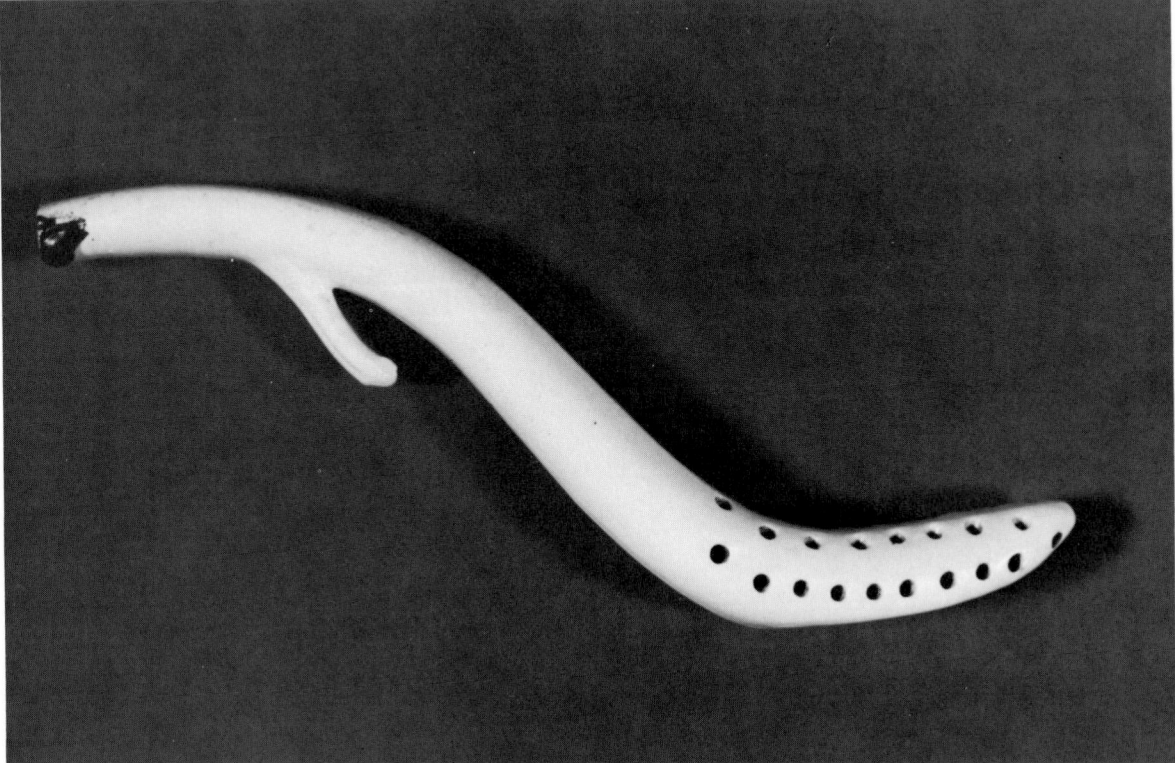

45. Sick syphon, 6½″ (16.5 cm.), mark illegible, c. 1770-1800. Wedgwood's sick syphon was actually a combination strainer and drinking straw through which the patient extracted liquid from a watery soup or stew. The S-curve shape of the instrument allowed it to rest on the edge of a porringer, while the hook attached it to the edge, making it convenient for the patient to use the syphon without holding it in his hands. Silver versions of this shape existed and had the added advantage of having the lower (pierced) end hinged, thus facilitating cleaning. The price of such a piece, however, would have far exceeded the 4d charge listed in Wedgwood's 1804 price book.

Three techniques of decoration that Wedgwood developed during his first decade of production, but that were used more extensively in bodies developed later, are illustrated here.

Lathe turning, the process of smoothing or decorating a piece by holding a cutting tool against it while turning it on the lathe, had been in use in the Potteries throughout the 18th century. Engine lathe turning, however, a process in which the lathe was made to turn with an eccentric motion and/or the cutting tool was moved longitudinally by a screw-thread, while not invented by Wedgwood, was introduced by him into the Potteries in the 1760s. During 1764 he experimented and read on the subject, having Bentley translate into English such works as Plumier's L'Art de Tourner, and by the summer of 1765, he felt confident enough of his work to include some engine-turned vases in a box of patterns he sent to the Queen.

The application of small molded decorative elements, or sprigs, had long been practiced in Staffordshire—and Wedgwood was to bring that art to its highest development in the decorative stoneware that he called Jasper—but during the 1760s he introduced the neoclassical taste into sprigging on Queen's Ware, substituting festoons and medallions for floral sprays. The decoration of a covered potpourri (plate III, p. 66), for instance, includes some of the vocabulary of neoclassical ornament that Wedgwood was to employ in all the bodies that he developed subsequently. The leafage surrounding the holes in the cover is applied as are the alternating acanthus and laurel leaves, and the ribbon and bellflower festoon. The third decorative style that was introduced in Queen's Ware, but exploited to the fullest extent in the stoneware bodies, was the unglazed or mat-finished exterior.

46. Garden pot, decorated with brown slip, green glaze, and incised and applied relief decoration, 5$^{11}/_{16}$" high (14.4 cm.), mark: "Wedgwood & Bentley," c. 1769-80. The incised decoration is both conventionally lathe-turned and engine-turned. The reeding on the green glazed bands or hoops is achieved by lathe-turning the pot in a conventional manner while a pointed tool is held against the bands. The vertical incisions are engine-turned, the cutting tool being drawn along the pot longitudinally. Places where the tool was drawn over the hoops by mistake can be seen in the illustration. Hooped garden pots with stands were made in many color combinations and were exceedingly popular, judging from the number of orders for them. The stands were slip decorated, engine-turned, and their tops were scalloped like the pots.

47. Vase, iron-red slip decoration, 6″ high (15.2 cm.), mark: "Wedgwood & Bentley,"
c. 1769-80. The vase is intended to hold flowers and is therefore glazed on the inside,
but it is unglazed on the outside, achieving the mat finish that Wedgwood was to ex-
ploit fully in the Cane and Jasper bodies.

2. *Variegated Ware*

The regular progress of cultivated life is from Necessaries to Accommodations, from Accommodations to Ornaments.

Sir Joshua Reynolds
Seven Discourses (1778)

Vases of carved and polished stone were among the many household decorations of classical times that designers of Wedgwood's period revived and reinterpreted to furnish the houses of the fashionable. Robert Adam and William Chambers were among the prominent domestic architects who designed not only houses but all the interior furnishings for them, from the furniture to the mantel ornaments, and, in collaboration with Matthew Boulton, the Birmingham manufacturer of decorative metal objects who was Wedgwood's friend and sometime competitor, they designed vases to be fashioned of colorful stones such as agate or blue john, a beautifully grained and colored Derbyshire stone, which Boulton then mounted in ormolu.

To meet this competition, Wedgwood transformed two standard techniques of the Staffordshire potters—that of combining clays of different colors to make pots with random-patterned marbling, and that of juxtaposing various colored glazes on creamware bodies to produce a mottled or tortoise-shell effect—into controlled, successful imitations of the costly stone ornaments.

Boulton had suggested that he and Wedgwood work together—Wedgwood making the vases and Boulton mounting them in ormolu—and Wedgwood considered the idea, discussing it in a letter to Bentley dated November 21, 1768: "Mr. Boulton . . . proposes an alliance betwixt the Pottery & Metal branches, Viz, that we shall make such things as will be suitable for mounting, & not have a Pott look, & he will finish them with the mounts. What do you think of it?" (Farrar, I, 233). Wedgwood decided not to join Boulton in the venture, but to compete with the metal-mounted ware by applying relief ornaments to his own vases and gilding them in imitation of ormolu. He called his imitation stone products "pebble ware."

Wedgwood imitated a variety of stones such as granite, agate, and various marbles, coloring them appropriately and using three different methods of achieving his effects. For striated stones such as marble and agate, he mixed different colored clays together in a process called "wedging," where the clays were blended—but not beyond the point where the stripes and patches of different colors remained distinct. The clays were tinted by the addition of minerals such as iron oxide, manganese oxide, or oxides of cobalt or copper. After blending and shaping, the ware was glazed with a clear lead glaze.

Wedgwood used another technique for achieving a striated effect, which he called "veining" or "marbling." The surface of the cream-colored ware was painted with slips of various colors, and while the effect was sometimes less dramatic, the problem of overmixing the colored clay bodies and producing a muddy effect was avoided. The slips were colored with the same minerals used in solid agateware.

The technique for imitating grained stones, such as granite, was to sprinkle powdered mineral colorants on the vases and then cover with lead glaze, or to sprinkle the powder onto the liquid lead-glazed surface before firing.

---

48. *Opposite page:* Vase, porphyry grey-blue glaze decoration with medallion of the three Graces, 11¾" high (29.8 cm.), mark: "WEDGWOOD & BENTLEY, ETRURIA," c. 1769-80.

While Wedgwood was modifying the old potting techniques to serve a new purpose, he was, at the same time, seeking inspiration for his new vase shapes from sources heretofore unknown in the potteries of Staffordshire. Through the generosity of his wealthy patrons, he was able to obtain antique vases from which to model, and both 17th- and 18th-century books of engravings depicting classical and Renaissance objects of art provided him with ideas.

The variegated techniques were used primarily on vases, but some variegated useful wares were also produced, although Wedgwood resisted it at first, writing on November 19, 1769: "Must we make pebble Teaware?" (Farrer, I, 311). Although Wedgwood strove for perfection in his useful ware manufacture, his creative energy seemed to direct itself more toward the ornamental, and there was a tension created between the two branches of his labors which he described to Bentley in the same letter: "We have got another Lathe up (the third) & I have committed a sad robbery upon my works at Burslem to furnish it. I have taken James Bourn to Etruria! . . . Poor Burslem —Poor Creamcolour. They tell me I sacrifice all to Etruria & Vases!" (Farrer, I, 308).

Not everyone was pleased with variegated ware vases, as a visitor to Etruria in 1771 complained: "but we know that they are not Antiques & that spoils them" (Farrer, II, 40). That seemed to be the minority opinion, however, because, as Wedgwood wrote to Bentley on May 1, 1769: "Mrs. Byerley is just return'd from London, & brings a strange acc^t of their goings on in Newport Street. No getting to the door for Coaches, nor into the rooms for Ladies & Gent^n & Vases, she says, Vases was all the cry" (Farrer, I, 261).

Although "vase madness," as Wedgwood called it, was at its height in the late 1760s and early 1770s, vases as well as other objects in variegated ware continued in high fashion throughout Wedgwood's career.

In a letter to Bentley dated September 27, 1769, Wedgwood suggested that it would be prudent for them to show only a few types of vases at one time so as not to "glut the curiosity" of their customers or offer their rivals too wide a field in which to imitate them: "By every new sort we invent, we inlarge their field of action, & give them another chance to rival us more effectually" (Farrer, I, 287). He goes on to suggest that they sell only four "species" of vases the following winter: "Blue Pebble, Variegated Pebble, Black Etruscan, & Etruscan Encaustic."

In his letters to Bentley, Wedgwood referred frequently to "blue pebble," and in a letter dated February 13, 1770, he decided to be more explicit, saying: "Pebble vases. Suppose we call those barely sprinkled with blue and ornaments gilt, granite. . . ." In the same letter, he described "variegated pebble" as being "with colours and veined" (as opposed to veined with black, which he called "veined granite"). He distinguished also between "variegated pebble" and "Egyptian pebble," the latter being "those with colours, and veined without any blue sprinkling . . ." (Meteyard, Handbook, 22).

49. Vase, decorated with blue and black lead glaze and gilded, molded and applied relief ornament, 12⁵⁄₁₆″ high (31.3 cm.), mark: "WEDGWOOD & BENTLEY ETRURIA," c. 1770-80. On August 29, 1770, Wedgwood wrote to Bentley: "Stellas book is an admirable one indeed! & the Roman Antiq⁵ is a very valuable addition to our books of Vases, many good things may be made out of both" (Farrer, I, 369). Stella's book was *Livre de Vases*, a compilation of fifty designs of ewers and vases by Jacques Stella (1596-1657). The etchings were done by Stella's niece Françoise Bouzonnet Stella (fl. 1657-67), and her sister Claudine Stella published the book in Paris before 1667.

This "blue pebble" vase with gilded masks and swags, and a fishtail top, was a literal ceramic interpretation of one of two vases decorating the title page of Stella's book. Wedgwood further dramatized it, however, by adding gilded scales to the fishtail. Wedgwood also made his plinth two or three times higher than the original and embellished the plinth with an anthemion design. The plinth is made in the Black Basalt body.

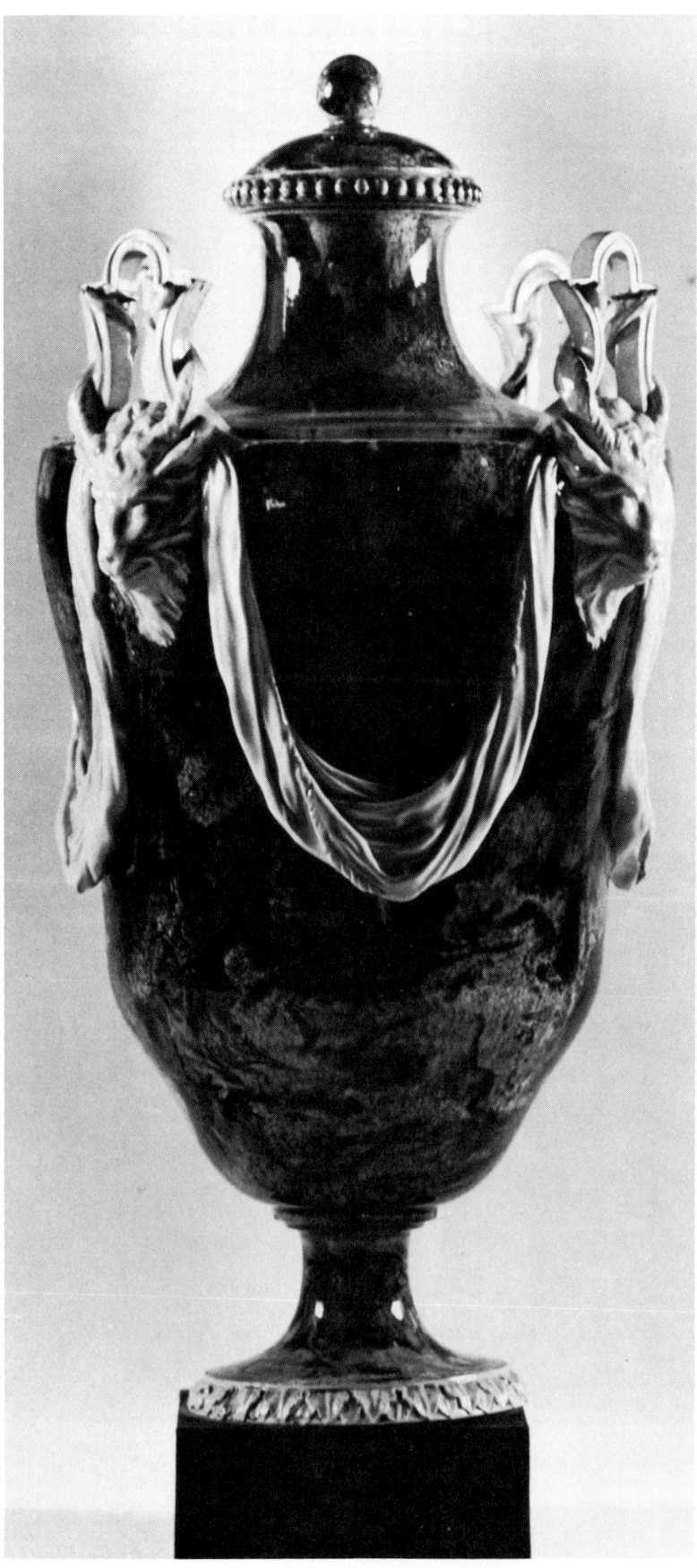

50. Vase with cover, decorated with molded and applied relief ornaments and blue, black, brown, and yellow glazes, 16 1/16" high (40.8 cm.), mark: "WEDGWOOD & BENTLEY ETRURIA" surrounding bolt, c. 1769-80. This speckled and marbled variation of the variegated or crystaline glaze fits Wedgwood's definition of "variegated pebble." The design of the vase, with goats' heads between swags, is similar to one on plate VI of della Bella's etchings. (Stefano della Bella [1610-1664] was a Florentine etcher who designed a series of vases and etched the designs on six plates that were first published in Paris about 1646. The prints were reissued as *A New Book of Vases & Urns, in 6 Leaves, By Della Bella* and bound in Robert Sayer's *Ladies Amusement; or Whole Art of Japanning Made Easy* [1760, 1762, 1771]). A cover has been added in Wedgwood's version of the vase, and the treatment of the arched finials with horns entwined around them differs slightly from della Bella's. Traces of gilding remain on the cream-colored relief ornaments.

Marbled variegated ware, or agate, was probably introduced as early as January of 1768, if indeed that is what Wedgwood was referring to in a letter dated January 3: "There is much sin to be committed in the Marble way, as you will guess by the patterns. L^d have mercy upon our old Stock say I!" (Farrer, I, 201). It was not on the market, however, until later that year.

In December of 1768 Wedgwood wrote to Bentley: "I have been at drawing two kilns this morning, a bisket & a Gloss [glaze] one. The latter is a bad one especially for Vases." Wedgwood explained that a new fireman had fired the ware too long and had ruined the vases. He continued: "The bisket oven is a good one. The small marbled Vases look delightfully, but the Gloss oven is the Purgatory, or something worse, which I am just now too polite to name, of these colours" (Farrer, I, 238). The biscuit ware referred to in the letter had already been colored, suggesting that it was solid agate. A letter dated January 27, 1776, definitely refers to solid agateware, saying ". . . when the Clays were perfectly mixt to produce a wildness & extravaganza in the Pebble, if the Workman gives the batts a twist edgways, instead of keeping them flatt when he puts them into the mould, a little stringiness is produc'd which shews the pott, instead of a finely variegated Pebble" (Farrer, II, 260).

Solid agateware can be distinguished from slip-decorated agate by identical color patterns appearing on the inside and outside of the piece, and sometimes by a break in the pattern at mold seams. Also, as is evident in plate VII (p. 69), the pattern continues over molded raised areas in a way that would be difficult to duplicate with brushed-on slip. Surface-decorated marbled ware was what Wedgwood referred to as "veining" or "marbling"; the first reference to "veining" in the correspondence is dated November 19, 1769.

51. Vase with cover, decorated with molded and incised relief ornament with brown, red, green, and white slip glazes under clear lead glaze, 9″ high (22.9 cm.), mark: "Wedgwood & Bentley," c. 1769-80. This vase differs from the solid agate one (plate VII, p. 69) in that the marbled effect is achieved not by mixing different colored clays in the body, but by painting different colored liquid clays, or slips, over the cream-colored body. The relief-ornamented handles, terminating in masks, were gilded to resemble vases fitted with metal handles, and the incised line between the shoulder and body was also gilded. The relief panels on the white stoneware plinth are decorated with paterae, which are oval or circular ornaments resembling a shallow dish of that name used in ancient Greece and Rome.

52. Pair of covered compotes, decorated with brown
and green slip glazes under clear lead glaze with molded and applied relief ornament, 5⅞" high (14.9 cm.),
mark: "WEDGWOOD & BENTLEY" on wafers, c.
1769-80. The compotes are examples of "marbled"
rather than "solid" agate. Although the robed seated
woman is a familiar finial figure in Wedgwood ware,
the use of cherubs, especially paired figures, as finials
or handles is uncommon. The plinth is of white
stoneware.

"Have you p.^d your visit yet to Ld Bessboro? I long to be molding from his Porphiry Vase" (Farrer, I, 369). This letter, which shows that Wedgwood had access to real porphyry models to copy if he wished, was written in August of 1770, but Wedgwood was thinking about the porphyry glaze as early as October of 1769 when he wrote to Bentley: "Porphiry Vases will be very Clever; but we must proceed with some method . . ." (Farrer, I, 303). By the following spring, he had started to produce it, writing to Bentley on May 12, 1770: "We shall send you some Green Porphiry Vases, Gilt, but I hope to make some true Porphiry, ungilt Vases soon, if you dare risque their spoiling the sale of your stock on hand" (Farrer, I, 345).

While the term "porphyry" in contemporary usage refers to rock texture rather than color, Samuel Johnson in his Dictionary of the English Language, published in 1755, defines porphyry as "Marble of a particular kind" and uses as one of his illustrative citations, "'Consider the red and white colours in porphyre . . .' Locke." So that by "true porphyry" Wedgwood probably meant an imitation of the dark red or purple porphyry found in Egypt and much used in Roman ornaments. The minerals that produced a red glaze, however, were far more difficult to control in the kiln than the ingredients of the green glaze, which is probably why "true porphyry" wasn't developed first.

The porphyry glaze was achieved by the application of ground mineral oxides (probably manganese or a combination of cobalt and manganese) to the translucent colored glaze to gain a speckled effect. The depth of color was controlled by the density of the sprinkling. Other variations, such as the running of the glaze on parts of the vases, were more difficult to control. Plate VI (p. 68) illustrates a candlestick vase of green porphyry. There are no traces of gilding on the laurel and berry festoons and mask-head handle terminals. They have been glazed with the translucent green glaze, but sprinkling has been avoided on these areas.

53. Oil lamps and candle holder, decorated with molded and applied relief ornament, blue-green and black
lead glazes, c. 1769-80. *Left,* 7½" (19 cm.), mark:
"Wedgwood & Bentley"; *center,* 9½" (24.1 cm.), mark:
"WEDGWOOD & BENTLEY" around bolt; *right,*
8¼" (21 cm.), mark: "WEDGWOOD & BENTLEY"
around bolt. The pieces on the left and in the center
are oil lamps. They would have been filled with fuel
(the decorative covers are removeable), and wicks
would have fitted inside the three pipes in each, the
outside ends of which can be seen in the photograph.
Remarkably, the fragile pipes are still intact. The floral
finials on the tripod lamp and the scroll-handled vase
served also as candle sockets. They would both have
been fitted with stoppers to give a finished appearance
when not being used as candle holders.

I. Jasper Medusa medallion, 5″ diameter (12.7 cm.), mark: "WEDGWOOD & BENTLEY," c. 1774-80.

II. *Above:* Early cream-ware. *Bottom row, left to right:* Tea canister with lid, 5⁷⁄₁₆″ high (13.8 cm.), unmarked, c. 1760-74; Tea canister, 4³⁄₁₆″ high (10.6 cm.), mark: "wedgwood," c. 1770-74; Pineapple-shaped cream jug with lid, 5³⁄₈″ high (13.6 cm.), unmarked, c. 1762-66. *Top row, left to right:* Cauliflower-shaped cream jug with lid, 5¾″ high (14.6 cm.), unmarked, c. 1763-70; Tea canister, 6″ high (15.2 cm.), unmarked, c. 1759-66; Rouletted teapot in the shape of a melon, 3½″ high (8.9 cm.), unmarked, c. 1762-66.

III. *Right:* Queen's Ware potpourri with relief and enamel-painted decoration, 13″ high (33 cm.), mark: "Wedgwood," c. 1770-1800.

IV. *Above:* Cane Ware teapot with enamel-painted decoration, 4″ high (10.2 cm.), mark: "WEDG-WOOD," c. 1780-1800.

V. *Left:* Queen's Ware jug with enamel-painted decoration, 8¹⁄₁₆″ high (20.5 cm.), mark: "WEDG-WOOD," 1790.

VI. Variegated por-
phyry candlestick
vase, 7$\frac{1}{16}$″ high (17.9
cm.), mark: "Wedg-
wood & Bentley," c.
1770-80.

VII. Variegated solid
agate vase, 15⅜″ high
(39.1 cm.), mark:
"Wedgwood & Bent-
ley," c. 1769-80.

VIII. *Above*: Queen's Ware sauce tureen with enamel-painted decoration, 8⅞" long (22.5 cm.), mark: "WEDGWOOD," c. 1770-1800.

IX. *Opposite*: Pearl Ware fitted castor frame with blue underglaze decoration, 6⅞" wide (17.5 cm.), mark: "WEDGWOOD" on frame, one castor, c. 1779-1800.

X. Bronzed Black
Basalt lions, 7⅞″ long
(20 cm.), mark:
"WEDGWOOD," c.
1780-1800.

XI. Encaustic-painted
Black Basalt plaque,
7⁵⁄₁₆ x 10³⁄₁₆″ (18.6 x
25.9 cm.), unmarked,
c. 1769-90.

3. Pearl Ware

As to the Blanching of our ware in general, when that step is absolutely necessary I hope it may be done. . . .

Wedgwood to Bentley
March 5, 1774

Although Wedgwood had been considering the advisability of producing a white-bodied earthenware at least as early as 1765 and was conducting "Experiments for Porcelain, or at least—a new Earthenware" by 1767 (Farrer, I, 168), the disadvantages seemed to have outweighed the advantages until, in all probability, his decision to capitalize on the prevailing predilection for underglaze-blue decorated porcelain led him to introduce the Pearl Ware body in 1779.

Pearl Ware is whiter than creamware, made so by the use of fine kaolinic Cornish clay in the body and the addition to the glaze of cobalt oxide, which acts like laundry blueing to whiten the glaze. The ware was not called Pearl Ware in the 18th century; Wedgwood referred to it as "pearl white." When he first reported its development to Bentley, on February 25, 1779, Wedgwood wrote: "Settled my white body and glaze (Pray give me a name for it . . .)" (Finer, 229), and on June 19 of the same year, he followed with: "I thank her majesty for the honor she has done to the *Pearl White* . . ." (Finer, 236).

Several factors delayed Wedgwood's decision to manufacture white ware. One was the greater cost of producing it. As Wedgwood explained to Bentley on July 2, 1770: "I have given over the thoughts of making any other color but Queens ware. The white ware wo^d be a great deal dearer, & I apprehend not much better liked . . ." (Farrer, I, 352). Higher costs would have probably resulted from the necessity of transporting raw materials from Cornwall to Staffordshire, and from increased fuel expenses, because high kiln temperatures were required to produce the desired whiteness and hardness of body. The possibility of producing a ware that "would be esteemed a degradation of *cream-colour* into *white stone ware*, rather than an improvement of it into Porcelain" (Finer, 121) had also to be reckoned with; and that problem was further complicated by the necessity of avoiding firing the ware to the point where it fused into a translucent body that would be considered porcelain, for a Bristol porcelain maker named Richard Champion held a patent for making porcelain out of the Cornish ingredients. Finally, Wedgwood had misgivings about introducing a white ware that might destroy his Queen's Ware business. That fear turned out to be unfounded. Queen's Ware and Pearl White ware coexisted successfully throughout Wedgwood's lifetime and afterward.

Despite his misgivings, Wedgwood kept the possibility of producing white ware open, asking on December 30, 1775 whether he "should be content still with the good old Creamcolor, painted & varied in every way we can invent. Or whether I should have a tryal in earnest at Porcelain, or white ware . . ." (Farrer, II, 253). Evidently Bentley urged Wedgwood to try white ware or porcelain (the Champion patent notwithstanding), for on January 14, 1776, Wedgwood wrote to Bentley: "But for usefull China, or such a whiteware as you mention I must beg a longer time." And ten days later he added: "I have given you my idea of the best plan for making perfect *Porcelain* with uniform success, and it is the plan I intend to proceed upon as time will permit, but I may probably make a *white ware* for Painting before the other plan is perfected into Manufacture" (Finer, 190).

The painting that Wedgwood envisioned was probably blue in imitation of the blue-and-white porcelain imported from China that had partially eclipsed in popularity even English porcelain wares. Just two years prior to the introduction of Pearl Ware, an auction sale of the possessions of

Sir Thomas Robinson, an acknowledged leader in London society, revealed that he owned no fewer than three Oriental blue-and-white table services, one of which consisted of eight oblong dishes, three dozen plates, fifteen soups, a terrine, a cover and dish, two boats, and two salts.

To serve his affluent and influential customers, Wedgwood almost had to enter the blue-and-white arena, and with a whiter ware than Queen's Ware, blue painting on cream-colored ware having a very different appearance even if it was applied under the glaze. That competition with blue-and-white porcelain motivated him is suggested in a letter from Wedgwood to Bentley dated March 8, 1779, in which he says: "to give the brat a name you may set a cream-color plate & one of the best blue & white ones before you, & suppose the one you are to name another degree whiter & finer still, but not transparent, & consequently *not china* for transparency will be the general test of china—Under this idea you may give it a name" (Farrer, II, 484). Another letter dated the following August 6th states: "Your idea of the *cream color* having the merit of an original, & the *pearl white* being consider'd as an imitation of some of the blue & white fabriques, either earthenware or porcelain is perfectly right . . ." (Farrer, II, 503).

The wares to which both men referred were probably tin-glazed earthenware and "scratch-blue" salt-glazed stoneware that was decorated, as Simeon Shaw said, "in rude imitation of the unmeaning scenery on foreign porcelain. . . ."

The technique of underglaze decoration (which is more durable in use than decoration applied over the glaze) was developed in China four or five hundred years before its popularity incited competition in Staffordshire. It was brought to stylistic perfection in the 15th century (during the Ming dynasty), and, although underglaze red was attempted at that time, it was largely abandoned because of the difficulty in controlling the pigment for red in the kiln. Cobalt blue was easier to use and remained virtually the only underglaze color until nearly the end of the 18th century.

Although blue was the earliest and (to judge from survivals and archaeological evidence) the most popular underglaze color in Pearl Ware, green and purple were also popular. Pearl Ware was painted in overglaze colors as well, and in underglaze slips of various colors.

Pearl Ware can be most easily distinguished from Queen's Ware by the bluish appearance of the glaze, particularly where it pools in crevices. The pooling of the Queen's Ware glaze typically has a greenish cast.

Although Wedgwood did not develop the Pearl Ware body and glaze until well over a decade after neoclassical trends began to dominate his production, some Pearl Ware pieces were closer in spirit to the more traditionally oriented incised salt-glazed stoneware decoration known as scratch blue in which cobalt oxide was rubbed into incised decoration. Potters produced scratch blue from the first through the third quarters of the 18th century, to judge from dated examples. Pearl Ware objects indebted to the earlier tradition for both shape and arrangement of decorative elements, as well as for style of decoration, are known.

54. Teapot, blue decoration painted under the glaze, 5½" high (14 cm.), mark: "wedgwood," c. 1779-1800. The random floral decoration is reminiscent of scratch-blue salt-glazed stoneware, although the decoration on such ware tended to be conventionalized, while the convolvulus depicted on the teapot is more or less realistically rendered.

55. Flask, molded and incised relief and blue painted underglaze decoration, gilding over the glaze, 6½″ high (16.5 cm.), mark: "Wedgwood," c. 1779-1800. The City Museum, Stoke-on-Trent, houses a scratch-blue salt-glazed stoneware flask similar to this Pearl Ware example in that flowers surround the circular panel, and the owner's name (and date of 1775) is inscribed—also at an oblique angle—within the panel. The shape and concentrically-banded decorative arrangement of both flasks are reminiscent of a Greek or Roman terra-cotta bottle shape. The relief ornamental elements of the Pearl Ware flask—laurel wreaths, ribbons with pendant flowers, and beaded molding—are classically inspired as well.

The name of the owner "R WEDGWOOD" is stamped with block letters and colored blue on the obverse, while on the side not pictured, the Wedgwood factory mark is stamped in a centered, smaller circular panel with beaded and molded frame. The panel on the back is surrounded with a laurel wreath in higher relief than that on the front, and there are ribbons with pendant flowers extending on the sides to the beaded border which surrounds the painted blue flowers. Traces of gilding remain on the relief decoration.

Wedgwood used his current Queen's Ware shapes for Pearl Ware production as well. Objects for general household use as well as table services were made in Pearl Ware just as they were in Queen's Ware, and the Pearl Ware services also enjoyed royal patronage. Wedgwood's letter to Bentley discussing the Queen's patronage, quoted earlier (p. 73), reported that "the dishes etc. to complete the service are gone to-day. . . ." The decoration, particularly in early Pearl Ware was mostly confined to monochrome painted under the glaze. The floral decoration on the Pearl Ware teapot, ewer, plate, and condiment bottles (figs. 54, 59, 60 and plate IX) are so similar in style that they may be by the same hand. Since the plate appears to have been made as a commemorative object in 1781, the possibility that all four objects were made near the beginning of Pearl Ware production is suggested.

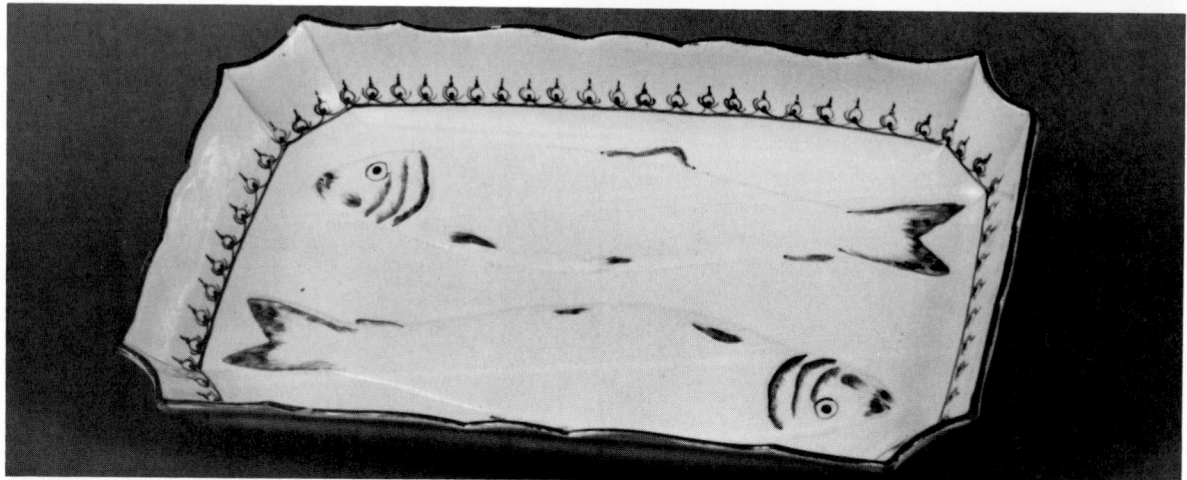

56. Argyle with cover, blue decoration painted under the glaze, 5¼" high (13.3 cm.), mark: "wedgwood," c. 1779-1800. Argyles were used to keep gravy warm with hot water, which was poured into the lipped spout. A false bottom located beneath the pouring spout separated the gravy from the heat source, and a steam hole in the cover kept condensation from watering the gravy. The "spiked onion" decorative motif is sometimes called the "mared" pattern, but the source of this term – and for the term *argyle* for that matter – is obscure. The pattern was illustrated in the first pattern book (1774), but the name *mared* is first known to have appeared in a 1920s Wedgwood ware catalogue. The term *argyle* is said to be connected to the fourth or fifth Duke of Argyll, members of the Scottish clan Campbell. The form first appeared in the 18th century.

The top edge of the warmer is painted blue, and the pigment can be seen to have run above and to the left of the handle. This would have occurred during the firing – a process more difficult to control in the underglaze decorative technique. Although it is tempting to suggest a date early in Pearl Ware production because of the fault, it may not be an accurate assumption because Wedgwood is known to have marketed "seconds."

57. Herring dish, molded relief and underglaze blue painted decoration, 11⅞" long (30.2 cm.), mark: "WEDGWOOD," c. 1779-1800. For the great variety of fish and shellfish that was served at the tables of Wedgwood's contemporaries, the potter produced a variety of casseroles and platters, but with the exception of waterzootjes (a Flemish fish stew), only that long-time staple of the English diet, herring, had a special dish manufactured for its service. Wedgwood's fish dishes, as illustrated in the 1802 shape book, were long thin oval platters. In addition, the first Queen's Ware catalogue (1774) stated that fish drainers could be supplied for all oval or round dishes. Herring dishes, on the other hand, were oblong with scalloped corners. Of the eight styles illustrated in the 1802 shape book, half were decorated with one or two fish that stretched the length of the platter – either "single" or "double", as they were listed in the first catalogue.

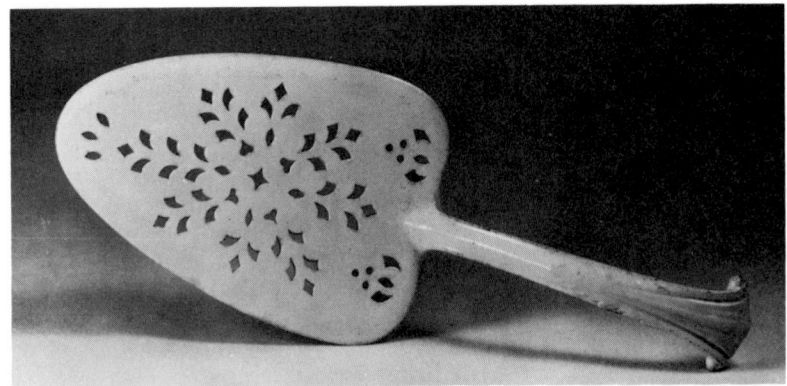

58. Fish slice, perforated decoration, 11⅜" long (28.9 cm.), mark: "WEDG-WOOD," c. 1779-1800. The implement was called a fish trowel in the 1802 shape book, in which the form is first illustrated. It was pierced so that the drippings would remain in the platter when the fish was served.

59. Ewer, molded relief and underglaze blue painted decoration, 11¼" high (28.6 cm.), mark: "WEDGWOOD," c. 1779-1800. "Wash-Hand Basons and Ewers, several sorts," are listed in the first Queen's Ware catalogue, and in the 1790-95 edition of that catalogue a similar helmet-shaped ewer without molded decoration is illustrated. The fluted model was in production by the time the 1802 shape book was compiled, but it was not illustrated with shell edge. A somewhat similar ewer, however, was offered either plain or with shell edge, suggesting that the fluted and shell-edged combination—a jaunty union of the neoclassical with the rococo—was no longer in production. The shell edge, usually painted in blue or green, seems to have been the most popular Pearl Ware border. The painting on this example, with the brush strokes drawn from the edges toward the center, highlights and conforms to the molded ridges and grooves of the pattern, although decorators sometimes cut corners, using the less time-consuming method of holding the brush to the edge of the plate while it revolved, producing an arbitrary stripe instead of a soft, feathery look. (*See* fig. 14.)

Although underglaze blue decoration predom-
inated in early Pearl Ware, Wedgwood did
branch out into using other colors. The color of
the Pearl Ware body, whiter than Queen's Ware,
provided a more neutral palette for the wide
range of colors available in overglaze enamels.

60. Plate, decorated in blue and brown underglaze colors, 9¾" in diameter (24.8 cm.), mark: "WEDGWOOD," 1781. On the back of the plate is an inscription painted under the glaze in blue, which reads: "S+E 1781." The fact that it is painted under the glaze indicates not only the date the piece was decorated but also that the plate was intended to be a commemorative piece, in contrast to pieces decorated in stock patterns and then personalized subsequently, because, while overglaze decoration can be added and fired onto the object at any time after the piece is glazed, underglaze decoration cannot. Several aspects of the decoration suggest that it might have been done by an apprentice decorator. The bordering varies in thickness and can be seen to run over itself at the upper left. Also, while the painter seems to have been practiced at painting flowers and insects, he was less skilled at bird painting – or possibly the birds were painted by another decorator.

61. Teapot, decorated over the glaze in polychrome enamels, 5" high (12.7 cm.), mark: "WEDGWOOD," c. 1779-1800. The parapet-shape teapot was illustrated in the Queen's Ware catalogue of 1790-95 along with a cylindrically-shaped one and an elongated round one. The spouts on all three are S-curved, while the spout on this teapot may be what Wedgwood's order book referred to as a "cannon spout." The olpe or high-arched handle is the same as that illustrated in the catalogue. The enameled painting shows a shepherd piping a tune for two young women. The same threesome is shown on the reverse side with the man reading to the women. Grapevines surround the paintings, and a floral decoration is painted on the inside and outside of the parapet.

The subject of eliminating rococo elements from his work cropped up repeatedly in Wedgwood's correspondence with Bentley during the autumn of 1769—although not in those words, the term "rococo" not having been coined until after Wedgwood's death. On September 13 Wedgwood wrote: "I left London with a full resolution to simplify, and you shall soon be convinced I was in earnest; as a first essay I have discarded the twiggen and flowered handles from the Terrines. . . ." He adds, however, that he would retain those elements on baskets (and presumably other objects) where "their apparent lightness, and real strength, and their similarity to the work of the vessels will induce me to retain them, but I am not determined, and should be glad of your opinion . . ." (Finer, 77).

The thoroughly rococo scrolled leafage and asymmetrically-tilted floral finials that remained on trellis-work Pearl Ware shapes (which could not have been produced sooner than ten years after the above letters were written) indicate that Wedgwood's opinion prevailed. This is most visible in the fitted caster frame illustrated in plate IX (p. 71). The specifically Greek fret borders that appear on this and other forms inject a neoclassical element, however, into the overall rococo designs.

That these and numerous other rococo designs remained in production along with the sternly neoclassical forms that comprised the greater part of Wedgwood's work serves to exemplify his determination to attract and retain customers of all tastes, from the conservative and traditionally-minded to those in the vanguard of fashion.

62. Sweetmeat dish, molded and painted blue decoration under the glaze, 7¾" wide (19.7 cm.), mark: "WEDGWOOD," c. 1779-1800. Wedgwood illustrated this form in the first Queen's Ware catalogue, calling it a sweetmeat dish or "croquant," a word that not only explains the derivation of the pottery form, but also illustrates the debt that potters owed to pastry chefs of earlier times when foods transformed into extravagantly fanciful creations were themselves the ornament of the table. After potters had started translating the elegant displays into more durable ceramic objects, Horace Walpole is reported to have noted the change: "Confectioners found their trade moulder away while toymen and china shops were the only purveyors of the last stage of polite entertainments." The croquante, used primarily for decorative purposes, was a pastry prepared by covering a mold with strips of almond paste arranged in a trellis or latticework fashion. The structure was baked, glazed with apricot marmalade, then set upon a decorated pastry base which was filled with rounds of puff paste stuffed with preserved cherries. The earthenware version would have served the same decorative function, holding pastries or other sweetmeats.

The jelly core mold or "pyramid," as it was called at the time it was produced, was a novel table ornament calling for collaboration between cook and potter. The mold was filled by inserting the decorated core inside the cover and pouring liquid gelatin through the holes into the space between the core and cover. After the jelly solidified, the cover was removed to reveal flowers, landscapes, or other designs shimmering through a coat of clear jelly.

It is not known when Wedgwood began production of the molds, but that they existed by 1782 and that Wedgwood was producing them before 1788 are confirmed by two contemporary references. Parson Woodforde's diary entry for March 28, 1782, records that dinner with a neighboring county family consisted of several main courses, including "a very pretty Pyramid of Jelly in the Centre, a Landscape appearing thro' the Jelly, a new Device and brought from London . . ." (Beresford, II, 15). Thomas Byerley, Wedgwood's nephew, was managing the London office when he wrote to his uncle on March 18, 1788: "You will remember the jelly pyramid that you make double—the inner one we paint upon—the smallest size of this sort 8½ inches. As it is a side dish we want some other pyramid to stand opposite to it—that is to be a comparison. It should be as high but not of the same form and may be single because this is not wanted to be painted. The base may be octagon or as may be more convenient to you" (Duff-Dunbar, 4).

Evidently, Wedgwood produced more than one size of at least one jelly core mold shape. They are known to have been made in three forms—the conical, the obelisk, and the wedge shape with canted corners. Byerley may have been referring to either of the last two shapes.

63. Jelly core mold and cover, polychrome enamel decoration over the glaze, 10″ high (25.4 cm.), mark: "WEDGWOOD," c. 1781-1800. The cover of the mold is shaped in a stepped, fluted, and gadrooned design that would further enrich the colorful table decoration. Jelly core mold covers were not all molded in relief designs; some were plain.

64. Jelly core mold, polychrome enamel and gilded overglaze decoration, 5″ high (12.7 cm.), mark: "WEDGWOOD," and inscribed on the bottom "Iron Bridge at Wearmouth, Helmsly Bridge Yorkshire," c. 1796-1800. In 1796 the Wear River was spanned at its mouth in Sunderland, Durhamshire, by what was then the longest single-span cast-iron bridge in the world. This jelly core mold might have been painted to celebrate that event, for on one side is shown the high modern bridge with fully-rigged sailing vessels speeding under it, and people on the shore watching. On the reverse side is depicted, by contrast, a traditional scene: a low stone bridge with a horseman walking over it and a fisherman angling in the quiet stream. The mold is wedge shaped with canted corners on the base. The cover would probably not have been fluted.

One of the reasons Wedgwood probably purchased ware from other potters was to satisfy requests from his regular customers for goods that he did not ordinarily produce. Such was probably the case with the earthenware statuettes known today as Staffordshire figures. There are no records, correspondence, or molds to indicate that Wedgwood ever did make such objects, but some marked with the factory name "Wedgwood," or with "Wedgwood" followed by a dot, do exist.

These were probably purchased from Ralph and Enoch Wood and perhaps others. In addition to stylistic similarities which link some marked Wedgwood figures to the Woods, there is documentary evidence that they did sell their ware to Wedgwood. An invoice exists for decorated figures, flower pots, and cups supplied to Wedgwood by Ralph Wood, Burslem. The invoice is dated 1783 and is receipted by Wood January 26, 1784. Frank Falkner quotes a letter from Ralph Wood to Thomas Wedgwood (manager of the useful works) dated October 19, 1784: "I should esteem it a great favour to settle the Note I delivered with the Flowerpots by the Week End . . . my Necessities oblige me or should not have ask'd so soon, at the same time I thank you for your goodness in promoting my Trade, hoping I may still be favored with your future orders in my Way. . . ."

Ralph Wood and his cousin Enoch, who had started a potting manufactory on his own in 1784, were in business together by 1786, according to Tunnicliffe's Survey of Staffordshire. They were described as making all kinds of useful and ornamental earthenware. The partnership had probably ended by 1790, according to Falkner, and Ralph Wood died in 1795. Enoch continued in business until about 1846. Wedgwood himself continued to patronize the firm into the 1790s.

65. Staffordshire figure, decorated over the glaze in black, brown, yellow, pink, and green, 9¾" high (24.8 cm.), mark: "WEDG-WOOD," attributed to Ralph Wood, the younger, c. 1785-95. The figure is impressed with the name "Simon" on the pedestal and is decorated in overglaze enamel colors, a process that superseded the more limited palettes of colored-glaze or underglaze decoration of Staffordshire figures and is thought to have come into practice near the end of the 18th century. The mold for the figure was probably made in 1783 or shortly thereafter, for its mold number (96), which was included in Falkner's list and description of known Ralph Wood figures, followed numbers 94 and 95, a stag and a hind, which were included in the aforementioned 1783 invoice. Both underglaze and overglaze decorated figures of Simon were described in Falkner's list. The figure's position on the list (96) would suggest that the mold was produced shortly before the practice of overglaze decoration came into style because all figures from molds numbered 99 or higher had overglaze decoration or were undecorated. "Simple Simon" was a popular 18th-century nursery rhyme character.

66. Staffordshire figure, decorated over the glaze in polychrome enamel, 21¾" high (55.2 cm.), mark: "WEDGWOOD.," attributed to Enoch Wood, c. 1790-92. The attribution of the figure to Enoch Wood is based on the existence of figures of "Fortitude" marked "E. Wood" and apparently made from identical molds or from the same one. Falkner stated that Enoch Wood's great-grandson also owned one that had descended in the family. This model of "Fortitude" descended in the Parry family of Philadelphia, and, according to family history, it was brought to America by Edward Parry, born in Wales, arriving first in Portsmouth, New Hampshire, in 1792, and subsequently settling in Philadelphia.

Vases to hold cut flowers, either with or without inserts with holes in them to separate the branches or stems, were called by Wedgwood "dressing flower pots" or "bough pots". He perceived that neither in use nor in placement within the house were such "pots" interchangeable with vases, and he wrote to Bentley on the subject July 25, 1772: "Vases are furniture for a Chimney piece — Bough pots for a hearth, under a Slab or Marble Table; I think they never can be used one instead of the other, & I apprehend one reason why we have not made our dressing flowerpots to please has been by adapting them for Chimney pieces where I think they do not place any pots dress'd with flowers. If I am wrong in this idea I should be glad to be set right as it is of consequence in forming these articles to know where they place them" (Farrer, II, 84). He also asked Bentley in a letter written two months later whether to call them "Beau pots" or "Bough pots" (Farrer, II, 98). In August he had referred to them as "Bow pots" (Farrer, II, 89).

67. *Below (left):* Bough pot, incised and applied relief, and underglaze brown and black colored slip decoration, 11⅞″ high (30.2 cm.), mark: "WEDGWOOD," c. 1779-1800. Although molded vases were more economical to produce than those with engine-turned or applied-relief decoration, Wedgwood still continued to produce individually-decorated earthenware vases as well as molded ones. The fluting on this object is engine turned; the festoons are molded separately in molds for small elements of applied decoration called sprig molds, and applied by hand or "sprigged" on. The incised, diced decoration may either be engine turned or pressed into the vase with a metal tool. John Wyke of Liverpool, who made metal punches for Wedgwood's pierced work, also made tools, which were probably roulettes, for this purpose. W. B. Honey, in *Wedgwood Ware,* illustrates a bough pot somewhat similar to this with a domed lid on it. Presumably the lid could be removed to add water so that the flower arrangement wouldn't be disturbed by removing the perforated insert, or perhaps the flower arranger would put a bough in the spout.

68. *Below:* Flower vase, molded and decorated with tan colored slip under the glaze, black stoneware base, 12¼″ high (31.1 cm.), mark: "WEDGWOOD," c. 1779-1800. This column vase is illustrated in the Wedgwood factory pattern books of ornamental ware that were still in use at Etruria in 1920. Although mold seams are not always visible on a well-finished piece, one can sometimes detect that a piece is molded by seeing or feeling the outside pattern reflected on the inside of the object. A thrown piece will be smooth on the inside.

George Stubbs (1724-1806) was one of England's preeminent painters of horses and hunting scenes, employing the traditional medium of oil on canvas, but in the late 1760s and 1770s he became interested in the use of enamel colors and started working with fired enamels on a copper base. By 1777 he had approached Wedgwood about making earthenware tablets for painting, possibly to offset the weight of working with large pieces of copper. Wedgwood started to make the biscuitware tablets for Stubbs in the autumn of 1777, and by May 30, 1779, he wrote Bentley with confidence: "We shall be able now to make them with certainty and success of the size of the 3 in this invoice and I hope soon to say as far as 30 inches, perhaps ultimately up to 36 inches by 24.... If Mr. Stubbs succeeds he will be followed by others to which he does not seem to have the least objection, but rather wishes for it; and if the oil painters too should use them they may become a considerable object" (Finer, 234).

Stubbs visited Etruria in the summer of 1780 to paint the Wedgwood family in oil on canvas. The painting was intended partly to pay Stubbs's bill for the earthenware tablets.

69. Vase with cover, 22" high (55.9 cm.), mark: "Wedgwood & Bentley," 1780. During the summer of 1780, when Stubbs visited Etruria to paint the Wedgwood family portrait, Wedgwood thought of having the artist try his hand at painting on vases. He wrote to Bentley on August 7, 1780: "We have been considering, and reconsidering some subjects besides tablets for Mr. Stubbs to paint in enamel, and are now making some large jarrs for that purpose" (Finer, 254.) Six days later Wedgwood addressed Bentley again: "I was telling Mr. Stubs that our vases would sell if they were painted with free masterly sketches but that our stippleing method was tedious beyond all bearing. He was of the same opinion, & will try his hand upon half a doz^n jarrs but these are only for himself & friends" (Farrer, II, 587).

There is strong evidence that this jar is one of those made for Stubbs. It is not a characteristic Wedgwood & Bentley product either in its ovoid unfooted shape, or in its lack of ornamentation. In another letter, Wedgwood implied that the jars were thrown, and he described them as large. This is a thrown jar, and it is among the largest of Wedgwood's vases. The fact that it is in the Pearl Ware body, rather than in Queen's Ware, is also noteworthy. Wedgwood would no doubt have used the more neutral body for a "canvas."

4. Black Basalt

> I am not without some little pain for our Nobility & Gentry . . . for what with the fine things in Gold, Silver & Steel from Soho, the almost miraculous magnificence of Mr. Coxes Exhibition, & the Glare of the Derby & other China shews—What heads or Eyes could stand all this dazzleing profusion of riches & ornament if something was not provided for their relief, to give them at proper intervals a little relaxation, & repose. Under this humble idea then, I have some hopes for our black, Etruscan, & Grecian vases . . . ."
>
> Wedgwood to Bentley
> April 11, 1772

Just as the introduction of Sadler's transfer-printing process coincided with Wedgwood's improvement in the creamware body—to the mutual benefit of both—so the flowering of the neoclassical impulse in English cultural life came at a time when Wedgwood had brought to perfection a ceramic body ideally suited to the interpretation of classical themes and designs. For it was while, as M. H. Grant states, "Friezes, urns, vases, fragments of tombs and pavements, flowed into this country with every tide," that Wedgwood's versatile imagination transformed "Egyptian Black," a traditional Staffordshire stoneware product, into "Etruscan," an ornamental ware that would subsequently be branded "Black Basalt" and that little resembled the familiar stoneware that had been produced throughout the century.

The colorant for Egyptian Black occurred naturally in a sediment from the drainage of neighboring coal deposits. According to Simeon Shaw, Wedgwood did use this ingredient, called locally "car," but by both mechanical and chemical experimentation he improved the color and produced a denser, finer-grained product. Of far greater importance, both to Wedgwood and to ceramic history, was his further departure from the casual design methods of Staffordshire. For while his efforts in variegated ornamental ware were directed toward meeting competition by emulating the semi-precious stone vases currently in fashion, and his design sources were the same books that the architects and interior designers were also using, he was trying actually to make reproductions of *antique* vases in the new black body, using the ancient vases themselves or pictures of them as models. The headings in the ornamental ware catalogues carefully distinguished between the two approaches, referring to the variegated vases as "Ornamental Vases of *antique Forms*," and the Black Basalt vases as "*Antique Vases*, Urns, etc. of Black Porcelain or Artificial Basaltes" [emphasis added].

This scholarly approach to design was an entirely new idea in Staffordshire, and Wedgwood was, for a time, alone in the effort. As he said to Bentley in a letter dated April 9, 1769: "I have got the start of my Bretheren in the article of V__s [vases] farther than I ever did in anything else . . ." (Farrer, I, 258).

The first Black Basalt ornamental wares were put on the market during the summer of 1768. They were unpainted black vases, which Wedgwood called "Etruscan," instructing his London

---

70. *Opposite page:* Bust of Robert Boyle, 18″ high (45.7 cm.), mark: "WEDGWOOD & BENTLEY," c. 1776-80.

staff to do so as well, referring in a note, dated September 3, to "the black (say Etruscan) vases sent the 27th" (Meteyard, *Life*, II, 69). At the same time, he sent to Liverpool "2 Etruscan bronze Vases" which Bentley was to give to a Miss Tarleton "as an offering of first fruits" (Farrer, I, 225).

The somewhat glossy appearance of the new ware, which Wedgwood likened to antique bronze, was completely different in effect from the traditional Staffordshire black stoneware product and had been arrived at through several years of experimentation. The effect had been achieved through alteration of the body itself rather than any surface coating. As Wedgwood explained to William Cox, his London manager, in a letter dated August 31, 1768: "Shew but a pair or two of the Bronze Vases at a time, if the price is found fault with they cannot be lower; I am really and truly a loser by them as I have not one in 6 good, the nature of the bronze clay to take a polish is so very delicate [·] NB the polish is natural to the Composition and is given in burning, they are never oiled etc." (Finer, 67).

By the following year, however, Wedgwood had evidently decided to improve on nature by applying to the ware a simulated bronze coating that contained gold powder. On October 30, 1769, he wrote to Bentley: "Say nothing of the Bronze Encaustic to anybody. It is accomplish'd—I bring it with me, & it will do your heart good to look at it. Trouble not yourself about the gold powder, that business is finished likewise—you shall have satisfaction in both" (Farrer, I, 305).

While he was pleased with the result of the new bronzing process, Wedgwood also feared that if the vases on which it was employed were not properly priced—more expensively than the uncoated vases—people might not recognize their superior value, "nay, may even be wicked enough to think of *black Potts* whilst they are looking at them" (Farrer, I, 238).

Wedgwood took out a patent in November of 1769 for the bronzing process and for a process that he had started two months earlier of painting on the black ware in thin mat colors that approximated the appearance of ancient Greek red-figured black vases. Some of these vases were being brought back to England from excavation sites in Italy, and familiarity with them spread among the cognoscenti in England through the publication of Sir William Hamilton's beautiful hand-colored, four-volume *Collection of Etruscan, Greek and Roman Antiquities* (1766-67).

The processes by which the ancient Greek ceramicists achieved their effects were unknown in the 18th century—unknown, in fact, until the mid-20th century, when sophisticated scientific equipment finally made analysis of the ceramics possible. The Greek red-figured wares were made with redware clay. The figures were depicted in the actual clay body and were surrounded by a slip coating made of clay similar to the body clay, but treated in a way that made it fuse at a lower temperature than the body, so that in the complicated three-part firing process, the figures, which were unglazed, turned red, then black, then red again, while the glaze turned red, then black, and stayed black in the third and final stage of the firing.

Wedgwood had seen Hamilton's book before he started to paint his vases, but he had not seen the actual antique vases. After he saw them, which was in September of 1769, he reported to Bentley: "The Etruscan Vases are arrived—I see how the mechanical part of the glaze & painting is perform'd, all which may be faithfullly imitated at any time" (Farrer, I, 297). He didn't imitate it, however. Instead he continued the decorating method he had already started, which was entirely different from the Greek method. He first fired the body to the biscuit state, which was black. Then he painted the red figures onto the black body in ceramic paints of his own invention, that could be applied thinly and accurately and had a mat rather than a glossy finish. Eighteenth-century ceramic painting enamels up to this point had tended to be glossy and to "run out of Drawing," as Wedgwood expressed it.

Although his method differed from that of the ancient Greeks (and Wedgwood knew that it did, distinguishing between "the true Etruscan manner" and his "Encaustic" method in a 1769 letter to Bentley), for advertising purposes he claimed to have rediscovered it, stating in the ornamental ware catalogues: "The Art of Painting Vases in the Manner of the Etruscans has been lost for Ages; and was supposed, by the ingenious Author of the Dissertations on Sir *William*

Hamilton's Museum [collection], to have been lost in Pliny's Time. The proprietors of this manufactory have been so happy as to rediscover and revive this long lost Art; so as to have given Satisfaction to the most critical Judges; by inventing a Set of Encaustic Colours, essentially different from common Enamel Colours, both in their Nature and Effects, . . . and by the Discovery of a Composition proper to receive them."

Although he used the term *encaustic* to describe his paints, Wedgwood did not use the word in the same sense that Pliny and such 18th-century writers on the art of the ancients as Count de Caylus, used it, meaning to paint with heated pigmented wax. Caylus's book, *Recueil d'Antiquites Egyptiennes, Etrusques, Grecques, Romaines et Gauloises*, which had been published between 1752 and 1767 and had made quite a stir in English art and literary circles, had made the word fashionable, so that Wedgwood would have wished to use the voguish term. Knowing, however, that Caylus had been mistaken in thinking that the technique was used on pottery, Wedgwood carefully distinguished in his catalogue between Caylus's explanations and his own, saying "The ingenious Experiments of Count Caylus to make *encaustic Pictures* had the same Object as ours, in Point of Taste; but his Use of *Wax* in compliance with the Letter of *Pliny*, had he succeeded ever so well in the Execution, must have rendered his Pictures very liable to be injured by any considerable Degree of Heat to which they might have been exposed; and the Manner of applying the Colours was liable to many Difficulties and Inconveniences. It is evident this Kind of Painting in *coloured Wax*, has little or no Resemblance to ours but in Name."

The catalogue goes on to make it clear that Wedgwood, at least by the time the first edition was published in 1773, no longer shared the widespread misconception that the ceramics that he was imitating were Etruscan (although he must have believed it when he named his new factory Etruria and took the motto "The Arts of Etruria are Reborn"), for in the catalogue, he states: "And it is evident the finer Sort of *Etruscan Vases*, found in *Magna Grecia*, are truly Greek workmanship, and ornamented chiefly with Grecian Subjects, drawn from the purest Fountain of the Arts; it is probable many of the Figures and Groupes upon them, preserve to us Sketches or Copies of the most celebrated Grecian Paintings; so that few Monuments of Antiquity better deserve the Attention of the Antiquary, of the Connoisseur, and the Artist, than the *painted* Etruscan Vases."

Wedgwood distinguished between his bronze appearance and painted black wares by calling them respectively "Bronze Etruscan" and "Etruscan Encaustic." While he retained the phrase "Etruscan Encaustic" by the time the first Wedgwood & Bentley ornamental ware catalogue was published in 1773, the name "Bronze Etruscan" had been changed to "Basaltes" and was used to describe bas-reliefs, vases, and small statues or figures.

Although Wedgwood had included figures in the list of articles the partnership would make when he wrote to Bentley on the subject in 1767, and in June, 1769, he discussed hiring figure-makers from the Derby porcelain factory—and he even went so far as to buy figure molds from Richard Parker in September of 1769—still he seemed hesitant to start on the figures. He wrote to Bentley October 1, 1769: "I believe *Vases* are much better articles, *for us*, than *figures* . . . Figures & other things may come in very well when we have no sale for all the Vases we can make . . ." (Farrer, I, 299). Bentley must have disagreed, however, for Wedgwood wrote again on November 19: "I have not seen these s^d black figures which have converted you again to a good Opinion of figure making . . ." (Farrer, I, 310).

By the publication of the first ornamental ware catalogue in 1773, however, there were twenty-three figures and busts in production, as well as bas-reliefs, cameos, and intaglios of "Chiefly Classical Subjects." The sources for these were often the antiques themselves, or reproductions of them in bronze or marble that could be cast in plaster to make molds from which the ceramic figures could, in turn, be molded. Such plaster molds were sold in London shops such as that of Hoskins and Oliver (later Hoskins and Grant), which Wedgwood patronized at least as early as September of 1769. Wedgwood often complained to Bentley about the poor quality of the molds supplied, and he employed modelers at Etruria to improve them and to sharpen and improve details on the ornaments after they had been molded.

Wedgwood was also on the alert to get models that were not already familiar through being sold in all the shops, urging Bentley in October of 1769: "I hope you will have an opportunity soon of getting some figures from the Cabinets of y.ʳ noble customers, which have not yet appeared in the shops . . . & I will endeavour to execute them in Terra Cotta" (Farrer, I, 303-304).

The first modelers at Etruria seem to have been Ralph Boot, C. Denby, and William Hackwood, of whom Wedgwood wrote to Bentley on September 20, 1769: "I hired an ingenious Boy last night for Etruria as a Modeler. He has modeled at nights in his way for three years past, has never had the least instructions, which circumstance considered he does things amazingly & will be a valuable acquisition. I have hired him for five years, & with Denby & him I shall not want any other *constant* modeler at Etruria. Palmer, & several others woᵈ fain have hired this Boy but he chose to come to me" (Farrer, I, 280). Even earlier, by the autumn of 1768, John Coward, a wood carver for Robert and James Adam, designed and drew copies of vases and other items for Wedgwood, and, according to Meteyard, in 1769 he was head of the modeling department.

In addition to vases, statuettes, busts, and other ornaments, more specifically useful products such as flower and bulb vases, lamps, and ink wells were all made in Black Basalt, and black teaware was one of Wedgwood's staple products. Teaware in "Egyptian Black" had been popular throughout the century because it flattered fair-skinned ladies by providing dramatic color contrast to their hands—which they went to a great deal of trouble to keep white. According to a letter Wedgwood wrote to Bentley in July of 1766 about discontinuing the production of dark color-glazed creamware, confidence in the continuance of the fashion for fair skin had encouraged him to experiment with the black ware in the first place: "I am quite clearing my Wareho. of Colour'd ware, am heartily sick of the commodity & have been so long but durst not venture to quit it 'till I had got something better in hand, which, thanks to my fair Customers, I now have & intend to make the most of it" (Farrer, I, 97). He expressed this idea more explicitly in a subsequent letter to Bentley (December 26, 1772): "Thanks for your discovery in favor of the black Teapots. I hope *white hands* will continue in fashion & then we may continue to make *black Teapots* 'till you can find us better employment" (Farrer, I, 123).

Teaware in Black Basalt, or in any other body, was not included in the articles that Wedgwood had proposed to Bentley that they make when they entered partnership together in June of 1769. Bentley evidently felt, however, that financial security was more assured if the partnership included the manufacture of tried-and-true black teaware. In reply to such a request, Wedgwood wrote to Bentley on August 29, 1770: "With respect to making some usefull Etruscan ware at Etruria, I shall *myself* have no sort of objection to it, but you know I have another partnership, in which it is stipulated that he [Thomas Wedgwood] shall have 1-8th share of the proffits upon all usefull ware, & he has bestow'd a great deal of attention for some time past upon China bodys for T:pots in brown, black, grey, etc., etc. so that though I believe he woᵈ not deny me if I ask him to give up the black T:pots etc. to us, yet I have some fear of its being a tender point with him" (Farrer, I, 368-69).

Bentley must have replied immediately and heatedly to Wedgwood's letter, perhaps harping sarcastically on the distinction between useful and ornamental wares to judge from Wedgwood's conciliatory reply which was sent September 3, and which is the only documentary evidence of anything more than mild disagreement between the two men. After again restating the terms of an agreement made a year earlier, he then described what he considered to be the difference between useful and ornamental wares. He negated *"fineness, or richness, or price, or colour, or enamelling, or bronzeing or gilding"* as criteria lest Thomas Wedgwood should stop short of making decorative improvements in his useful ware products for fear that they might be transferred to the ornamental works. Wedgwood continued: "May not usefull ware be comprehended under this simple definition, of such vessels as are *made use of at meals*. This appears to me the most simple and natural line, and though it does not take in Wash-hand basons and bottles or Ewers, Chamberpots, and a few such articles, they are of little consequence, and speak plain enough for themselves; nor would this exclude any superb vessels for sideboards, or vases for deserts [table decoration] if they could be introduced, as these articles would be rather for *shew* than *use*" (Finer, 95-96).

The argument was decided to Bentley's satisfaction—as evidenced by the note penned in his handwriting at the end of the letter: "Mr. B received this letter a few Days before he set out for Etruria. The Difficulty was easily settled, and the Etruscan Tea Pots made by ye Company at Etruria. The Company very much wanted some such constant selling Article" (Finer, 97). Evidence also lies in the fact that there are Black Basalt tea and tablewares marked "Wedgwood & Bentley." It is not known whether Thomas Wedgwood received any of the profits from the sale of Black Basalt and, later, Jasper useful wares.

Ornamental as well as useful wares continued to be produced in Black Basalt throughout the century, but between the appearance of the 1779 and 1787 editions of the ornamental wares catalogue, Jasper had superseded Black Basalt in at least one class. In 1779 the wording in the Bas-Reliefs, Medallions, Cameo-Medallions and Tablets category had read, "The articles in this Class may be made either in the *black Basaltes*, which has the Appearance of antique Bronze, or in the *blue and white Jasper*." In the 1787 catalogue, however, the wording was changed to "These bas-reliefs, chiefly in the jasper of two colours. . . ."

From the first ornamental ware catalogue (1773) to the last one (1787) published before Wedgwood's death, Wedgwood acknowledged his debt to Sir William Hamilton, citing his collection of antique works of art as the major source from which the Etruscan Encaustic designs were copied. The catalogues state: "The Vases of this Class . . . as well as the Paintings are copied from the antique with the utmost Exactness; as they are to be found in Dempster, Gorius, Count Caylus, Passerius, but more especially in the most choice and comprehensive Collection of Sir William Hamilton; which, to the honour of the Collector, and of this Nation, and for the Advantage of Artists, is now placed in the British Museum." (The collection had been sold to the British Museum in 1772).

Certainly at first, and probably always, it was Hamilton's book of engravings, with text by P. H. d'Hancarville, Collection of Etruscan, Greek and Roman Antiquities, rather than the collection itself that was consulted. The design of the Cupid and Lion plaque (see plate XI, p. 72) is derived from an antique sardonyx gem which was widely illustrated in the 18th century. It is copied directly from volume III, p. 211 of Hamilton, where the vignette, enclosed in an oval frame within a rectangular frame, is used to fill space on the last page of a chapter. The engraving, signed "Ed. Beaulieu del." and "Aniello Lamberti inc.," also includes the same reel and bead border, the Vitruvian scroll border, the inner border of running anthemion design, and the ground upon which the lion is walking.

Although the hand-colored plates in Hamilton's book copied the Greek ceramics accurately, using unshaded colors, Wedgwood, with the intention of improving on the original art, did shade his colors to give the illusion of volume that 18th-century patrons were accustomed to seeing in painting. In the ornamental ware catalogues, he described his set of encaustic colors that were not only "sufficient completely to imitate the Paintings upon the Etruscan Vases; but to do much more; to give to the Beauty of Design, the Advantages of Light and Shade in various Colours. . . ."

71. Vase with cover, decorated with mat ("encaustic") enamel in shades of red, 10" (25.4 cm.), unmarked, 1769. This is one of the so-called "First Day Vases" produced by Wedgwood and Bentley at the inauguration of their manufactory at Etruria during a pot-making ceremony, in which Wedgwood threw six Black Basalt vases while Bentley turned the wheel. The ceremony took place on June 13, 1769.

The shape of the vase, including the protuberances on the handles and on the shoulder between the handles, is shown in Hamilton's *Antiquities* as part of an engraved illustration on p. iii of the preface to volume I. Plate 109 is a scaled drawing of the vase with the difference that the pointed bumps on the shoulders are more complicated ornaments—female heads with pointed caps. The decoration is also from the first volume of Hamilton's publication and is a copy of the three figures on the left side of plate 129, which illustrated the legend of Hercules in the Garden of the Hesperides. On the reverse side is written the inscription: "JUNE XIII .M.D.CC.LXIX./One of the first Days Productions/at/Etruria in Staffordshire,/by/Wedgwood and Bentley."

72. Vase with cover, decorated with orange and white mat ("encaustic") enamels, 9¼" high (23.5 cm.), mark: "Wedgwood & Bentley" around bolt, c. 1770-80. The design on this urn is taken directly from plate 48, volume I of Hamilton, and is a scene identified as a bacchanal. Wedgwood used the same decorative borders on the vase as appear in Hamilton, but in the book the ivy wreath design is found between the chevrons and the figures.

73, 74. Vases, 20¼" high (51.4 cm.), mark: "WEDGWOOD," c. 1780-1800. *Below (left)*: decorated with mat ("encaustic") enamels of orange and white; *below (right)*: decorated with mat ("encaustic") enamels of iron red and white. The shape of these vases is presented in a scale drawing, with dimensions, in plates 80 and 81 of Hamilton's *Antiquities*, volume III. They are in the form of a lekythos, an ancient Greek pouring vessel, sometimes used to hold oils and unguents, and sometimes used in funeral rites. The decoration of both vases is also taken from Hamilton. They are decorated on one side only, making them left- and right-handed vessels respectively.

The decoration of fig. 73 is illustrated in color on plate 122 of volume I, and is described as a domestic sacrifice. One of the figures holds a patera and dips a staff into the altar. The other figure seems to be about to pour the sacrificial wine into the patera from a wine pitcher.

Fig. 74 is taken from plate 82, volume I. The subject of the engraving is not identified in the text, as D'Hancarville only discussed the plates that he felt he could identify with some confidence.

75. Cup and saucer, decorated with orange mat ("encaustic") enamel, cup – 2" high (5.1 cm.), saucer – 5" in diameter (12.7 cm.), mark: "WEDGWOOD," c. 1780-1800. The same factory books of stock Greek-figure designs were used for Black Basalt teaware as for Queen's Ware, and at least one order included both Greek-figured plates and teaware "Black Greek painted" (MS 9626-11).

The seated figure on the saucer is from design number 162 in the factory design book, while that of the cup, even including the small rosette to the right of the figure, is from design number 112. These, in turn, are from volume I of Hamilton. The saucer design is from plate 74, and is the central figure in what is described as a marriage ceremony. The cup design is in the lower right corner of plate 130, in which there are dancing figures and horse-drawn chariots. The picture is identified as "The Race of Atalanta and Hippomenes."

76. Plaque, decorated with mat ("encaustic") enamels in orange, sepia, and white, 10″
long (25.4 cm.), unmarked, c. 1770-1800. This plaque copies exactly plate 35,
volume II of Hamilton, except that there is some blue on the drapery in the colored
engraving. D'Hancarville interpreted the figure to be a genie leaning on a symbolic
column: "if beauty is an indication of goodness, this ought to be the good genie
Agathodaemon, to whom the Athenians raised statues, and according to Pausanias
there was a chapel in Lebedos dedicated to him and to Fortune, of whom this column might be the symbol."

XII. Encaustic-painted Black Basalt canopic urn, 14³⁄₁₆" high (36 cm.), mark: "WEDGWOOD & BENTLEY," c. 1769-80.

XIII. Jasper statue of
Venus Rising from
the Sea, 6½″ high
(16.5 cm.), mark:
"Wedgwood & Bent-
ley," c. 1775-80.

XIV. Jasper three-color diced cachepot and stand, 4¾″ high (12.1 cm.), mark: "WEDGWOOD," c. 1780-1800.

XV. Jasper vases with Cupid figures, 8¾″ high (22.2 cm.), mark: "WEDGWOOD," c. 1785-1800.

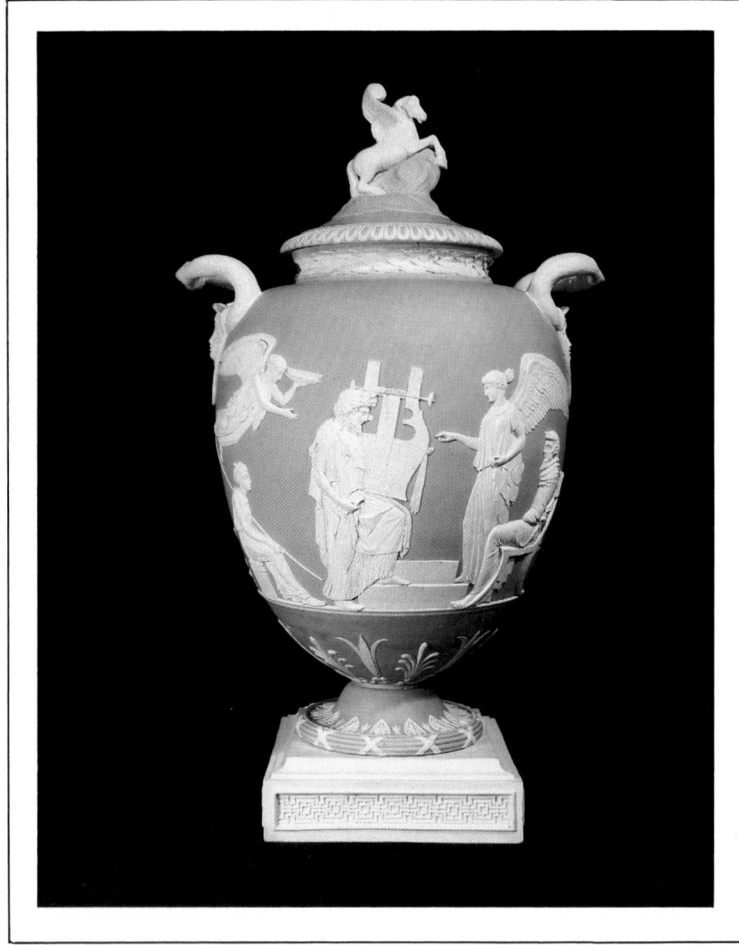

XVI. Jasper vase with Pegasus finial and bas-relief decoration depicting the Apotheosis of Homer, 18½″ high (47 cm.), mark: "WEDGWOOD," c. 1785-95.

XVII. Jasper three-color diced candle-stick vase, 10″ high (25.4 cm.), mark: "WEDGWOOD," c. 1780-1800.

XVIII. **Jasper custard cups.** *Clockwise from top*: dark blue, 2½″ high (6.4 cm.); lilac, 2¹⁄₁₆″ high (5.2 cm.); pale blue, 3¹⁄₁₆″ high (7.8 cm.); pea green, 3″ high (7.6 cm.). All impressed "WEDG-WOOD," c. 1780-1800.

XIX. Cane Ware
tureen with cow finial
and enamel-painted
decoration, 11¾″
wide (29.8 cm.), mark:
"WEDGWOOD," c.
1780-1800.

XX. Teapot and bulb
pot in Rosso Antico.
Teapot: 4″ high (10.2
cm.), unmarked, 1769-
80. Bulb pot: 7½″
long (19.1 cm.), mark:
"Wedgwood & Bent-
ley," c. 1769-80.

The sources of some of the "encaustic" decorations are not yet identified and may be from prints or other unpublished material such as drawings about which Wedgwood wrote to Hamilton on November 4, 1773: "It is our present Duty to express our great Obligation to you for the Continuance of your Favour . . . & for the excellent Drawings that the Writer of this Letter has this Day been delighted with: for tho' they arrived three or four weeks since in London, he was then in Derbyshire, & they being sent immediately to Mr. Wedgwood our TB [Thomas Bentley] could not see them before.

"We think them perfectly chaste & in the true Antique Style; & shall avail Ourselves of them as soon as we can: & for this Favour we beg Leave to repay your Excellency with—our most grateful thanks" [Buten Museum Archives].

Greek motifs such as the anthemion and stylized laurel that decorate some Black Basalt tea and tablewares could have been taken from many 18th-century sources, including Hamilton.

77. Pair of vases, decorated with mat ("encaustic") enamels in white, orange, and blue, 8⅜″ high (21.3 cm.), mark: "WEDGWOOD," c. 1780-1800. At the auction sale of ornamental ware that took place in 1781, after Bentley's death, the lots of "encaustic" painted vases were frequently offered in suites of five or seven for mantel decoration or as pairs "for niches," or a single one was occasionally included with Black Basalt figures or candelabra for "chimney ornaments." An example of the combinations offered was lot 1184: "One vase with encaustic painting; Cupids wrestling; two boys, from Fiamingo; pair of sphinx candelabra."

The subject on the right-hand vase is "The Dipping of Achilles." The scene on the other vase may also be from an Achilles series—perhaps "Individual Combat Before the Walls of Troy," a subject that Wedgwood also used in relief decoration along with other Achilles subjects, as Carol Macht has pointed out.

78. Plaque, decorated with mat ("encaustic") enamels in blue, orange, sepia, and white, 13⅜" long (34.6 cm.), unmarked, c. 1770-1800. "Encaustic"-painted tablets of this sort were used either as framed free-hanging pictures or for installation in furniture, or in mantel pieces. Sets included a central plaque, two flanking friezes, two oval or square inserts at the corners, and sometimes two vertical side panels. Architect Robert Adam was known to use Wedgwood "encaustic"-painted tablets in his chimney piece designs. As Wedgwood wrote to Bentley on the subject, July 8, 1775: "The fame of your painted chimney piece is not confined to London only. We are asked much of them here and if you can spare us a good sett to show here this summer now our season is commenced it will be a treat at least to our visitants if we do not sell them but I think the later is very probable. . . ."

79. Bowl, decorated with relief molding and mat ("encaustic") enamels in blue, green, iron red, and tan, 3" in diameter (7.6 cm.), mark: "WEDGWOOD," c. 1790-1800. To judge from its size, the bowl was probably for sugar, and a cover would have been supplied. The bright blue anthemion border with vividly contrasting green lilies is a departure in style from the more entrenched "encaustic" colors—iron red shading to white—found on many other pieces. It might have been the more vibrant type of decoration to which Josiah Wedgwood, Jr., was referring when he wrote to his brother Tom in 1790: "Your black tea ware with lively colors I dare say will please the foreigners, but the English I am afraid will not admire them. We are not bold enough to adopt at once anything that is new and beautiful but require the sanction of fashion to give it value" (Farrer, III, 117).

Wedgwood, Sr., evidently used an "in house" name for the Greek anthemion, which often incorporated a stylized honeysuckle. He wrote to Bentley on October 29, 1770: "I have glazed some black Vases but do not like them at all. You must paint & border & honeysuckle them all over to hide the glaze or you will never sell them" (Farrer, I, 380).

Sometime before the publication of the first ornamental ware catalogue in 1773, Wedgwood had introduced lamps into production. He made both simple shapes with painted decoration, and more elaborate shapes with molded decoration, taking his inspiration, as he did in vase-designing, from both the antique objects themselves and from prints.

Wedgwood's conscientious efforts to copy precisely the originals were recognized and appreciated in America, as a 1790 letter written to Thomas Jefferson from John Rutledge of Charleston indicates. Rutledge had sent a Wedgwood lamp to Jefferson as a gift, and he wrote: "Since my arrival here, I have received from Mr. Wedgwood, in England, some of his imitations of etruscan and roman antique lamp vases &c. Amongst the lamps he has sent me, one is fashioned and painted after an etruscan candelabras I saw at his manufactory. His copy I find a very exact one, and he has made it much more complete than the original by fitting to it Keirs patent hydrostatical lamp" (Boyd, 52).

Peter Keir patented a device by which oil could be raised to the wick and sustained there by the weight of a column of salt water, which has a greater specific gravity than oil. The patent was one of a number that appeared soon after the 1784 appearance of the Argand patent in which combustion in the oil burning lamp was improved by the introduction of air through a hollow wick. Wedgwood was quick to adapt his lamps to these improvements.

80-82. Oil lamps. *Above:* decorated with mat ("encaustic") enamels in orange and white, 5⅛″ wide (13 cm.), mark: "WEDGWOOD," c. 1780-1800; *overleaf (above):* single molded relief decoration, 10⅜″ wide (26.4 cm.), mark: "WEDGWOOD & BENTLEY ETRURIA" around bolt, c. 1770-80; *overleaf (below):* double molded relief decoration, 9½″ wide (24.1 cm.), mark: "WEDGWOOD & BENTLEY ETRURIA" around bolt, c. 1770-80.

In the ornamental wares catalogues published during the Wedgwood and Bentley partnership, Wedgwood distinguished between lamps designed for "Chambers, Halls, Stair-Cases, &c" and lamps designed for "the finest Apartments." Although embellished with the classical anthemion, stylized laurel, and tongue motifs, the simple shape of the painted lamp—also classically derived—would probably place it in the first category. "The Tripod Lamps," he said, "with several Lights, are highly enriched, and will be suitable Ornaments for the Finest Apartments." Although the partners did make lamps with three supports, they might also have included in the category of tripod lamps relief-decorated lamps with three-sided bases.

The single-wick lamp with relief decoration has neoclassical decoration, but its asymmetrical design of a kneeling figure seemingly ready to pour oil, and the twisted fluting and scalloped spout suggest something of the rococo; the double lamp is thoroughly neoclassical.

An early and continuing source of design inspiration for Wedgwood was the engraved plates from Le Antichità Di Ercolano Esposte, which Wedgwood copied in many different forms, with both relief and painted decoration. Le Antichità was an eight-volume work depicting and interpreting the art and artifacts excavated from the ruins of the ancient Roman seaside resort Herculaneum, which had been buried in a volcanic eruption in 79 A.D. The book was written by a group of anonymous scholars gathered together for the purpose under the name of Accademia Ercolanese by the future Charles III of Spain, who was, at the time the first volume was published in 1757, King of Naples and Sicily. After conquering the kingdoms in 1734, Charles had proceeded to squirrel away the excavated treasures belonging to Naples and Sicily for his private enjoyment, allowing few people to see them. Until the publication of the illustrated volumes, between 1757 and 1792, the objects remained almost as remote to the world as they had been when buried under the ashes of Vesuvius.

Wedgwood was a subscriber to the English translation of the work, acquiring the first volume in the spring of 1773. By 1770, however, he owned the first six volumes of the Italian edition. The first volume was devoted to wall paintings, and it was in this volume that the sources for the three following decorations appeared.

83. Plaque, decorated in molded relief with ground painted in dark red mat ("encaustic") enamel, 14½" in diameter (36.8 cm.), unmarked, c. 1771-1800. The plaque is one of two described in the bas-relief section of the first ornamental ware catalogue as "A Bacchanalian Figure from Herculaneum, upon a round Tablet, 15½ inches." They were among sixteen bas-reliefs taken from the Herculaneum wall paintings, but, unlike some of the others that were figures taken out of the context of the painting, they were actually painted tondos set beneath the main painting, as depicted in *Le Antichità*, plate VIII. Although Wedgwood could have, and probably did, see the tondos in the book before the time the reliefs were executed, the actual bas-reliefs plus the fourteen other Herculaneum bas-reliefs accompanying them, were molded from bas-reliefs brought home after a tour of Italy by the Marquis of Lansdown. Alison Kelly, in *Decorative Wedgwood*, quotes a 1770 invoice from plaster mold-makers Hoskins and Oliver for "Making Molds on sixteen round Basso-relievos," which are undoubtedly the Herculaneum subjects.

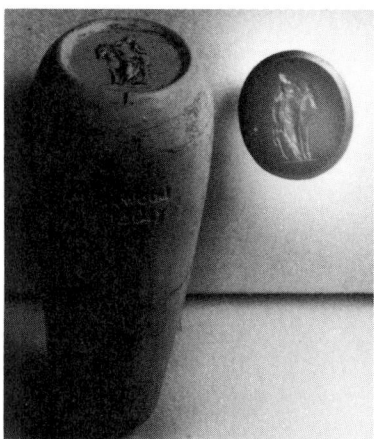

84. *Above (left)*: Plaque, decorated with mat ("encaustic") enamels in blue, iron red, and white, 13¼″ wide without frame (33.7 cm.), unmarked, c. 1770-80. The plaque is a close copy of plate XIV from volume I of *Le Antichità*, which is described in the text as "a domestic supper." The subject is said to have been listed in the unillustrated catalogue of King Charles's collections of Herculaneum treasures (1755) and was a wall painting in a house. The painting was in color, and it measured 2 feet, 5 inches square. The plaque, or tablet as it is described in the 1781 Christie's auction sales catalogue, was sold in the "encaustic painted pictures" section in Lot 540 which was a suite of five tablets to be installed in a mantel piece. In the same lot was included the Cupid and Lion (*see* plate XI, p. 72).

85. *Above (right)*: Seal and mold, seal decorated in intaglio formed by the relief molding on the mold, seal – ⁹/₁₆″ in diameter (1.4 cm.), mold – ⅝″ in diameter (1.6 cm.), mold marked: "Wedgwood & Bentley, 110," impressed, c. 1775-80. The mold is made of dense, hard, off-white ceramic, probably stoneware. A comparison of the size of the working end of the mold with the seal shows how much (or how little) shrinkage there was in the Black Basalt body – only about one-sixteenth of an inch. This was one of the qualities Wedgwood was working toward, as he wrote to Bentley on January 13, 1771: "Some of my present views are . . . To make a black body, that shall shrink little or none in burning." The purpose of this effort, he declared, was "to make Tablets & figures &c without cracking . . ." (Farrer, II, 3). The ornamental ware catalogues – under Class I, Cameos and Intaglios – state that the "Intaglios in artificial Basaltes" are "exact Impressions from the finest Gems; and therefore much truer than any engraved Copies can be. . . ." However, this intaglio, or rather the mold, is an exact copy of part of an engraving on p. 15 of *Le Antichità*, which, according to the text, depicts a marble relief. Wedgwood introduced the design in the 1779 catalogue as "A figure from Herculaneum" so that if he did take the impression from a gem, it was one that was a copy of the marble, or vice versa.

86. Pair of cups, decorated on the inside with cream-colored slip and glazed on the inside only, brick-red and white mat enamels, relief decoration on handles, 2½″ high (6.4 cm.), mark: "Wedgwood & Bentley," c. 1770-80. The dotted line on the inside of the cups is brick red, while the trophies and edging on the feet and handles are white. The handles are embellished with a molded relief of laurel leaves and berries. Wedgwood kept a factory book of stock trophy designs which could have been copied from many published sources. Montfaucon (*see* p. 111) showed pages of trophies, as did others. Each of these cups has three trophies, musical instruments on the sides, and implements of war or hunting on the fronts. None of the instruments are repeated, and, just as it was necessary to have different designs for each plate in dinner and dessert services, so this entire tea and coffee service probably had no repetition of trophies.

*Unlike Hamilton's publications and Le An-
tichità, the engravings of which were drawn from
observations of actual antique objects, L'Antiquité Expliquée et Representée en Figures, by
Bernard de Montfaucon (1655-1741), was a compilation of illustrations of the works of art
previously published by other artists and authors.
The scholarly text, published in five two-part
volumes in 1719, followed by a five-volume supplement in 1724, dealt with the ancient history,
culture, legend, and myths that were represented
in the art, sometimes pointing out disparities between the stories as written and as depicted.*

*Since Montfaucon used engravings that had
been published elsewhere, it is not possible to say
with certainty in any given instance which source
Wedgwood used. The "encaustic"-painted ornament pictured in plate XII of this book (p. 97) was
painted to approximate the relief decoration of the
canopus shown in Montfaucon, plate CXXXII,
volume II, part 2. Montfaucon reproduced the
engraving from La Chausse; Wedgwood might
have used either work. For statuettes and bas-
reliefs the probability is great that Wedgwood
would have had access to bronze or stone reproductions of the originals that were depicted in Montfaucon or in other publications, and that he would
have had molds made from the reproductions.*

*That he did rely upon Montfaucon for design
sources is certain, as he made frequent references in
his correspondence to the books. On April 5,
1788, Josiah, Jr., who was managing the factory
while his father was in London, wrote to
Wedgwood: "By todays waggon I send the 2nd vol.
of D Hancarville & I will very soon send you
copies of what you want out of Montfaucon &
Count Caylus" (Farrer, III, 62).*

87. Candlestick, molded decoration, 11½" high (29.2 cm.), mark:
"WEDGWOOD & BENTLEY," c. 1770-80. The candlestick closely
approaches the shape illustrated in Montfaucon, although
Wedgwood inserted a slender waisted foot and the Greek anthemion
panel in the base. The highly-polished surface may illustrate a technique that Wedgwood told Bentley about in August of 1770: "I am
trying another method to render the surface [of black vases]
smoother in general when no accidents happen in the fireing, which
is to burnish them when they are pretty hard, with steel burnishers,
'till they have the polish of a mirror; but as this is done by hand, it is
very tedious work, but they take an admirable polish if the fire does
not destroy it . . ." (Farrer, I, 360).

Before the publication of the ornamental ware catalogue of 1775, Wedgwood and Bentley had introduced an inkwell that was a mechanical improvement on others in several ways. There was a cone-shaped holder for the pen when not in use that did not open into the ink reservoir, so that the ink would not evaporate through the aperture, thereby keeping "the Ink from growing thick and Spoiling, as usual in common Ink-Stands." The opening through which the pen was dipped was so small that the pen point would not be blunted by striking the bottom of the well, and the hole through which the well was filled had a stopper—also to prevent evaporation.

The inkwells, while always the same mechanically, were produced in a myriad of shapes, from the plainest round or square vessels to the most elaborate creations imaginable. Diagrams of the mechanism were included in the catalogues, with careful explanations, and, as the 1775 catalogue stated: "These Ink-Vessels are sold separately, as they are represented in the above Engraving; or with a Sand-Box, &c in a Stand, forming a compleat Ecritoire."

Sales evidently were slow to begin with, for in October of 1776, Wedgwood wrote: "P.S. Our Ink Pots being the best in the World, & every Body wishing to have one of them—Why do not we sell an immense number? These & the Cyphers, when ready, are two articles that will merit our attention to set them a going in a wholesale manner" (Farrer, II, 320).

88. Desk set, applied and molded relief decoration, 7⅞" long (20 cm.), mark: "Wedgwood & Bentley," c. 1775-80. Late in 1777 Wedgwood wrote to Bentley: "I am fully sensible of the propriety of your observation that too great a variety in the ink stands distracts your customers choice, & will sin as little as possible, but vagaries in this article are so tempting that I cannot but indulge a little" (Farrer, II, 398).

The inkwell in this desk set has only two holes—one for filling the well and the other for dipping the pen—because the pen holders are in the center section next to the candle holder. The spaniel is the handle for the cover of a box which would have been used for seals and sealing wax. Both the spaniel and the textured surface with acorns and entwining oak branches were used by Wedgwood and Bentley on other objects in Black Basalt, the dog appearing as a finial on rum kettles, and the oak motif on tankards.

89, 90. Inkwell *(left)* and inkwell and sander set *(below)*, molded relief decoration, c. 1780-1800. Inkwell: 3⅜″ wide (8.6 cm.), mark: "Wedgwood"; set: 5¾″ long (14.6 cm.), mark: stand – "Wedgwood," sander – unmarked. In both inkwells, the large opening in the center is where the pen was dipped into the ink. In the round inkwell, there are four holes: one for filling the well, and three to hold pens. The other inkwell has two pen holders. The stoppers for the filling holes are missing on both. The sander is perforated like a salt cellar (the cover is removable). Sand was sprinkled onto the page to blot the ink. The two-handled vase served both as a handle and a quill holder.

The inkwell and the inkwell and sander set are decorated with two of the most important decorative motifs of the 18th century: the baluster and the vase. The shapes appeared everywhere, especially in the splats of chair backs – sensitive barometers of fashion changes – which were more often than not baluster-shaped or vase-shaped until the Adam urn-shape gained ascendency.

The play of curves on the body of the vase and the ends of the ink stand make it clear that Wedgwood was enjoying himself designing inkwells, as he wrote to Bentley on October 22, 1777: "As they [inkwells] do not sell in pairs like Vases I think we may indulge ourselves & the public with a little variety without much risque" (Farrer, II, 388).

The Reverend Joseph Spence, like Montfaucon, was interested in comparing ancient art with its literary sources, but he confined his study to the writings of the Roman poets. His book, Polymetis, was published in 1747, and, in its subtitle, he described the purpose of the work as "an Enquiry Concerning the Agreement Between the Works of the Roman Poets, and the Remains of the Antient Artists Being An Attempt to illustrate them mutually from one another."

A number of Wedgwood's customers and friends, such as Lord Gower and John Blagrave, were subscribers to the book, and if Wedgwood did not own it, he certainly had access to it, for it was another source of the "encaustic" paintings.

91. Vase, decorated with mat ("encaustic") enamels in iron red and white, 11½" high (29.2 cm.), mark: "WEDGWOOD," c. 1780-1800. The shape of the vase is that of an ancient Greek vessel for mixing wine and water called a krater. The handles terminate in four serpents' heads. The painting is copied from an engraving in *Polymetis* and depicts Venus riding on the backs of sea horses.

Small semi-precious or precious engraved stones, or gems, were used in the ancient world as seals and marks to identify one's possessions. The gems depicted, just as pottery did, the same subjects that were used in painting and sculpture. They were treasured by the ancient Greeks and Romans and heavily collected by 18th-century connoisseurs. Gem collections—belonging to patrons of Wedgwood, such as Lord Bessborough—and publications illustrating antique gems, such as those of Maffei and Agostini, were pregnant sources of designs for Wedgwood. He wrote to Bentley (August 24, 1770) about being advised that they should look at "Maffie's [sic] & Agostini's gemms" (Farrer, I, 364).

Earlier (September 30, 1769), Wedgwood had discussed antique gems with Bentley, asking, "Has L.ᵈ Bessborough sold all his casts from Antique Gems, or the Gems themselves to the Duke of Marlborough? I am, & so are you, much interested to know this as we had leave from L.ᵈ B: to take casts from all his Casts, but if the D. of M: has bo.ᵗ them we shall have that leave to solicit again." He continued: "Though the Gems from Italy may be too small to apply to the Vases themselves, they will make very good Studys & we can have larger modeled by them much better than from prints, we can likewise paint after them. Gems are the fountain head of fine & beautiful composition, & we cannot you know employ ourselves too near the fountain head of taste" (Farrer, I, 294).

92. Pair of medallions, decorated with mat ("encaustic") enamels in iron red and white, 3½" long (8.9 cm.), unmarked, c. 1770-1800. The dolphin holding a ribbon in its mouth was copied from an antique gem in nicolo, a variety of onyx having a faint bluish layer over black. The sea horse was after a gem of green quartz. Wedgwood did not copy the gems themselves, however, but copied illustrations of them from Maffei's book of gems. They were sold with three other tablets in a suite of five for a chimney piece in the 1781 auction sale at Christie's, and were described as "Cavallo Marino, Delfino, from Maffei's gems."

Evidently the same engravings were published in Lionardo Agostini's *Gemmae et Sculpturae Antiquae* (1685), for Wedgwood's paintings were exact copies of plates 211 and 212 which have black-and-white line engravings. The text in Agostini describes the dolphin as a heavenly sign, and the sea horse as a symbol of Neptune as well as a heavenly sign.

93. Pair of plaques, molded relief decoration, with gilded wood frames, 20¼″ high (51.4 cm.), unmarked, c. 1770-1800. The plaque *(right)*, which depicts a child reaching for poppies, was copied from an antique gem illustrated in plate 116 of Agostini and identified as "Venus and Cupid." While writers on Wedgwood, such as Macht, have also identified the subject as "Venus and Cupid," Wedgwood himself used it for his bas-relief entitled "Night," which was number 79 in the catalogues; "Day" was number 80. The dimensions of both were given as 20 by 14½ inches.

Since Wedgwood added "or 'Ceres and Triptolemus'" to the 1779 catalogue listing of the cameo "Night Shedding Poppies" (and, in the Ceres and Triptolemus legend, Ceres gives poppies to the infant Triptolemus), it is probable that "Night" was a larger version of that cameo.

While not an exact copy, the design source for "Day" was probably Agostini's plate 115, which shows a nude female figure holding a ring or wreath in front of a baby. According to Samuel Smiles, the sculptor John Bacon (1740-99) modeled "Day" as a companion piece to "Night" in 1770. It is not known who modeled "Night," but while it was a literal copy of the engraving, an artist such as Bacon may have been called upon to "improve" upon plate 115 by clothing the figure and adding a lyre and a rectangular structure behind it.

"I was going to say when I left Etruria that I liked much your plan of havᵍ the Bronze figures from Rome, provided they are fine, & have not been hackney'd here." So Wedgwood wrote to Bentley on September 13, 1769. Just as tourists through the ages have brought home souvenirs of their trips —sometimes original works of art, but probably more often reproductions of works they have seen in museums—so 18th-century Englishmen returning from the Grand Tour brought home antique sculptures, vases or bas-reliefs, or marble or bronze copies of them, such as the *Venus de Medici,* one of the most popular attractions at the Uffizi Museum in Florence; copies of Roman busts from the Capitoline at Rome; or a copy of *Mercury,* the masterpiece of contemporary sculptor Jean Baptiste Pigalle.

Wedgwood, in turn, copied these acquisitions in Black Basalt. As he wrote to Bentley in 1771, *"If you could borrow some good bronze or marble busts for us to mold off wᵈ be the best and cheapest way."* "Egyptian Lions, from the Capital" (see plate X, p. 72) were modeled after bronze lions lent him by the architect Sir William Chambers. The bronzes, in turn, were copies of "real" basalt lions that had been placed at the foot of the monumental staircase that approached the Capitoline in Rome.

That Wedgwood regarded himself as a preservationist is evident in the ornamental ware catalogues in which he states: ". . . when Bronzes are rusted away, and all the excellent Works in Marble dissolved, then these Copies, like the antique Etruscan Vases, will probably remain, and transmit the Works of Genius, and the Portraits of illustrious Men to the most distant Times."

94. Statuette, molded figure of a pug dog, 11⅛" long (28.3 cm.), unmarked, c. 1774-1800. This image of a pug dog, modeled as if caught in an alert moment, is the portrait statue of Trump, a favorite pet of William Hogarth (1697-1764), the English painter who defined the rococo in his writings on the "line of beauty"—the S-curve. In style the statuette embodies the rococo and is the antithesis of the classical idea of timelessness in portraiture customarily found in Wedgwood's sculptural portraits. It is modeled after or perhaps cast from a terracotta figure by Louis François Roubiliac (1695-1762), the French sculptor who lived in London and was one of the leaders in bringing the rococo style across the Channel.

The Wedgwood version first appeared in the ornamental ware catalogue of 1774 as "a pug dog." "Two pug dogs" are listed in the 1777 and subsequent catalogues, and in the 1781 auction sale at Christie's, they are identified as "a pair of pug dogs, from a favourite dog of Hogarth's."

95, 96. Statuette, molded figure of a Grecian sphinx, 12″ long (30.5 cm.), mark: "Wedgwood & Bentley," c. 1770-80; statuette, molded figure of a woman, 17¾″ high (45.1 cm.), mark: "WEDGWOOD," c. 1780-1800. The Grecian sphinx figure was in production by the time the 1773 ornamental ware catalogue was issued. Also available then was an Egyptian sphinx with a man's head and royal headdress. The standing female figure was called "Zingara" and first appeared in the 1779 ornamental ware catalogue, the mold for it having been billed to Wedgwood by Hoskins and Grant on May 5th of that year.

The Zingara ("gypsy" in Italian) was modeled after a statue that was illustrated in Maffei's *Raccolta di Statue antiche*, and described by the author as having a combination of marble head and bronze feet. Maffei said it was located in the Borghese garden. In late 1773 or early 1774, a bust also called "Zingara" had been made for Wedgwood by Richard Parker, a plaster cast maker, and comparison shows that the head of the standing figure is a reduced version of the bust. Kelly has pointed out in *Decorative Wedgwood* that the Zingara bust is identical in details such as the pose of the head, the veil under the chin and others, to a white marble copy of a classical original by Italian sculptor Antonio Canova (1757-1822), and it seems very likely that the original that inspired Canova was the Zingara illustrated in Maffei.

The sphinx and Zingara are shown together because the resemblance between their faces is too great to be ignored; the same modeler might have made both figures.

97, 98. Statuettes, unmarked, c. 1770-1800. *Above:* molded figure of the god Morpheus, 26⅜" long (70 cm.); *left:* molded figure of the infant Hercules strangling snakes, 10½" high (26.7 cm.). Two of Wedgwood's largest undertakings in Black Basalt figures were also among his earliest. Both listed in the 1773 catalogue, they were number 8 ("Morpheus, a reclining figure") and number 10 ("Infant Hercules, with the Serpent, 20 inches high, by 21 broad.") Kelly, in *Decorative Wedgwood*, describes a bill dated May, 1770, from Hoskins and Oliver that includes charges for both of these figures: a "Mould for the Morpheus for Pressing, cutting the model in pieces and joining it together again after it was moulded," and "finishing the Infant Hercules for moulding," and making the mold for it.

The wording of the invoice suggests that a mold for Morpheus was supplied to Hoskins and Oliver. The question then becomes: did they make the molds themselves, and, if not, who did? An invoice to Wedgwood from Theodore Parker dated October 7, 1769 (Meteyard, *Life*, II), may provide the answer. For on it are included "A Statue of Hercules" and "A Boy A Couch" [sic], "Time from the 7th above in Casting." It is possible that Parker cast from bronze or marble reproductions of the antique originals. The original for Morpheus was a sculpture found in the Borghese vineyard in Rome and illustrated in Montfaucon (supplement I, plate 214). A Hellenistic statue (now in the collection of the Kunsthistorisches Museum, Vienna) was probably the inspiration for Hercules.

99, 100. Statuettes, c. 1780-1800. *Above (left):* molded figure of Mercury tying his sandal, 19½″ high (49.5 cm.), mark: "WEDGWOOD"; *above (right):* molded figure of Venus with a pair of birds, 21″ high (53.3 cm.), mark: "Wedgwood." Hoskins and Grant billed Wedgwood for "a Setting Figure of Venus" and "a Setting Figure of Mercury" on June 28, 1779. Both are copies of life-sized marble originals by the French sculptor Jean Baptiste Pigalle (1714-85).

The marble sculptures were signed "J.-B. Pigalle Fecit, 1748 Parisiis." Wedgwood copied the Mercury exactly, but he took liberties with the Venus, changing her position slightly and transferring the two doves from her left side, as Pigalle had placed them, to her right side. Although the Black Basalt statues face each other, just as they did in the Pigalle originals, perhaps Wedgwood required the added symmetry of balancing the sandal-tying on Mercury's left with the doves on Venus's right.

101. Statuettes, molded figures of Cupid and Psyche, Cupid—8⅛″ high (20.6 cm.), Psyche—8½″ high (21.6 cm.), mark: "Wedgwood," c. 1780-1800. "Cupid Sitting Pensive" and "Psyche to Match," as Wedgwood called the figures in the 1787 catalogue, are copies of two works by Étienne-Maurice Falconet (1716-91), a sculptor who was appointed director of the atelier at the Sèvres porcelain factory in 1757. Among the many soft-paste porcelain biscuit figures produced there during Falconet's tenure, which lasted until 1766, were reproductions in miniature of some of his large marble sculptures. The Cupid was originally executed in marble in 1757 and was about three feet high; the biscuit figure followed the next year in several sizes ranging from about six to about thirty inches. There was no companion marble figure of Psyche, but a biscuit figure was made in 1761. It was called the "Little Girl Hiding Cupid's Bow" or, occasionally, "Nymph" or "Psyche."

Except for the addition of slightly thicker anthemion-decorated bases, the Black Basalt versions appear to be identical copies of the biscuit pieces and may well have been cast from them.

102. Ewer, molded, 11½″ high (29.2 cm.), mark: "WEDGWOOD," c. 1780-1800. The ewer is in the form of an ancient Greek, Roman, or Etruscan prochous, a sacrificial vessel from which libations of wine were poured. The human head was not the most common shape for the form in ancient times, and Wedgwood did not produce many pitchers like it. Those that were produced were undoubtedly for ornament rather than use. (The head-shaped pitcher, of course, reached total secularization in the Toby jug in the mid-18th century.) One example of this Wedgwood ewer is in the collection of the British Museum, and, as Hugh Tait has pointed out, it is modeled after a bronze original that is probably Etruscan, made about 400 B.C. and now in the Louvre.

103, 104. Plaque, molded relief decoration of "Bacchanalian Sacrifice," 19⅜" long (49.2 cm.), mark: "WEDGWOOD," c. 1780-1800; plaque, molded relief decoration of "Bacchanalian Triumph," 20" long (50.8 cm.), unmarked, c. 1770-75. These two plaques were introduced in the 1773 ornamental ware catalogue as numbers 70 and 71, respectively. The "Bacchanalian Sacrifice" *(top)* was modeled after a bas-relief by the French sculptor Claude Michel, called Clodion (1739-1814), who modeled numerous nymphs, satyrs, and bacchanalian scenes both in sculpture and bas-relief. A bronze example of the Sacrifice bas-relief signed by Clodion is in the collection of the Buten Museum. It is inscribed on the lower right corner " A Monseigeur [sic]/Le Prince de Rohan/Hommage de Centaur M.C. 1787." The original Clodion model from which subsequent bronzes were cast had to have been made before 1773, when its Black Basalt copy appeared in the catalogue. A "bronzed" example of the plaque marked "Wedgwood & Bentley" is in the British Museum.

There are minor changes in Wedgwood's version in that more foliage has been added on the sides and some foreground landscape has been added. Another small but significant change can be seen in the second figure from the left in both the Clodion and the Wedgwood plaques. She is a female satyr child in the Clodion, and, in the Wedgwood, the sex has been obscured. Similar precautions have been taken in three succeeding versions of the other plaque, "Bacchanalian Triumph," the source of which may also be attributed to Clodion on the basis of style, although the exact source is not known.

105, 106. Vases, molded relief decoration with applied bronze coating (mounted with French ormolu of the late 18th or early 19th century); *above (left)*: 15½″ high (39.4 cm.); *above (right)*: 15⅞″ high (40.3 cm.), mark: "WEDGWOOD," c. 1780-1800. The vases, one decorated with a satyr seated on the shoulder of the vase and holding the horns of a ram's head, and the other decorated with a triton holding the tail of a dolphin, are known respectively as the "wine" and "water" ewers or vases, and were itemized on an invoice sent to Wedgwood by J. Flaxman, March 25, 1775. The modeling for the pair has traditionally been described as the first work that John Flaxman, the sculptor, did for Wedgwood. As Harry Barnard has pointed out, however, the bill was receipted "for my father," and signed "John Flaxman, Junr.," supporting the possibility that the senior Flaxman supplied plaster molds for the ewers to Wedgwood.

   If John Flaxman, Jr., who was 20 years old at the time, had anything to do with the ewers, it would have been to cast them from the originals that have been attributed to Clodion, who designed for the Niderviller pottery and porcelain factory. The satyr-handled ewer, of which the "wine" is a very close copy, was in the Musée des Beaux-Arts, Orleans, when Thirion wrote *Les Adam et Clodion* in 1885. Thirion lists the pair of "wine" and "water" vases in the sales of Clodion's works in 1780. "Wine" and "water" ewers with grape-vine decoration are seen more frequently than the ewers pictured here with figural reliefs.

107, 108. Rum kettles, marked: "WEDGWOOD & BENTLEY"; *left:* decorated with engine turning and applied relief ornament, 11″ high (27.9 cm.), c. 1776-80; *below:* decorated with engine turning and applied and molded relief ornament, 11⅛″ high (28.3 cm.), c. 1776-80. Wedgwood wrote to Bentley on June 21, 1777: "You'll tell us when to stop making Bassrelief pots & bowls for punch. D⁰ [ditto] for Tea & Coffee. They are much admir'd here by everybody who sees them . . ." (Farrer, II, 363). Rum kettles, which were used to heat and serve hot beverages, can sometimes be distinguished from hot water kettles used for tea by the presence of perforations on the inside, such as teapots have, to act as strainers. Recipes for some hot mulled wine or rum beverages required sticks of cinnamon, bread crumbs, or citrus fruit slices or gratings, making strainers desirable in pouring the drinks.

The round, three-dimensional effect that is achieved both by undercutting and by extending parts of the relief over molded parts can be seen on the pot with the cupids carrying garlands. The pot probably dates after 1776 when Wedgwood wrote of having solved the difficulty of applying relief figures to the Black Basalt body.

109. Bulb pot, decorated with applied relief and mat ("encaustic") enamels in orange, violet, and white, 9″ long (22.9 cm.), mark: "Wedgwood," c. 1780-1800. "Root flowerpots [bulb pots] of various sorts, ornamented & plain" were the first item on the list of things they would make that Wedgwood sent to Bentley on November 9, 1767, in anticipation of the commencement of their partnership (Farrer, I, 188). Evidently Bentley didn't know what they were, for, having received one from Wedgwood, he pressed it into service for holiday wassailing, causing Wedgwood to write to him on New Year's Eve: "Your *punch bowl* is a *Winter flowerpot*, not to be fill'd with *water, & branches of flowers*, but with *sand & bulbous roots* & is to those baubles made in Glass for growing one bulbous root, what a *Garden* is to a *flowerpot*, however I must acknowledge, that seeing you did not find out the original intention of the vessell, you have hit upon a tolerable succedaneum, this cold weather, & I beg leave to tender you my best thanks for the honour you have done the maker in remembering him at your festive board" (Farrer, I, 199).

110. Tankard, decorated with engine turning and applied and molded relief ornaments, 4½″ high (11.4 cm.), mark: "Wedgwood," c. 1780-1800. One of the most effective ways that Wedgwood kept ahead of his competition in Staffordshire was to nurture connections that would make available to him fresh sources of design so that he would not have to buy hackneyed models off the rack at the plaster shops. The bas-reliefs on the tankard and the rum kettles are from the same series—one that was introduced by the time of the publication of the 1775 catalogue and that was listed as: "84 Hunting, 85 ditto, 86 Music, 87 The Arts." In the 1787 catalogue, the description of 85 was more explicit: "Bringing home the game."

Sculpture, especially ancient Greek and Roman sculpture, was copied in "encaustic" paintings as well as in Black Basalt figures, busts, and bas-reliefs. It is overwhelmingly likely, however, that painters at Chelsea and Etruria worked from prints depicting the sculptures rather than from the originals themselves.

111. Plaque, decorated with mat ("encaustic") enamels in sepia and white, 14⅝" long (37.1 cm.), unmarked, c. 1770-1800. The painting is a copy of the Hellenistic statue "The Gaul Falling Backward," commissioned in the third century, B.C., by Attalus I, ruler of the Pergamenes, to commemorate his victories over invading Gauls. This sculpture was one of the several groups that Attalus dedicated on the Acropolis of Athens, probably during his visit to the city in 200 B.C.

112, 113. Plaques, decorated with mat ("encaustic") enamels in iron red and white, 13⅜″ in diameter (34.6 cm.), unmarked, c. 1771-1800. A letter from Wedgwood to Bentley indicates that the partnership started to produce plaques molded in one piece with their frames in 1771. Several varieties of frames were used, the usual kind being the ones pictured with bound reed inner borders and fluted outer borders.

One of the twelve labors of Hercules is illustrated on the left. The figure may be derived from a statue of Hercules strangling Antaeus that was in the courtyard of the Grand Duke of Florence in the early 18th century when Paolo Alessandro Maffei wrote his descriptive work on sculpture, *Raccolta di statue antiche*, in which the statue was illustrated in plate 43. The subject of the other plaque is "the Rape of Helen," the legend in which Paris persuaded Helen, wife of Menelaus, King of Sparta, to elope with him to Troy—the mischief that started the Trojan War.

From 1774 until the end of the decade, figure-making played second fiddle to the production of busts. Wedgwood, writing to Bentley on September 11, 1774, made the new direction explicit: "I must send you a few of the new model'd figures as they are, for Hackwood, if he is capable of giving character to their faces, & improving the draperies, which I have some doubt of, though I am perswaded he would mend them considerably, he has not time for it at present. The Busts will employ him for a year or two before our collection is tolerably complete, & I am much set upon having it so, . . . I hope in time to send you a collection of the finest Heads in this World" (Farrer, II, 196).

Four busts are listed in the 1773 catalogue—Cicero in two sizes, Horace, and King George II. Twenty-nine more were in production in time to be included in the 1774 catalogue, and, by 1779, thirty-six new subjects had been added. Most of the busts were of Greek and Roman statesmen, writers, and mythological figures; others included Englishmen—and a few Frenchmen—prominent in literature and science. Of the five new busts added by the time the last ornamental ware catalogue was published in 1787, four were portraits of eminent Dutchmen.

The impetus for the production of busts may have come from Bentley, for on March 2, 1774, Wedgwood wrote to him: "If we are not so expeditious in completing orders my Dear Friend will please to bear in mind the reduction of our hands the last year . . ." (Farrer, II, 175). Nevertheless, he wrote three days later—perhaps in response to persuasion: "You may send some Busts from Parkers [Hoskins], and put all you send us into the Catalogue" (Finer, 159). These were sent, and, as Wedgwood reported to Bentley, "To make the moulds . . . will be a great & long piece of work" (Farrer, II, 184).

114. Bust of Venus, 17″ high (43.2 cm.), mark: "Wedgwood & Bentley," c. 1774-80. A bust of "Venus de Medicus" appeared on a lengthy invoice including mostly busts, dated March 21, 1774, from Hoskins and Grant. The original statue was the Hellenistic statue housed in the Uffizi Gallery, Florence.

The bust was listed in the 1774 catalogue as number 43 "Venus Medicis." The addition of an "s" was not surprising. In the 18th century, spelling was casual—but evidently Bentley did find some names impressed upon the busts themselves that were unacceptable. In reply to whatever comments Bentley had made, Wedgwood wrote on July 3, 1775: "Bad spelling—very true, our Head makers had taken it into *their Heads* that nothing bad could come from London, therefore when the Plaister Busts had names upon them our People boldly copied them without consulting Mr. Cox or anybody else, & this accounts for the *Saffo* &c." (Farrer, II, 231).

115. Bust of young Marcus Aurelius, 15$^{1}/_{16}$" high (38.3 cm.), marks: "Wedgwood &
Bentley" on both bust and socle, "MAR AURELIUS" on bust, c. 1774-80. Hoskins
and Grant supplied two sizes of molds in 1774, one for the "young" figure and the
other a "large." In the catalogue that was published the same year, three were listed:
"38 Young Marcus Aurelius, ditto [a bust]," "47 Marcus Aurelius, large, ditto," and "49
Marcus Aurelius, ditto, 2d size." Since in subsequent catalogues there are only two
such figures listed, it would appear that either the third listing was a mistake or that
one size was discontinued, although there are no other examples of that having being
done.

   The bust is copied from the original in the Capitoline Museum, Rome. The plinth
of the marble bust is inscribed "M. Aurelio."

While authors of books on ancient art such as Hamilton/D'Hancarville, Agostini, and Montfaucon were illustrating actual objects from the ancient world, designers during the same period were inventing and publishing their own designs of vases, furniture, and all manner of decorative devices, often using the classical vocabulary of ornament, but combining elements of design in a way that bore the stamp of their own time. The architect-interior designers, and the manufacturers who supplied them—such as metalworkers, potters, pressed stone and plaster ornament makers, and woodworkers—all used these design books as sources of artistic inspiration so that relatively classical and distantly classical interpretations lived side by side in the houses of the fashionable.

Wedgwood had hit upon the perfect medium for interpreting the chaste forms of the Greek figured vases in his "encaustic" technique, but the more contemporary designs were often elaborate creations that required a different approach. Wedgwood wrote to Bentley on June 6, 1772, while he and Mrs. Wedgwood were visiting Bath: "I have been surveying the Bath stone Vases for Piers &c and am rather sorry to tell you that they make them much cheaper than we can do in clay." Faced with this, Wedgwood said: "I think all the chance we have in competing with this Manufacture must be by introducing Bass relief figures upon the Vases, or some ornaments which they cannot execute so well in their course-grained stone" (Finer, 124). This Wedgwood did, but it took him several years to master the technical problems of applying bas-reliefs to the Black Basalt vases.

116. Ewer, molded relief decoration, 11¹¹/₁₆″ high (29.7 cm.), mark: "Wedgwood & Bentley," c. 1770-80. Wedgwood and Bentley designed a number of ornamental items from the engravings of Jacques Stella's *Livre de Vases*. Although relatively simple in shape, this ewer with trefoil lip was intended to be ornamental. As Wedgwood wrote, "You know I never had any idea that *Ornamental ware* sho[d] not be of *'some use'*. . . I co[d] wish therefore that you had not repeated this idea so often, & ask'd me if my Partnership with T:W [Thomas Wedgwood] wo[d] exclude our making Stellas Ewers" (Farrer, I, 371).

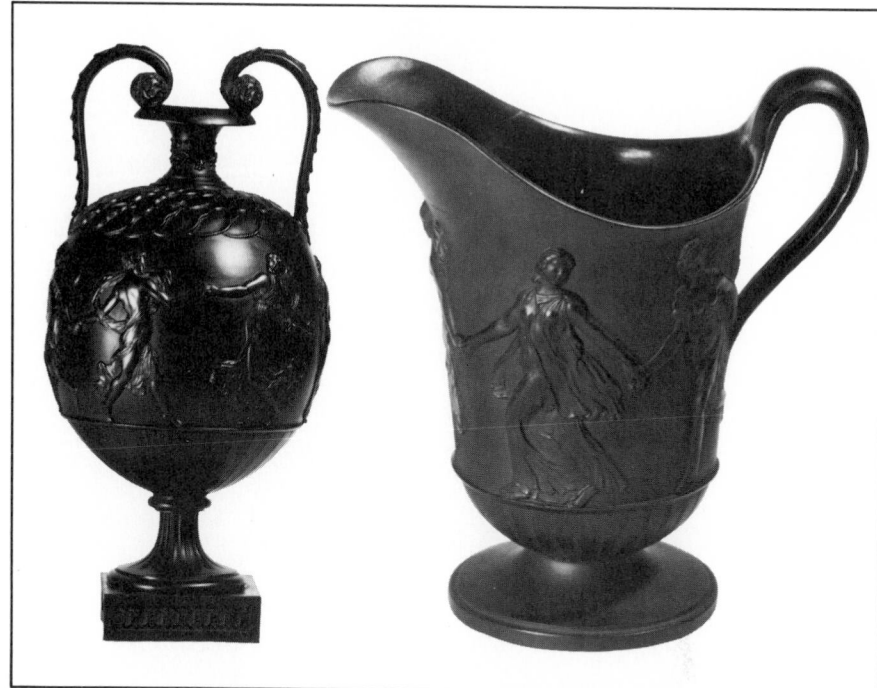

117. Bough pot, engine-turned, molded and applied decoration, 10¹¹/₁₆" high (27.1 cm.), mark: "Wedgwood & Bentley," c. 1776-80. The removable pottery disc inserted in the top of the vase was a device to make it easier to arrange flowers, equivalent to a present-day frog placed at the bottom. Wedgwood made bough pots in all of his ceramic bodies and in a great variety of shapes, but none was more fantastic than this, with two mermen seated upon a giant oyster shell. As Timothy Clifford has stated, the vase is copied from one designed by the sculptor Edme Bouchardon (1698-1762) and published as plate 11 of the second part of a volume containing etchings of Bouchardon's vase designs by Gabriel Huquier (1695-1772). The updated work was entitled *Premier Livre de Vases Inventes par Edme Bouchardon* and *Second Livre de Vases Inventes par Edme Bouchardon*. Other than adding engine-turned vertical fluting where Bouchardon's vase was plain, Wedgwood and Bentley's major change to the design was to convert mermaids into mermen.

118, 119. Vase, engine-turned, molded, and applied relief decoration, 14" high (35.6 cm.), mark: "Wedgwood & Bentley," c. 1776-80; Cream jug, engine-turned and applied relief decoration, 4¾" (12.1 cm.), mark: "Wedgwood," c. 1780-1800. The vase and cream jug have in common probably the most well-known of Wedgwood's designs, the "Dancing Hours," conceived by John Flaxman (1755-1826), who designed and modeled for Wedgwood from about 1775 to 1787. A pair of ewers in the Wedgwood Museum, Barlaston, which may be designed after plate 11 of Stella's *Livre de Vases*, were probably designed en suite with the two-handled vase. They have similar handles, and both have the scale-like decoration on the shoulder, and the grape vine around the neck. Although the Wedgwood ewers have Cupid bas-reliefs applied, the Stella ewer has a dancing procession with male and female figures, the female figures being quite similar to Flaxman's design in their drapery, fluidity of movement, and the way in which they alternate directions.

The source for most of the figures, however, has been identified by Kelly in *Decorative Wedgwood.* She attributes the design to the frieze of a white marble chimney piece from the Borghese Palace in Rome that is now in the Lady Lever Art Gallery at Port Sunlight, England. It was brought to Hertfordshire in the 1760s by Sir Laurence Dundas, a patron of Wedgwood.

There are two versions of the "Dancing Hours"—the 18th-century one designed by Flaxman, in which navels and legs are freely exposed, and a remodeled version by Hackwood, in which the dresses are lengthened and arranged more discreetly. That the nudity of classical figures would offend his customers was always a worry to Wedgwood.

120. *Above*: Vase with cover, engine-turned, molded and applied relief decoration, 7⅝″ high (19.4 cm.), mark: "Wedgwood," c. 1780-1800. Wedgwood's fluted urn supported by three caryatids attached by hose-like protuberances from their heads, and to each other by a garland of laurel, is an interpretation of an incense burner designed by the French painter Joseph Marie Vien (1716-1809). It was engraved by his wife Marie Therese Reboul in a volume entitled *Suite de Vases Composée dans le Goût de l'Antique*, dated 1760. The Black Basalt interpretation faithfully reproduces the Vien caryatids, but the engine-turned vertically-fluted body and cover are more severely neoclassical than Vien's design, which has spiral reeding and a large guilloche surrounding the body. Vien's simple knob on the cover is replaced by Wedgwood's seated figure finial. The Chelsea porcelain factory also produced a thoroughly rococo flower-bedecked version of the Vien design.

121. *Left*: Watch stand, molded and applied relief decoration, 8¾″ high (22.2 cm.), mark: "WEDGWOOD & BENTLEY ETRURIA," c. 1770-80. The watch stand vase was used to hold a pocket watch when it was not in use. The shelf that held the watch would center it in the aperture, thus converting the vase into a clock. A laurel wreath and festoons hanging from masks that are satyrs' heads with rams' horns decorate the vase, which, as Clifford has pointed out, is copied from an undated etching by Friedrich Kirschner (1748-89), a German miniature painter. Kirschner's vase design had a fluted cover with acorn finial, as did, probably, the watch stand, and it was perhaps the blank oval reserve in Kirschner's vase design that suggested to Wedgwood the idea of making it into a watch stand. He copied the design also as a vase (without the reserve) in Black Basalt with engine-turned fluting and in Variegated Ware.

Although potters had traditionally followed the lead of silversmiths in designing their more elegant pottery forms, by the late 18th century the debt was mutual, for silversmiths were following the potters' (particularly Wedgwood's) lead in designing matched tea sets as well as vases copied from his wares. It is hard to say who copied whom in some of the objects that appeared about the same time, but it is clear that pottery and silver were competing in ways that would have been unthinkable twenty-five years earlier.

As an admirer told Wedgwood—and Wedgwood repeated the compliment to Bentley in a letter (August 24, 1770)—"When Roman luxury increas'd, Etruscan ware gave place to Plate [silver]: but when English luxury seems at the height, your elegant taste has put to flight Gold & Silver vessels, & banished them from our Tables . . ." (Farrer, I, 364).

122. Teapot, molded, 4¼″ high (10.8 cm.), mark: "WEDGWOOD," c. 1780-1800. Just as silversmiths were designing tea sets à la Wedgwood, Wedgwood was designing tea sets in traditional silver shapes, such as this severely plain but elegant example.

123. Stirrup cup, molded, 4¾" long (12.1 cm.), mark: "Wedgwood & Bentley" behind the ear, c. 1770-80. The stirrup cup, or rhyton, usually in the form of an animal or occasionally a human head, is made without a flat bottom so that, once filled, it cannot be set down until emptied. The form is ancient and is derived from the drinking horn—a hollow animal horn used as a cup (*see* fig. 85). Stirrup cups were made in pottery and porcelain, and in metal. A foxhead form exactly like the Wedgwood example is known in Sheffield silverplate also. Whether one was molded from the other, or both were copied from a third source, is not known.

124. Stirrup cup, molded, 7¾" long (19.7 cm.), mark: "Wedgwood," c. 1780-1800. On July 11, 1775 Wedgwood wrote to Bentley that "Mr. Tebo has had a cast of a Hares Head before him some time, *but it is not a likeness.*—The wet plaister in Casting presses down the hair upon the face, & makes it like the head of a drown'd Puppy; & Mr. Tebo cannot model anything like the face of a Hare—he has made many attempts at sundry times, but they generally turn out to be full as like Pigs as Hares. Besides we cannot tell what to do with the Ears . . ." (Farrer, II, 233-34).

"Tebo" was probably an anglicized spelling of Thibaut, a modeler of French origin who worked in England. Little is known about him other than that he probably worked at the Bow porcelain factory about 1750-65, and subsequently at the Plymouth, Bristol, and Worcester porcelain factories. Wedgwood had hired him by November of 1774. He stayed at Etruria until the following October or November, during which time Wedgwood rarely seemed pleased with his work.

Although Wedgwood's letters, his catalogue descriptions, and the objects themselves indicate that Black Basalt and neoclassicism were fairly wedded in Wedgwood's mind, the exotic attraction of the Orient never really subsided during the 18th century and crept even into the Black Basalt in the form of objects shaped to resemble bamboo. For two reasons it seems likely that bamboo-shaped Black Basalt wares went into production at the very end of the Wedgwood & Bentley partnership. One reason is that there are few marked Wedgwood & Bentley pieces of this sort. The other is that bamboo is not mentioned in the catalogues produced during Bentley's lifetime, appearing for the first time in the 1787 catalogue.

125. Teapot, molded decoration, 3¼″ high (8.3 cm.), mark: "Wedgwood & Bentley," c. 1779-80. While Wedgwood & Bentley teapots are not common in the bamboo design, other tea accessories in this design marked "Wedgwood & Bentley" seem to be unknown. The shape might have been newly introduced to the market shortly before Bentley died, and it would have been natural to try it in teapots first. Although tea sets were popular, teaware was by no means produced exclusively in sets. Factory orders and invoices indicate that many more teapots were sold than other parts of the tea service.

Intaglios were among the smallest, but most numerous, of Wedgwood & Bentley's types of ornamental ware that were introduced in the 1773 catalogue. These were minutely and precisely detailed "so that Gentlemen may have a great Variety of Seals at a small Expense; or have an Opportunity of making Collections of perfect and durable Copies of the choicest Gems." The seals were not only kept on the desk with other writing materials, but were worn on watch fobs as decorative accessories.

Portrait medallions of eminent personages, past and present, were another important product of the ornamental ware department. They were meant to be displayed in boxed sets of drawers, much like those used for coin collections. As Wedgwood wrote to Bentley on January 2, 1773: "We shall do all we can to make your several Classes as complete as may be . . . & if you please to reconsider the subject of makeing a little completeish Historical Cabinet of Medals . . . 400 Eminent Men might be created for about £ 5 if a good number of setts wo.d be sold" (Farrer, II, 127).

By the time the 1775 catalogue had been published, Wedgwood & Bentley was also offering a custom-order service in which portraits of any individual would be produced in wax, and then molded in Black Basalt as either a cameo or intaglio. These were to be set in jewelry or (if intaglio) used as seals.

126. *Center*, seal, intaglio of cypher, mirror image of the letters "BN," ⅞" long (2.2 cm.), mark: "Wedgwood & Bentley," c. 1775-80; *left*, portrait medallion of Pope Eugenius III, molded relief, 1¼" in diameter (3.2 cm.), mark: "Wedgwood & Bentley, 170," c. 1770-80; *top*, self-shanked seal, intaglio, number 328, "A Lion Seizing a Horse," 1" long (2.5 cm.), unmarked, c. 1775-80; *right*, portrait medallion of King Edward VI of England, relief decorated on both sides, portrait on obverse, bas-relief design and birth, coronation, and death dates on reverse, 1⅜" in diameter (3.5 cm.), unmarked, c. 1770-80; *bottom*, seal or stone to be mounted in jewelry, intaglio decoration, unidentified portrait, ¾" long (1.9 cm.), mark: "Wedgwood & Bentley," c. 1773-80.

The portraits of the Pope and King Edward were modeled after medals made by John Dassier (1677-1763), a Swiss engraver of medals. Wedgwood lists Eugenius as the 170th pope, while according to Vatican records, he was actually the 165th. Wedgwood can perhaps be forgiven, however, as even the *Catholic Encyclopedia* lists him as number 167. The self-shanked seal is after a painting by George Stubbs, while the portrait seal illustrates an attempt to imitate black-and-blue onyx or nicolo.

127. Plaque, molded relief of Peter the Great, 16¾″ high (42.5 cm.), unmarked, c. 1770-1800. Included in the category called "miscellaneous heads" was the largest of the portrait medallions, "Peter the Great of Russia, a fine Medallion, 17 inches by 14." Evidently the partners had considered, but decided against, producing a bust of Peter the Great, for Wedgwood mentioned the possibility during the winter of 1776-77.

128. Medallion, molded relief portrait of Josiah Wedgwood, 5″ high (12.7 cm.), unmarked, design attributed to Joachim Smith, c. 1773-74. Before the publication of the 1774 catalogue, Wedgwood had made an arrangement with Joachim Smith, a portrait modeler, whereby Smith would charge for the wax models and Wedgwood would charge for the cameo or intaglio copies. The Wedgwood portrait, which shows the pockmarks that remained on his face from a childhood attack of smallpox, is attributed to Smith on the basis of a listing in the catalogue of the Liverpool Art Club *Loan Collection of the Works of Josiah Wedgwood* (1879), which states: "1039 Josiah Wedgwood, Potter 1730-1795. *In light-coloured pottery, ground and back painted a reddish brown.* The portrait is signed on the shoulder 'Jo Smith, fecit.' " Elsewhere, the work has been attributed to Flaxman.

5. Jasper

. . . I am making new experiments . . . first To make a white body, suc-
ceptible of being colour'd & which shall polish itself in burning
Bisket. . . .

Wedgwood to Bentley
January 13, 1771

Even the most ardent of Josiah Wedgwood's biographers acknowledge that his experiments were directed toward perfecting clay bodies that were already in use by other Staffordshire potters rather than towards attempting entirely new clay combinations. His Queen's Ware, Basalt, and other clay compositions discussed in this book are examples of his ability to improve upon the work of his predecessors. The one exception to this was the effort he made toward developing something quite original, a new clay composition—easily tinted in many colors—which was capable of holding very sharp details and of being fired with relief decoration in another color in order to achieve a cameo effect. When he finally succeeded in perfecting this new composition, Wedgwood named it "Jasper," and it became his best-known product.

Records of actual trials at the Wedgwood factory and notations in Wedgwood's experiment book indicate that more than 5,000 different attempts were required to perfect the Jasper body. This series of experiments extended over a period of several years and had to be accomplished while Wedgwood was running his already successful firm. He complained to Bentley in August, 1774: "If I had more time, more hands, and more heads I could do something . . . A Man who is in the midst of a course of experiments should not be at home to anything or anybody else but that cannot be my case. Farewell—I am almost crazy" (Farrer, II, 193).

When he began the experiments in January, 1771, Wedgwood outlined his goals in a letter to Bentley. First, the body had to turn white during the firing process; this was necessary in order to achieve the light color he was looking for in the cameo effect. Second, the composition had to be capable of being tinted in the wide variety of colors that occurred in natural cameos. And, finally, the body had to "polish itself in burning Bisket," by which Wedgwood meant a process of vitrifi-cation that eliminated the need for a glaze.

Several events inspired Wedgwood to start working on the new composition at this time. The improved Black Basalt body was by now perfected to a stage where it could be manipulated into many different shapes—such as vases, medallions, and intaglios—as well as in a wide range of sizes from the tiniest cameo to statues two feet in length. But, although Wedgwood had successfully achieved black relief decoration on a black background, he perceived that this somber effect limited the ware's acceptance to only a small audience. Though interest in Etruscan and Egyptian decoration was to persist throughout the 18th century and into the early 19th—Thomas Hope, for example, included an Etruscan room in his home in London which was famous as a showplace of interior design in about 1815—the neoclassical aesthetic was moving away from a literal rendition of classical styles to a new freer, and more creative interpretation. Also, the two-toned effect of one-color relief decoration on a different colored background was much more popular in England at the time. Ancient gems made from stone and shell, collected avidly by the well-to-do, were of two colors. Robert Adam, a trend-setting architect, decorated interiors of his buildings with white plaster relief decoration on painted, usually pastel, backgrounds. Wedgwood was also prompted to begin his experiments by the success of the work of James

129. *Opposite page:* Vase, "Venus in Her Car," solid pale-blue Jasper with white relief and snake handles, 15¾" high (40 cm.), mark: "WEDGWOOD," c. 1784-1800.

Tassie, a Scotsman, who made reproductions of ancient gems from a glass substance of his own invention. These newly-made gems could be produced in quantity and sold cheaply.

Wedgwood's earliest objects in the new body were in the form of small cameos, as popular a form then as it proved to be in succeeding years. The process of producing them required careful molding, manipulation, and firing. The round or oval clay background was first molded, and then set aside. A second batch of clay was forced into a "pitcher mold," a fired earthenware block into which the desired design had been formed. After this step the clay was removed with the use of a flat pallet knife, and the clay now bore the design from the mold. The relief was dampened on the undecorated side with water and positioned carefully onto the background piece. The "leather-hard" combination was then fired at a high temperature, the result being a finished stoneware piece.

Initially Wedgwood fired these cameos white on white and referred to the finished objects as being of "waxen bisquit," not Jasper. In fact, when he first began his experiments on the new body he was using the term "Jasper" to refer to a species of variegated ware; only much later did he adopt the term to describe the clay of his two-toned cameos. Many of these early cameos were sold in the white-on-white combination, but some were given painted backgrounds in order to achieve the sought-after two-toned effect. White on white cameos continued to be made after Wedgwood had perfected two-toned cameos.

By 1775 Wedgwood had made considerable progress in his experiments and was able to include Jasper – again, not by that name – in his sales catalogue of that year. "The Cameos will be made of a new Composition as fine as Parian Marble," he wrote, "but infinitely more durable, with burnt-in Grounds of various Colours . . . ." The "burnt-in Grounds," unlike the painted backgrounds produced earlier, were subjected to the firing process, which made them much more resistant to damage.

Wedgwood, however, was still unsatisfied. His goal was to achieve a uniform tint throughout the body rather than merely a surface application. This he regarded as necessary in order to effectively imitate natural cameos, and in order to allow high polishing on a lapidary wheel. The problems he encountered, however, were enormous. The color after firing was very inconsistent in hue and quality and the body cracked and blistered. The addition of coloring matter often changed the properties of the body, making it incompatible with the uncolored white clay used for the relief; consequently, the relief decoration would not fuse to the background. Frequently, the relief would adhere properly, but the background color would stain the white decoration. Adding to Wedgwood's problems was his concern for absolute secrecy. In January, 1775, just as he felt he was making a breakthrough in his efforts to perfect the body, Wedgwood wrote to Bentley saying, "The only difficulty I have is the mode of procuring & conveying *in Cog[nito]* the raw material . . . I dare not have it the *nearest way*, nor *undisguis'd* . . . Could not Mr. More set some poor Man to work upon it in some of the uninhabited buildings at the Adelphi. – Everybody knows him to be a Conjurer, & this may well pass for an Ore for him to operate upon" (Farrer, II, 215).

By 1775, Wedgwood thought his trials were over and, in a letter to Bentley dated January 1 of that year, he claimed victory in his quest: "I am glad you think the white body of sufficient fineness & have no reason to doubt of being able to continue it so. The blue body I am likewise *absolute* in of almost any shade, & have likewise a beautifull Sea Green & several other colors, *for grounds* to Cameo's, Intaglio's &c, & shall be able to make almost any of our Cameo's in figures from the Herculaneum size to the least Marriage of Cupid &c, & in heads from Peter the Great to the smallest Gem for Rings . . ." (Farrer, II, 214). His boast, however, was to prove premature, for in a letter to Bentley dated January 25, 1777, Wedgwood complained: "We cannot, by any means devised, make the blue Seals all alike either in color or texture – The deepest, & the palest are made from the same lump of Clay & fired not only in the same Kiln, but in the same Sagar [sagger] at the same time" (Farrer, II, 338-39). Jasper was to prove equally recalcitrant in progressing from the production of small cameos to larger-scale objects, and it took several more years of experimentation before Wedgwood was able to fire the body in "the Herculaneum size," 15½ by 12½ inches.

In addition to the technical problems affecting the color of Jasper, there were aesthetic considerations. Wedgwood was most anxious to convert prominent architects of his time to the use of Jasper rather than imitation stone and plaster, but the gentlemen of fashion were difficult. In a letter dated October 6, 1778, Wedgwood wrote to Bentley: "Both Mr. B [the architect Capability Brown] & Ld. Gower objected to the blue ground, unless it could be made into Lapis Lazuli. I shew'd them a sea green, & some other colors, to which Mr. Brown said they were pretty colors, & he should not object to them for the ground of a room, but they did not come up to his ideas for the ground of a tablet, nor would any other color unless it was a copy of some natural, & valuable stone . . . if we could not make our colour'd grounds imitate marble, or natural stones, he advised us to make the whole white, as like to statuary marble as we could. — This is certainly orthodox doctrine, & we must endeavour to profit by it" (Farrer, II, 454).

By 1779 Wedgwood had conquered almost all the problems associated with Jasper production. He felt comfortable including the material — with its new name — in the sales catalogue published that year. "It may be proper to observe here," he wrote in the catalogue, "that this artificial Jasper is made in two Colours; the Relief of one Colour, and the Ground of another, which is not laid upon the Surface like Enamel, but goes thro the whole Mass; and that the Grounds admit of a good Polish . . . ." Objects made in this way, with the color penetrating the body, are known today as "solid" Jasper, in order to distinguish them from "dip," "laminated," and "slip-decorated" examples. Jasper dip is essentially a layering process in which an unadorned background piece is given a surface application of a second color before the bas-relief decoration is applied. Alternatively, wafers of Jasper can be sandwiched together to achieve a similar layered effect; this is known as laminated Jasper. In slip-decorated objects, the bas-relief decoration is applied to the background piece and then the colored slip is painted on around it. The term "slip-decorated" should not be used when referring to objects in which the colored layer is enameled, but only when describing objects in which the color was applied as slip or liquid clay.

These several techniques for working Jasper arose through a variety of technical or aesthetic considerations. Jasper dip was less expensive than solid Jasper because it required a lesser amount of costly coloring agents such as cobalt to achieve a colored background. Also, Wedgwood may have tried the dip process as a way to produce a more uniform and consistent color. Laminated Jasper was invented to mimic the striations found in natural cameos. After sandwiching the layers together, Wedgwood often beveled the edges to expose the various colors, and he sometimes polished the edge as well, making the object even more like the gems he was emulating. Wedgwood occasionally faked this effect by simply painting a band of colored slip around a solid background piece. Slip-decorating was used most frequently when working with black Jasper as a way to eliminate or control the tendency to stain the white relief decorations that was characteristic of that color.

When he first developed Jasper, Wedgwood utilized many of the shapes and subjects that had already proved successful in other bodies, particularly Black Basalt. Designs taken from ancient gems and statuary were common and, as was the case with the Basalt designs, new subjects were primarily acquired through print sources or from mold makers such as Hoskins & Grant. Later, particularly after the death of Bentley, Wedgwood designs exhibited less reliance on the source books that had figured so prominently in the development of Basalt subjects. Though the influence of classical art was still very strong, the motifs were more freely rendered, and new artists such as Elizabeth Templeton, Emma Crewe, and Diana Beauclerk introduced sentimental themes inspired by popular novels and idealized views of daily life. The invention of Jasper opened up a whole new world to Wedgwood's fertile imagination. On May 15, 1776, he wrote to Bentley, ". . . we are but just beginning, to make something of our Bass-reliefs — I have many ideas, & visions crowd in upon me, not only quicker than I can execute them, but faster than I can find time to lay them to rest a while in my Common place Book" (Farrer, II, 284). From buttons to teapots, vases to inkpots, Wedgwood's Jasper is astounding in its variety, versatility, and vitality.

When Wedgwood began his experiments with Jasper, he could at first successfully fire only small items, mostly cameos and intaglios which, like their Basalt counterparts, he considered "fit for Rings, Buttons, Lockets, and Bracelets; and especially for inlaying in fine Cabinets, Writing-Tables, Bookcases, &c." Vast quantities of these were sold for framing, forming historical cabinets, or for other uses. "The Ladies may display their taste a thousand Ways in the Application of these Cameos," Wedgwood wrote in his 1775 catalogue, "and thus lead Artists to a better Style in ornamenting their Works."

In addition to cameos and intaglios, Wedgwood later produced somewhat larger objects in Jasper, which he referred to as bas-reliefs, medallions, and cameo-medallions. Intended for "inlaying, as Medallions, in the Pannels of Rooms . . . or for hanging up, as Ornaments, in Libraries," objects of this size had earlier been offered in Black Basalt, as well as in a type of "polished Biscuit, with brown and grey Grounds," which cannot now be accurately identified. Soon after the publication of his 1775 sales catalogue, however, Wedgwood mastered the firing of large-size Jasper objects. Efforts toward this goal evidently commenced in 1775, for, in August of that year, Wedgwood wrote to Bentley: "I am going upon a large scale with our Models . . . I hope to bring the whole in compass for your next Winters shew & ASTONISH THE WORLD ALL AT ONCE, for I hate piddling you know" (Farrer, II, 239). By the time he published his 1779 catalogue, Wedgwood could confidently offer blue-and-white Jasper "from the Size of a Ring to that of a large Chimney-piece Tablet or Cameo Picture."

130. Cameo, "Judgment of Hercules," black Jasper dip on pale blue with white relief showing dark staining, 1¼" long (3.2 cm.), 1¹⁄₁₆" wide (2.7 cm.), mark: "Wedgwood & Bentley," c. 1775-80. The formation of entire collections or "cabinets" of mythological and historical subjects was one of the chief uses of Wedgwood cameos, and Wedgwood arranged to have special display cases made for them. On November 13, 1778, he wrote to Bentley regarding blue cameos in particular: "We sh^d give them a little curled gilt frame which would look very well . . . The whole assemblage of white–blue–gold & black drawers would have a striking effect, & be very pleasing. I hope your visitors will think them what they really are, a most liberal, & noble collection of such subjects, which we know are very rare & difficult to come at" (Farrer, II, 467). In his 1779 sales catalogue, Wedgwood specifically advertised "Cameos; made of the artificial Jasper . . . at a very moderate Price, for those who wish to form mythological Cabinets." The cameo pictured here shows Hercules choosing between Fame and Pleasure and can be compared to a later, larger version of the same subject in fig. 139.

131. Cameo, "Isis," light-blue Jasper with white relief, 2⅜" high (6 cm.), 2" wide (5.1 cm.), mark: "Wedgwood & Bentley," c. 1775-80. In his 1773 sales catalogue, Wedgwood listed two versions of "Isis, wife of Osiris," one specified as "with the flower Lotus." By the time he issued his 1779 catalogue, Wedgwood had added "Isis, with the Cistrum" to the above. The new design was copied from a well-known gem illustrated in both Agostini's *Gemmae et Sculpturae Antiquae* (plate 68) and in the first volume of Montfaucon's *L'Antiquité Expliquée* (plate 108). Although Agostini and Montfaucon both picture Isis from the waist up and show her holding the sistrum, Wedgwood chose to use the head only; thus, the sistrum appears floating in the field near her shoulder.

132. Cameos, "Four Seasons," dark-blue Jasper dip on grey-blue with white bas-relief decoration, polished edges, 2½" high (6.4 cm.), mark: "WEDGWOOD," c. 1780-1800. Although these four winged figures are not listed in the Wedgwood sales catalogues, their fluttering draperies and their floating poses identify them as aurae or sylphs, female aerial beings frequently used as subjects for ancient ceiling paintings. The figures are occasionally called the "Four Winds"; that title, however, is inappropriate since, as Joseph Spence points out, the winds are properly depicted as male. Somewhat more suitable as a title is the "Four Seasons." Upon close inspection it can be seen that the figures vary in drapery from the most covered up (*third from left*), who presumably represents winter, to the bare-armed figure of summer (*far left*).

133. Monogram seals, each 1" long (2.5 cm.), unmarked, c. 1775-1800. *Left:* solid-blue Jasper; *right:* solid-blue Jasper with white Jasper dip face. In addition to flat intaglios that were meant to be framed or set like cameos, Wedgwood made self-shanked intaglios for use as seals. In his 1779 sales catalogue he advertised "Seals . . . with Shanks of the same Stone, highly polished, and particularly a complete Set of Cyphers, consisting of all the Combinations of two Letters: these require no mounting, but may be finished with gold or gilt Ornaments, according to the Taste of Purchasers." These objects were an attempt by Wedgwood to halt what he called the "terrible depredations" that James Tassie and former employee John Voyez had made upon his Black Basalt seal trade, the former "by making them more beautiful," and the latter by offering cheap copies of Wedgwood's designs upon which he forged Wedgwood & Bentley's trademark. Wedgwood's solution to the situation was "to sweep our Cabinet of the Black, & fill them with White, Blue, & other color'd Seals," which his competitors could not imitate (Farrer, II, 272).

134. Medallion, "Pan Teaching Daphnis to Play the Shepherd's Pipes," light-blue Jasper dip on grey-blue with white relief, 4⅜" high (11 cm.), 5⅜" wide (13.6 cm.), mark: "WEDGWOOD & BENTLEY," c. 1775-80. The subject is taken from a full-length, widely copied statue attributed to Heliodoros in about 100 B.C. Wedgwood probably knew it from the first volume of Montfaucon's *L'Antiquité Expliquée* (plate 49). The original statue is a "symplegma," that is, a closely-knit composition of two figures. Though Wedgwood chose to use only the heads from the original design in his bas-relief version, he retained the spirit of the symplegma in the intertwined limbs and psychological closeness of Pan and Daphnis.

135. Medusa medallions. *Top:* white glass paste composition by James Tassie, 3½" wide (8.9 cm.), unmarked, late 18th century; *left:* solid light-blue Jasper with white relief, 3⅛" wide (7.9 cm.), mark: "Wedgwood & Bentley," c. 1775-80; *right:* solid-white Jasper, 3⅛" wide (7.9 cm.), unmarked, c. 1775-80. As early as 1769, Wedgwood purchased "70 impressions in Sulfer" from James Tassie for the purpose of copying the designs in Black Basalt (Meteyard, *Life*, II, 92). Later, the two men were to become serious rivals, Tassie objecting to Wedgwood's published claims in the 1779 catalogue that Jasper cameos were "far above all other Imitations or Copies of antique Gems." According to Tassie's biographer, John M. Gray, Tassie pointed out that his glass paste composition actually provided much more accurate casts of gems because, unlike clay, it was not subject to shrinkage.

   Wedgwood produced several portraits of Medusa; his 1779 catalogue listed at least four different models varying in size from five to two inches. The design for the version illustrated here was probably cast directly from one of Tassie's paste medallions, the difference in size caused by the characteristic shrinkage of the clay. Tassie himself issued over 100 versions of Medusa. The one shown here is illustrated in his sales catalogue and is identified as number 8897, "Medusa . . . cameo from a bas-relief of Card. Albani's" (Raspe, II, 523).

136. Medallion, "Urania," laminated light and dark-blue Jasper with white bas-relief decoration, bevelled edges, 3⅜" high (8.6 cm.), 2¾" wide (7 cm.), mark: "Wedgwood & Bentley," c. 1777-80. In addition to avoiding any nudity which might offend his customers, Wedgwood also strove to make certain that his subjects were deemed appropriate. In a letter to Bentley dated October 6, 1778, he wrote: "I took the liberty of waiting upon [Lord Gower and the architect Capability Brown] with a tablet & two frises . . . the frises being Apollo & the nine muses, they both agreed that it would be very proper for his [Gower's] Library . . ." (Farrer, II, 453). This opinion echoes the evidence presented by Joseph Spence, who pointed out in *Polymetis* (1747) that the Muses were a popular decorative motif in ancient libraries. Wedgwood, as Carol Macht indicates, is known to have owned Spence's book.

In his 1779 catalogue Wedgwood listed "Nine Muses and Apollo, separate . . . 3½ inches by 2½." The standing version of Urania was probably introduced about that time, as the seated example (fig. 138) would not have matched the others in the suite. The new figure was most likely taken from the "Sarcophagus of the Muses," illustrated in volume I of Montfaucon's *L'Antiquité Expliquée* (plate 59).

137. Medallion, "Charlotte at the Tomb of Werther," marbled dark-blue Jasper dip on white with white relief, 3³⁄₁₆" high (7.9 cm.), mark: "WEDGWOOD & BENTLEY," c. 1774-80. In 1774 the German poet and writer Johann Wolfgang von Goethe (1749-1832) published his famous work *The Sorrows of Young Werther*. Wildly popular, it was read in all fashionable circles and was considered to be wonderfully "affecting." The medallion illustrated here owes its inspiration to Goethe's story. Its design of a woman weeping over a funerary urn is well within the usual mourning iconography found in the work of many artists, including John Flaxman, Angelica Kauffmann, and others. Although the subject of Charlotte at the tomb of Werther does not appear in the Wedgwood sales catalogues until 1787, it is evident from the Wedgwood & Bentley mark that it was produced long before that time. If, as is generally believed, Lady Elizabeth Templeton is responsible for the medallion's design, the mark on the medallion would indicate that she was providing designs for Wedgwood as early as 1780, several years earlier than the date usually given of 1783.

The medallion perhaps represents an experiment on the part of Wedgwood to make his Jasper more nearly resemble natural stone, such as lapis lazuli. Intentionally or not, the blue background is very uneven, resulting in a marbled effect that is quite attractive. Although this design is occasionally identified as "Antonia at the Urn," the latter subject properly depicts a woman standing with an urn at her feet.

With the acceptance of his cameos, intaglios, and medallions fairly well established, Wedgwood turned his attention toward still larger objects, primarily plaques—or, as he called them, "tablets" —to be used in architectural settings. The introduction of these articles to the architects of the day proved to be fraught with unexpected setbacks. Though Wedgwood felt that his plaques rightly had "a Place amongst the finest Ornaments the Arts have produced," they were not immediately accepted by the architects and builders whose approval Wedgwood regarded as essential to his ultimate success. Capability Brown complained that the Jasper did not look sufficiently like natural stone and James Wyatt, too, must have voiced some objections, since in a letter dated October 16, 1778, Wedgwood begged Bentley to visit the architect to "try . . . to root up his prejudice & make him a friend to our jaspers." To drive home his point Wedgwood remarked: "If we could by any means gain over two or three of the current architects the business would be done" (Farrer, II, 458-59).

Perhaps one reason for the architects' reluctance was the relatively high price of Wedgwood's Jasper plaques. Wedgwood compared his wares to marbles and found them in "every way better," but conceded that "people will not compare things which they conceive to be made out of moulds, or perhaps stamp'd at a blow like the Birmingham articles, with carving in natural stones where they are certain no moulding, casting, or stamping can be done" (Farrer, II, 458). Rather, the architects compared Wedgwood's plaques to similar objects in artificial stone, and found the latter preferable. "It is a pity the builders should be so stupid," Wedgwood wrote to Bentley in April, 1778, "but I am told they apply a great number of artificial stone tablets & other decorations of the same material in the new buildings in London, particularly in the fine houses in Portman Square" (Farrer, II, 425). Despite Wedgwood's best efforts, use of his Jasper plaques never became as popular as he would have liked and competition in the form of artificial stone, stucco, and other ornaments prevented his domination of the market.

138. Plaque, "The Nine Muses" *(from left to right:* Erato, Euterpe, Clio, Terpsichore, Polyhymnia, Melpomene, Thalia, Calliope, Urania), solid-blue Jasper with white relief, 6½″ high (16.5 cm.), 25¼″ wide (64.1 cm.), mark: "WEDGWOOD & BENTLEY," c. 1777-80. The plaque is a compilation of figures from a variety of sources. According to Macht, John Flaxman, Sr., is known to have provided casts for Melpomene, Thalia, Terpsichore, and Euterpe in 1775, and two years later his son, John Flaxman, Jr., was asked to complete the suite. The younger Flaxman evidently turned to Montfaucon's *L'Antiquité Expliquée* for inspiration; the figures of Erato and Urania appear to be derived from statues illustrated in plates 57-58, while Polyhymnia can be seen in the so-called "Sarcophagus of the Muses" shown in plate 59. It has recently been suggested that the two remaining figures, Clio and Thalia, are variations of the Dancing Hours figures *(see* figs. 118 and 119) that Flaxman was working on about this time. Their flowing draperies, which contrast markedly with the costumes of the other figures, support this conclusion.

139. *Top:* Plaque, "Judgment of Hercules," solid-blue Jasper with white bas-relief decoration, 21½″ wide (54.6 cm.), 10½″ high (26.7 cm.), mark: "WEDGWOOD," c. 1785-1800. The modeler of the plaque is not known. Meteyard states that "it cannot be with any probability referred to Flaxman" and suggests that "it may be Tebo's work as he excelled in large bas-relief figures" (*Life*, II, 337). Several versions are known, the first issued as early as 1773. The sales catalogue for that year lists it as an oval measuring 18 x 13 inches. At that time it could have been made only in Black Basalt. In the 1779 catalogue the plaque is still listed as an oval, but many more sizes were available, and Wedgwood noted: "The articles in this Class may be made either in the black Basaltes . . . or in the *blue and white Jasper.*" By the time the 1787 catalogue was issued, the design had been reworked "agreeably to Lord Shatsbury's idea of representing this subject." Although the plaque shown here is considerably larger than the dimensions given for the "Judgment of Hercules" in the 18th-century catalogues, it displays the vitality in modeling and attention to detail that characterize production of that period.

140. *Above:* Plaque, "War of Jupiter and the Titans," solid pale-blue and white Jasper, 10″ wide (25.4 cm.), 7½″ high (19.1 cm.), including frame, mark: "WEDGWOOD," c. 1780-1800. Like the "Judgment of Hercules," this subject was issued in both Jasper and Black Basalt. This was by no means an unusual practice for Wedgwood since the two compositions had obvious similarities in texture and finish. Sometimes the mold was used without alteration; on other occasions it was changed slightly or reworked. Known examples of the "War of Jupiter and the Titans" in Black Basalt show hills and cities in the background.

In his 1773 sales catalogue, Wedgwood listed "Class X: Heads of Illustrious Moderns, from Chaucer to the present Time." Included in this category were forty-six luminaries such as Shakespeare, Galileo, Inigo Jones, Martin Luther, Alexander Pope, and Sir William Hamilton. The designs for these subjects were drawn from a wide variety of sources, including portrait waxes by Isaac Gosset and other artists, medals, ivory carvings, paintings, and engravings. Although both were certainly talented enough to do so, William Hackwood and John Flaxman did not work from life when designing for Wedgwood. Often, of course, the subject was no longer living, but even in the case of living celebrities, Wedgwood generally chose to use an already existing, preferably famous, portrait. Thus, most of the portrait subjects that appeared in Wedgwood's catalogues and were intended for public sale were not designs original to the firm.

In contrast, small editions of original works which were intended only for private circulation were produced. In his 1775 catalogue, Wedgwood offered his "Plan for the Production of Original Works" by which the nobility and gentry could have their portraits modeled for production as ceramic cameos or intaglios. "Mr. Joachim Smith, an excellent Modeller, in Berner's-street," wrote Wedgwood, "proposes to model the Portraits of those who may please to employ him, in Sizes proper for Rings, Seals, Bracelets, or small Pictures. . . ." Evidently this scheme met with some success, for a similar offer is included in the 1779 catalogue as well.

Contemporary portrait medallions were undoubtedly one of Wedgwood's most important items. As he wrote to Bentley on July 2, 1776: "such subjects will be the most likely to go in quantities, for People will give more for their own Heads, or the Heads in fashion, than for any other subjects, & buy abundantly more of them" (Farrer, II, 294).

141. Double portrait medallion, "King George III and Queen Charlotte," light-blue Jasper with dark-blue dip top and bottom and white relief, 1¼" high (3.2 cm.), 2" wide (5.1 cm.), mark: "WEDGWOOD," 1789. The portraits of the king and queen used on this octagonal medallion are unusual variations of Wedgwood's more common versions. Among the many portraits of the monarchs illustrated in Robin Reilly and George Savage's *Wedgwood Portrait Medallions*, none are identical to those shown here. The medallion depicts the royal couple facing each other, but separated by an impressed inscription in Latin—"SAL PEREN ESTO"— meaning "Health Restored." The phrase refers to George III's recovery in February, 1789, from a period of temporary insanity caused by porphyria, a disease that was to permanently impair his faculties by 1810.

142. Medallion, "Thomas Bentley," dark-blue Jasper dip over pale blue with white relief, mark: "WEDGWOOD & BENTLEY," 4⅛" longest dimension (10.5 cm.), c. 1778-80. Four different portraits of Thomas Bentley are known to exist and a fifth, a "twenty-one inch head," is documented in the company's oven books, but is currently unknown (Reilly & Savage, 61). The earliest portrait of Bentley was modeled in 1773 by Joachim Smith. It shows Bentley in contemporary dress and is considered a pair with the Smith portrait of Wedgwood (*see* fig. 128). The other known portraits all show "Mr. Bentley Al antique," as described in a letter from Wedgwood to Bentley dated November 8, 1778 (Farrer, II, 466). It has been suggested that the version shown here was designed in 1780 as a memorial portrait, but the existence of the Wedgwood & Bentley mark on the piece would seem to indicate that it was produced before his death. None of these portraits are listed in the company's 18th-century sales catalogues.

Josiah Wedgwood was very much a man of his times, and he liked to keep abreast of current issues. American independence, the abolition of slavery, the improvement of roads, canal building, and better housing for workers were just a few of the issues that caught his attention and earned his approbation. His voracious appetite for information was fed by a constant stream of books, pamphlets, and newspapers. He was a critical reader, one not likely to believe everything he saw in print, and he enjoyed Bentley's reports on the latest gossip and rumors in London.

Wedgwood was politically aware and was active in a variety of causes, but often he found it expedient to underplay his role. Although he donated a generous amount to a fund for the relief of Americans taken prisoner during the War of Independence, he insisted that it be done anonymously. "I have more reasons than one why my name should not appear in the list," he wrote to Bentley in this regard on December 22, 1777. He continued: "In the mean time be so good to subscribe 10 guineas for me, or double that sum if you think proper, because I think it is a charity that should not be postpon'd . . ." (Farrer, II, 290).

Earlier that year Wedgwood had issued a Jasper intaglio with a design of the American rattlesnake and the legend "Don't tread on me," a common motif in American propaganda. On August 8, 1777, he wrote to Bentley to report "the Rattle Snake is in hand," and he cautioned Bentley about disposing of the intaglios, saying, "I think it will be best to keep such unchristian articles for Private Trade," by which he meant friends sympathetic to the cause (Farrer, II, 375).

Jasper commemorative items frequently took the form of portrait medallions, particularly memorial medallions; allegorical scenes, however, were used as well. For the latter, Wedgwood drew upon his own vast knowledge of classical art as well as the many authoritative source books that were available to him.

143. Plaque, "Mercury Uniting the Hands of France and England," solid-blue Jasper with white relief, 14⅞" high (37.8 cm.), 14³/₁₆" wide (36 cm.), mark: "WEDGWOOD," c. 1786. Issued to commemorate the signing of a commercial treaty which Wedgwood supported, this tablet is one of a pair of bas-reliefs modeled by John Flaxman after preliminary drawings by Henry Webber, an artist employed at Etruria. In his letter to Flaxman commissioning the designs, Wedgwood suggested that one of the pair should depict the burning of the implements of war, with Hercules representing Virtue. This was ultimately changed to "Peace Preventing Mars from Opening the Gates of Janus." The other design, "Mercury Uniting the Hands of France and England," did follow Wedgwood's initial specifications, and shows the god of commerce presiding over the reconciliation of the two countries. In describing this design, Wedgwood cautioned Flaxman "not to shew that these representations were invented by an Englishman [;] as they are meant to be conciliatory, they should be scrupulously impartial [;] the figures . . . should be equally magnificent and important . . ." (Finer & Savage, 301).

Presumably the designs for these commemorative tablets were composed from imagination, rather than being drawn directly from antique sources. It is evident, however, that Wedgwood did some research before presenting his suggestions to Flaxman; the idea of using Hercules to represent Virtue came from Wedgwood's reading of Montfaucon's *L'Antiquité Expliquée*, and he carefully cited the volume and page numbers in his letter to Flaxman.

144. Slave medallion, solid-white Jasper with black relief, inscribed "Am I Not A Man And A Brother?," 1¼" high (3.2 cm.), unmarked, c. 1787. In the summer of 1787 Wedgwood, one of the ardent founders of the Society for the Suppression of the Slave Trade, directed William Hackwood to model a medallion appropriate to the abolitionists' cause. Thousands of these medallions were made and distributed free of charge to anyone concerned with the issue, and the wearing of the medallions set as hatpins, bracelets, rings, and buckles became quite the fashion. On February 29, 1788, Wedgwood sent some of the medallions to Benjamin Franklin in Philadelphia, enclosing with them a letter saying: "This will be an epoch before unknown to the world, and while relief is given to so many of our fellow creatures immediately the object of it, the subject of freedom itself will be more canvassed and better understood in the enlightened nations" (Finer & Savage, 311-12). Franklin responded, saying that the medallions would be as effective as the best written pamphlet in calling attention to the issue. Although at this time Wedgwood did mark the great majority of his wares, the first slave medallions were not marked. The unmarked example illustrated here is probably from the first edition of the design.

145. Medallions, white applied-relief portraits and borders, all marked "WEDGWOOD." *Top row, left to right:* Jean Sylvain Bailly, 2⅜" (6 cm.), c. 1789-90; Jacques Necker, 2⅜" (6 cm.), c. 1788; Duc d'Orleans, 2³⁄₁₆" (5.7 cm.), c. 1788; *bottom row, left to right:* Comte de Mirabeau, 2⅜" (6 cm.), c. 1789-90; Louis XVI, 2⅜" (6.7 cm.) c. 1785; Marquis de Lafayette, 2⅜" (6 cm.), c. 1789-90.

Each of the subjects of the anthemion-bordered portraits was a major force in the events of the French Revolution. Unlike the portraits of the revolutionary heroes, those of Louis XVI and Jacques Necker are both framed with the fleur-de-lis, the royal symbol. The portrait of the Duc d'Orleans is surrounded by a border of laurel, setting him in yet another class.

The events of July, 1789, inspired Wedgwood to make timely use of portraits of popular figures already in production. To these he soon added the "anthemion" series. Though it was timely, the series soon went out of fashion. On December 23, 1791, Wedgwood received a letter from one Burley (probably employed at the Manchester warehouse), who stated that he was returning "1 box of such cameos that are least call'd for" (MS 11263-12). Heading the list are two cameos of Louis XVI, but also included are those of Orleans, Bailly, Lafayette, and Necker.

146. Medallions, dark-blue Jasper Dip on white with white bas-relief decoration, all marked "WEDGWOOD," 1790. *Upper left:* "Leopold the Lawgiver Supported by Wisdom & Benevolence," 1⅞″ high (4.8 cm.); *upper right:* seal of the German Empire, 1″ high (2.5 cm.); *center:* "Coronation of Leopold," 2″ high (5.1 cm.); *lower left:* "Grieving for Elizabeth," 1¾″ in diameter (4.4 cm.); *lower right:* "Turkey & Russia & the two Belligerant powers consulting upon peace, & Germany the Mediator between them," 2³⁄₁₆″ in diameter (5.6 cm.).

Among the many series issued by Wedgwood—the Popes, Kings of England, French series, and others—there was an enigmatic group of subjects issued in about 1790 and intended specifically for the German market. All of the cameos in the series appear to commemorate events concerning or surrounding the coronation of Leopold II, who succeeded his brother Joseph II. Despite a good deal of documentary evidence, however, the series remains a mystery, with neither the exact subject matter nor the full extent of the series known with undisputed accuracy.

According to Harry Barnard, an invoice sent to Thomas Byerley, dated September 11, 1790, lists a consignment of 186 cameos of seven different designs, some available in more than one shape or size. At the time, Byerley, together with Wedgwood's eldest son Josiah, was in Frankfurt, which was one of several stops in a whirlwind tour of the Continent undertaken to display the Portland Vase and secure new orders. The list, which describes the cameos as having a "fine blue ground," defines the *minimum* number of subjects in the series; it is evident, however, that the series was much larger. At least five other designs are known which have motifs indicative of similar German subjects, and still more may exist.

147. Medallions, dark-blue Jasper dip over white with white bas-relief decoration, all marked "WEDGWOOD," c. 1790. *Top:* 2″ high (5.1 cm.); *left:* 2⅛″ in diameter (5.4 cm.); *right:* 2³⁄₁₆″ in diameter (5.6 cm.). The subjects of the three cameos are as yet unidentified. None appears in the 1790 invoice. It is evident, however, from the designs—each incorporating symbols of the German Empire—that they should be included as part of Wedgwood's series of medallions on German themes. The figure of Minerva, used to represent Germany, appears on each of the cameos. The symbolism is made explicit in the medallion to the left: Minerva's shield bears the German eagle rather than the expected head of Medusa.

148. *Left*: Medallion, dark-blue Jasper dip on white with white bas-relief decoration, 2″ in diameter (5.1 cm.), mark: "WEDGWOOD," 1790. This cameo is listed in the 1790 invoice as "Germany, in the Character of Minerva present^g Leopold with a Civic band as a reward for his code of Laws."

149. *Below*: Medallions, dark-blue Jasper dip on white with white bas-relief decoration, all marked "WEDGWOOD," c. 1790. *Left*: "Fame inscribing Vase to the Memory of Elizabeth," 1⅞″ high (4.8 cm.); *center*: "Mars present^g a Crown to the Genius of Germany," 2⅛″ in diameter (5.4 cm.); *right*: "The Genius of the Empire holding the Bust of Leopold while a priestess is officiating at an Alter [sic]," 2⅛″ in diameter (5.4 cm.). The design at left was issued to commemorate the death in February, 1740, of Elizabeth, the favorite niece of Joseph II, Leopold's predecessor. The design on the cameo at right was taken from a bas-relief in the Villa Albani illustrated in volume I of Winckelmann's *Monumenti Antichi Inediti* (plate 186). Wedgwood adapted it slightly to fit his own purposes.

150. *Left*: Medallion, "Memorial to Salomon Gessner," white Jasper relief on blue with black slip, 4¾″ long (12.1 cm.) excluding frame, mark: "WEDGWOOD," c. 1790. Salomon Gessner (b. 1730) was a Swiss poet and painter, whose works embodied the pastoral ideal that was sweeping England and the Continent in the latter part of the 18th century. His death in 1788 was an occasion for international mourning, and Wedgwood decided to issue a commemorative portrait medallion. Progress on the design proceeded slowly, and it was not until January 23, 1790, that Wedgwood could write to Bentley: "I have since got two sizes of the head modelled in wax, one proper for rings and other small ornaments and the other larger for bracelets, girdles, pictures etc" (Whieldon, 7). Shortly thereafter, Wedgwood designed another medallion (illustrated here) incorporating an architectural monument designed by the sculptor Michel Brandoin. The pose of the figures can be compared to the mourning iconography of "Charlotte at the Tomb of Werther" (*see* fig. 137). In all, Wedgwood produced four different designs for memorial medallions in honor of Gessner.

Although he sold some ready-mounted objects such as bracelets and framed cameos in his showrooms, by far most of Wedgwood's wares were sold unset. Wedgwood did no mounting of cameos and medallions at Etruria, but he did make use of the services of various mounters in England and France. Brass, copper, foilstone, ormulu, mother-of-pearl, precious metals, and many other materials were used, with mounters generally specializing in a particular type of work. London and Uttoxeter, for example, were the centers for gold work, while Wolverhampton and Birmingham were famous for cut steel. Wedgwood patronized or supplied a great number of firms including Thomas Copestake of Uttoxeter, John Vernon and William Hasselwood in Wolverhampton, and the firms of William & Richard Smith, Green & Vale, and Bolton & Scale of Birmingham.

Among the many materials used for mountings, cut steel is perhaps the most interesting and attractive. Prized for its diamond-like sparkle, cut steel was popular for setting buttons, buckles, and a wide range of other ornaments or "toys," as they were called in the 18th century. Although the material was inherently inexpensive, the detailed workmanship required made cut-steel objects very costly—sometimes more expensive than gold. Good-quality 18th-century cut steel is distinguished by the large number of facets per bead or stud, frequently as many as fifteen on a single large stud. It is also usually dense in design and relatively heavy. Unlike precious metals, which were often melted down and reworked when styles changed, much of the cut steel that survives has retained its original form.

151. Patchboxes, marks not visible, c. 1780-1800. *Above:* ivory with silver and gold inlaid decoration and tri-color Jasper dip cameos, 3⅝" long (9.2 cm.), 1½" wide (3.8 cm.); *below:* blue glass and metal with cut-steel beads and tri-color Jasper dip cameos, 3⅝" long (9.2 cm.), 1⅛" wide (2.9 cm.). Between wearings, decorative silk patches, used to draw attention to the beauty of the wearer's complexion or to cover blemishes, were kept in tiny, elegant containers made especially for the purpose. Tri-color cameos in lilac, dark blue, and white decorate both objects. In the second of the two boxes, the cameos are set under small glass domes like those found on watches. Earlier, when the colored backgrounds on Jasper objects were simply painted on, such domes were necessary for protection. In this case, the colors are fired and the use of the glass domes is an aesthetic choice rather than a strict necessity.

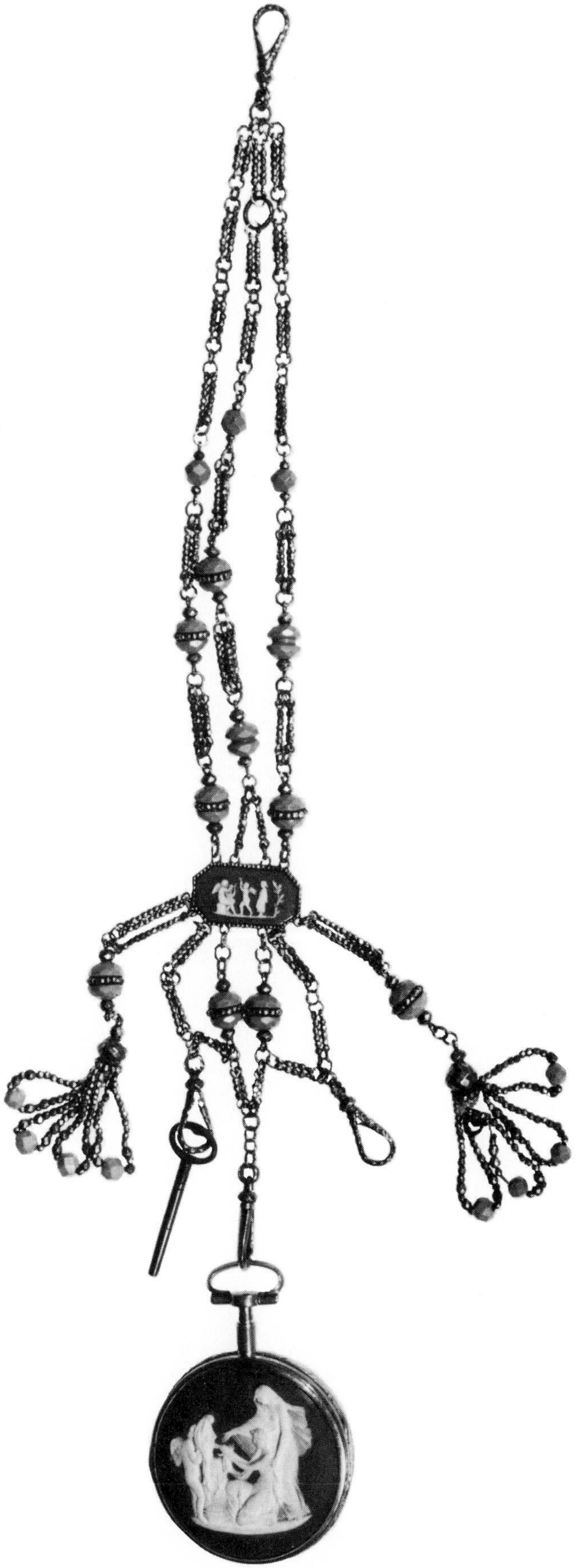

152. *Left:* Chatelaine with removable watch, cut-steel and solid medium-blue Jasper beads with center double-faced cameo and dark-blue Jasper dip watch back, 13⅞″ long (35.2 cm.), including watch, mark: not visible, c. 1775-1800. The word *chatelaine* originally referred to the mistress of a household who was responsible for the keys to various cupboards and safes. Although the object was first used only for carrying keys, eventually its use expanded to include scissors, watches, and other personal and household items. By the 18th century, chatelaines had become quite elaborate and were intended as much for show as for use. The remarkable Jasper beads shown here demonstrate the fineness and hardness of the body, which could be polished to a high sheen on a lapidary (gem-cutting) wheel. Attached to the chatelaine is a watch made by Abraham Louis Breguet (1747-1823), a Swiss-born craftsman who worked in Paris. Wedgwood made curved medallions designed specifically to fit watch backs; the subject used here is known as "Cupid Masked."

153. *Above:* Telescope, dark-blue Jasper dip tube with white bas-reliefs set with ivory, brass, and cut steel, 2¾″ long (6.9 cm.), 2″ (5.1 cm.) at widest point, mark: not visible, c. 1780-1800. This small low-powered telescope was intended for use at plays, the opera, or similar entertainments. The bas-relief decorations depicting two charioteers, male and female, were most likely taken from plates 190 and 192 in Agostini's *Gemmae et Sculpturae Antiquae* (1685), which show similar figures. The female charioteer in particular became a very common Wedgwood motif; the design is now usually known as "Aurora," although that name is not given by Agostini. Floral swags and an anthemion border complete the design.

154. *Left:* Brooch, dark-blue and white medallion (probably Jasper dip) set in cut steel, 4″ long (10.2 cm.), 2½″ wide (6.4 cm.), mark: not visible, c. 1790-1800. This object was probably originally used as a shoe buckle, but was subsequently modified with the addition of a silver pin so that it could be worn as a brooch. The cut-steel setting is of good quality, although the studs do not exhibit the variety of sizes and density in packing that characterize the very best examples. The twelve small cameos were produced especially to be set in this way and were made with a center hole to accept the wire shanks of the studs. The subject of the central medallion is unknown, and the existence of the expected Wedgwood trademark is unverifiable without dismantling the setting. Because the setting covers all but the face of the medallion, it is difficult to determine whether the piece is solid Jasper or dip; the dark-blue color, however, seems to be somewhat more prevalent in the latter process.

155. *Above:* Sewing box, rosewood inlaid with cut steel and dark-blue and white jasper cameos and central medallion, 13¾″ long (35 cm.), 10¼″ wide (26 cm.), 3⅛″ high (7.9 cm.), mark: not visible, c. 1785-1800. The sewing box, which has a matching stand, was made for Anna Turiet, whose name appears on a steel plate set within the central medallion. Inside the box are the original ivory-and-cut-steel sewing implements with which it was equipped, including crochet hooks, bobbins, and other tools for fancy work. The central medallion is surrounded with cut-steel beads and is decorated with the signs of the zodiac. Additional steel work, both faceted and inlaid, and eight small cameos adorn the top rim. The small cameos, which depict Hebe and the Eagle, the muses, and similar subjects, are of Jasper dip, and it is likely that the large medallion is also dip. The stand (not illustrated) is decorated with several small cameos, as well as with a large cameo depicting "the Marriage of Cupid and Psyche" after a celebrated gem in the collection of the Duke of Marlborough, from whom Wedgwood had obtained a cast.

Regarding Wedgwood statues, figures, and animals in general, Eliza Meteyard stated that "less is known of Wedgwood's labours in this class of ornamental ware; than in any other; fewer examples survive; and in some cases they appear to have wholly perished" (Handbook, 212). While true for Basalt statues and figures, this statement is doubly true for such objects in Jasper. In the latter cases we do not have even adequate documentary evidence; most of the Jasper figures were produced after Bentley's death, and Wedgwood's correspondence of this period never again attained the richness and intimacy of those earlier letters.

"Class XII: Busts, Small Statues, Boys, Animals, &c." appeared in Wedgwood's first sales catalogue with twenty-three subjects. Two years later, the category was expanded to include fifty-five subjects. These were produced predominantly in Black Basalt, with some examples made in Rosso Antico and Cane Ware. The latter bodies were particularly difficult to work with, and in the late 1770s it must have seemed to Wedgwood that only the Jasper body held the promise of ever being as aesthetically satisfying as the Basalt had proved to be. To this end, he began experiments on Jasper busts and statues virtually as soon as he was assured of the success of that material in cameos and tablets. As early as November 5, 1778, Wedgwood wrote to Bentley describing "a head of Voltaire in white jasper upon a basaltes pedestal richly ornamented," which he had succeeded in making (Meteyard, Handbook, 216). This early success, however, was but a first step in a long process of trials and experimentation which was necessary before Wedgwood could attain the consistency and quality he required for successful mass production. Though there do exist some Jasper figures marked "Wedgwood & Bentley," they are very rare and are not included in the 1779 catalogue.

By 1787 Wedgwood had overcome the problems of firing Jasper busts and figures, and his catalogue of that year announced that "a small assortment of the figures is now made in the jasper of two colours, the effect of which is new and pleasing." Still, by comparison to Basalt figures, which could be made up to two feet in length, the Jasper figures were very small, rarely more than six or seven inches tall.

156. Bust of Plato, solid-white Jasper, 15″ high (38.1 cm.), mark: "WEDGWOOD & BENTLEY," c. 1778-80. This fine bust has had a difficult career—at one point being completely covered over with a coat of dark paint. Though beautifully modeled, it is a problematical piece. The body is quite uncharacteristic of Wedgwood's production, lacking the fine-grained, semi-vitreous quality that one would expect to find in Jasper. It is perhaps an early trial. A second unusual feature is the way in which the bust is affixed to the plinth. On pieces of this size, it was Wedgwood's custom to fire the bust and plinth separately and then screw them together; in this case, however, the bust was fired directly onto the plinth.

Perhaps the most surprising feature is the appearance of the words "Plato No 31" incised into the front of the plinth. This inscription does correspond to the listing of the subject in the 1775 sales catalogue, but it was far more common for Wedgwood to inscribe identifying names on the backs of busts. Numerals indicating catalogue class and number are generally only found on cameos and medallions. That the legend is impressed on the front of the bust of Plato has given rise to the suggestion that the object was perhaps never intended for sale, but rather was an example kept at the factory for reference.

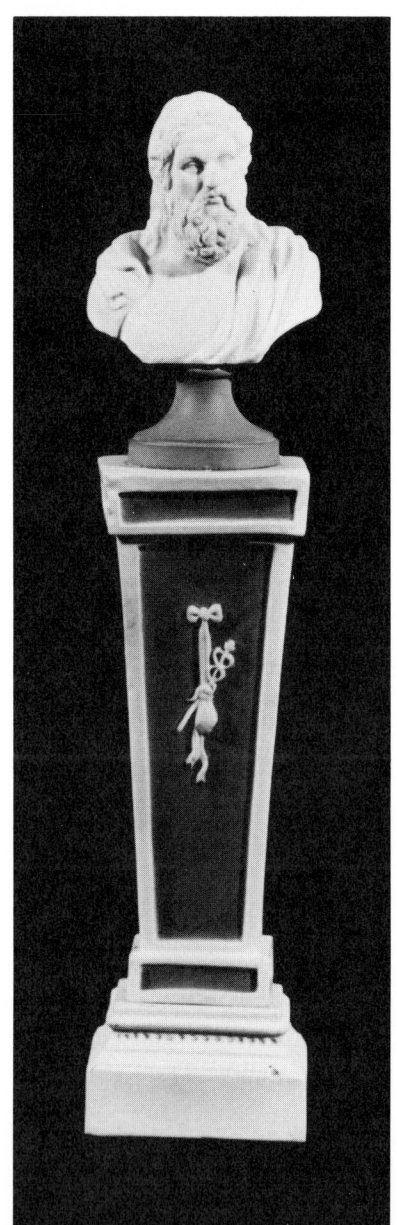

157. *Left:* Bust of Aristophanes, solid-white Jasper bust on blue base with white relief, 5½" high (14 cm.), marked on back of bust: "Aristophanes, Wedgwood," on base: "Wedgwood," c. 1780-1800. An object such as this may have been what Wedgwood had in mind when he listed in his 1787 catalogue the availability of "small busts with emblematical terms," the word "term" meaning a pillar or pedestal.

Petro Bellorio in *Veterum Illustrium Philosophorum Poetarum Rhetorum et Oratorum* (1685) illustrates a virtually identical bust of Aristophanes, though without a term. It is not known whether Bellorio's book was part of Wedgwood's library, but he probably had access to it. He may, of course, have had the bust modeled directly from Bellorio's illustration, but it is much more likely that he purchased the mold for this, and its companion Pindar, ready-made.

158. *Below (left):* Figures of Hebe (*left*) and Cupid (*right*), white Jasper figures on solid pale-blue bases with white relief, 6⅞" high (17.5 cm.), both marked "WEDG-WOOD," c. 1782-1800. Wedgwood's 1787 catalogue contains adjacent listings for "CUPID, *on a pedestal*" and "HEBE, *ditto*." While the two subjects are not given specifically as a matched pair, in size and attitude they complement each other. Both figures, representing eternal youth, are on bases decorated with Jasper swags, masks, and trophies. Meteyard attributes the figures to Henry Webber, who worked as chief modeller for Wedgwood during 1782-84.

159. *Above:* Figure, Sphinx, white Jasper figure and base with black slip decoration and white relief, 6⁹⁄₁₆" long (16.6 cm.), 4" high (10.2 cm.), mark: "WEDGWOOD," c. 1780-1800. The modeling on this couchant winged sphinx is of the highest caliber, so good that the object almost seems to be sculpted rather than molded. The wings are beautifully feathered; the face is full and carefully detailed. The animal vitality of the subject is evident in the tense musculature of the forearms and in the undulating ribs and flesh of the flanks. Only the tail betrays the true nature of the material from which the piece was formed; it retains the hand-rolled, plastic quality of clay.

The smooth waxen finish of the white body is enhanced by contrast with the inky-black slip, which was painted on the rectangular stand after the bas-relief decoration had been applied. This technique was commonly used by Wedgwood in early objects of black Jasper as a way of circumventing the tendency of this color to stain the white relief when the dip process was used.

Elaborate, finely-detailed candlesticks are among the most exquisite objects produced by Wedgwood in the Jasper body. Thus, it is surprising to find the following comment in a letter Wedgwood wrote to Bentley on November 4, 1778: "If one may confess a disagreeable truth . . . it seems to me that metal is the only proper candlestick material. Clay serves only to gratify caprice or poverty" (Farrer, II, 465). Bentley had forwarded to Wedgwood some sketches of designs for candlesticks, but the latter replied, "I really despair of the article in pottery of any kind." Though he admitted that "something pretty might be made in blue & white Jasper," Wedgwood was concerned that such objects might "vulgarise the material," which he was using primarily for imitations of antique gems. Later, Wedgwood evidently changed his mind, for in his 1787 sales catalogue he included "Various kinds of Lamps and Candelabra, useful and ornamental," noting that "some are made in the jasper of two colors."

Eighteenth-century candlesticks made entirely of Jasper are very rare. More commonly Wedgwood supplied Jasper components to be mounted in ormolu or other such material and fitted with metal candle sockets. Occasionally, however, Wedgwood transformed Jasper figures or vases into candlesticks, just as he had done earlier with Basalt. Perhaps because of their scarcity, little is known about these objects, and their shapes and designs are not given in the sales catalogues. The large dramatic candelabra all date from the years after Bentley's death, since before that time Wedgwood could not successfully fire objects of that size.

160. Candlesticks, Minerva (*left*) and Diana (*right*), white figures with candle holders of solid deep-blue, bases of solid pale blue with applied bead and laurel-leaf decoration in white, 13¾" high (35 cm.), unmarked, c. 1780-1800. Skillful contrasts in color and texture make this pair of candlesticks particularly effective visually. The detailing on these pieces is extraordinary. Minerva's plumed helmet is enriched with a figure of a sphinx and with rams' heads in relief on the visor; Diana's coiffure is enhanced by a tiny crescent moon. Even fingernails and toenails are carefully delineated. Although the candlesticks are generally attributed to Henry Webber, some authorities have recently credited John Flaxman with the design. The original molds are still in the possession of the Wedgwood factory.

161, 162. Triton candlesticks, solid-white Jasper figures with blue dip bases and
holders, both marked "WEDGWOOD," c. 1780-1800. *Left:* 10¾" high (27.3 cm.);
right: 10" high (25.4 cm.). Appearing in Wedgwood's first catalogue (1773) as a "Pair
of Tritons, from Michael Angelo, 11 inches high," these candlesticks initially were
produced only in the Black Basalt body. By 1787, however, Wedgwood was able to
announce in his catalogue that "a small assortment of the figures is now made in the
jasper of two colors, the effect of which is new and pleasing." Presumably the Triton
candlesticks were produced in Jasper about that time. Examples in both solid Jasper
and in Jasper dip are known.

    There appears to be no agreement upon the question of who modeled the pieces.
Various authorities attribute the work to John Flaxman, Mary Landre, Thomas
Boot, and William Keeling. In a letter to Bentley dated September 20, 1769,
Wedgwood wrote that "Boot is making Tritons & Sphinx's, & does them very well,
better than I expected" (Farrer, I, 280). Considering that these shapes were very
popular and evidently in production for many years, it seems possible that many different modelers worked on them at various times. Certainly there do exist many
small differences in the treatment and handling of the figures among the extant examples.

163, 164. Candlesticks, solid-white Jasper figures with solid-blue bases and holders, both marked "WEDGWOOD," c. 1780-1800. *Left:* "Ceres, 12½" high (31.8 cm.); *below (left):* "Cybele," 12¹³⁄₁₆" high (32.5 cm.). The elaborate abundance of an 18th-century feast is admirably reflected in these two candlesticks, which represent two related goddesses of classical mythology. Ceres, the goddess of the harvest, is identified by a sheaf of wheat at her side and a crown of wheat in her hair. Cybele, goddess of agriculture and civilization, was worshipped as the procreative power of all things in nature. Accompanied by a lion, Cybele wears the "corona muralis," a crown fashioned to represent the walls of a city. Each figure bears a cornucopia as a convenient holder and socket for a candle.

165. *Above:* Candlestick vases, "Birth of Achilles" (*left*) and "Dipping of Achilles" (*right*), white with black slip decoration, 10½" high, (26.8 cm.), both marked "WEDGWOOD," 1780-1800. Camillo Pacetti, one of a small group of artists who worked in Rome and provided Wedgwood with designs, is credited with the modeling of a series of bas-reliefs depicting events in the life of Achilles. According to Macht, the source for the Achilles reliefs was a marble disk or "puteal" that was probably originally intended to encircle the rim of a well. The disk was given to the Capitoline Museum sometime during 1740-58, and it is likely that Pacetti saw and sketched it there. The Achilles series was used by Wedgwood on many different forms including tablets, vases, and other shapes.

The candlestick vases are composed of three parts. When the entire lid is removed, a vase is created. When the finial alone is removed and re-inserted upside down, a candlestick is the result. When the lid and finial are left in place, the object is intended to be used as a decorative urn.

Bentley's death in 1780 had a profound effect on Wedgwood's business. The entire ornamental ware stock had to be sold at public auction in order to satisfy the claims Bentley's widow had upon the company's assets, and there was much speculation on the part of Wedgwood's customers whether Wedgwood, single-handedly, would be able to keep up the high level of quality he had attained with Bentley's help and encouragement (Meteyard, Handbook, 283). To allay those suspicions, Wedgwood rushed a new line of vases into production utilizing the Jasper body. These were featured at the gala reopening of his showrooms in Greek Street in 1782.

Although the vases were introduced early in the 1780s, there is no official mention of them until the 1787 catalogue in which Wedgwood listed Jasper vases, tripods, and other ornaments, noting: "As these are my latest, I hope they will be found to be my most improved work." Evidence of Wedgwood's pride in this new line of ornamental ware is seen in his presentation of a tri-color Jasper Pegasus vase to the British Museum in 1786 (see plate XVI, p. 100, for a similar example). In a letter to Sir William Hamilton, he described it as "the finest and most perfect I have ever made" (Meteyard, Handbook, 286).

Since Wedgwood was of the opinion that "verbal descriptions could give but an imperfect idea of the delicacy of the materials, the execution of the artist, or the general effect," his Jasper vases, bulb pots, and similar objects are not well described in the 1787 sales catalogue, and potential customers were instructed to examine the objects in person. From the pieces that survive, however, it is evident that Wedgwood continued to draw inspiration from classical antiquities, while at the same time obtaining new designs from contemporary artists such as Lady Elizabeth Templeton, Emma Crewe, and others. Toward the close of the 18th century, Wedgwood's use of classical motifs became freer and less literal, some of the late Jasper pieces becoming virtually "over-decorated" by Wedgwood's early standards.

166. Vase, "Bacchanalian Triumph," solid-blue Jasper with white bas-relief decoration, 18⅝" high (47.3 cm.), mark: "WEDGWOOD," c. 1780-1800. Copied from a 5½-feet tall marble vase found on the Quirinalis in the 16th century, the design depicts a Dionysiac or Bacchanalian celebration. After its discovery, the vase became one of the most famous treasures in the collection of the Villa Borghese and was illustrated in Bartoli's *Admiranda Romanarum Antiquitatum* and in Montfaucon's *L'Antiquité Expliquée*. In this case, however, Wedgwood did not have to rely on printed sources for his design. "Bacchanalian Triumph" was modeled for him in Rome by John Devaere and touched up by John Flaxman. In 1788, Flaxman wrote to Wedgwood, saying, "Mr. Davaere has been at work with the utmost diligence . . . on the bas-relief of the Borghese Vase, in which he has succeeded very well, but it will take him some weeks to finish, and after he has done, I shall have something to do to it" (Rathbone, 190).

The Wedgwood vase is similar in shape and design to the original, which is now in the Louvre, but a lid was added and the double masks below the frieze were replaced with looped handles. The central figure represents Bacchus who wears, according to Montfaucon, a "feminine coiffure" and leans on the shoulder of a muse.

167. Vase, "Procession of the Deities," lilac Jasper dip over white with white bas-relief decoration, 13⅛″ high (33.3 cm.), mark: "WEDGWOOD," 1780-1800. Macht describes this design as taken from the "Puteal of the Twelve Gods," formerly in the collection of Cardinal Albani and now in the Capitoline Museum. The source, according to Macht, is thought to be Athenian and from the first century B.C., although it repeats earlier types. Wedgwood may have known the design from Winckelmann's *Monumenti Antichi Inediti* (1767), where it appears in a group of plates following page 103.

The use of lilac Jasper 18th-century object of this size is extremely rare. Occasionally Wedgwood used lilac Jasper for teaware (*see* fig. 179), and the color is also seen in tri-color and five-color Jasper combinations.

168. Vase, "Sacrifice to Hymen," solid-blue Jasper with white relief, 20″ high, (50.8 cm.), mark: "WEDGWOOD," c. 1780-1800. According to Macht, the frieze design of cupids and masks was taken from the cinerary urn of D. Lucellus Felix, now in the Capitoline Museum. The design shows several cupids or *erotes* dancing, playing musical instruments, and carrying torches as they presumably proceed to the temple of Hymen, the Greek god of marriage.

The Wedgwood vase does not resemble the original early-empire octagonal urn in shape, nor in its over-all decoration which displays the tendency toward greater elaboration that is characteristic of late 18th-century Wedgwood production. The modeler of the design is unknown; in *Memorials of Wedgwood* Meteyard first assigned it to John Flaxman, but later felt some uncertainty on this point.

169. Portland Vase, solid black Jasper with white relief, 10″ high (25.4 cm.), numbered with graphite pencil on the rim of the interior: "3", c. 1790-1800. The shape and decoration of this vase were taken from a cameo glass vase brought to England from Italy in 1783 by Sir William Hamilton, who sold it to the Duchess of Portland. The Portland Vase (also known as the Barberini Vase after its previous owners) was probably the most celebrated classical artifact of the 18th century, and gentlemen and scholars vied with each other in attempting to explain the meaning of the enigmatic relief decoration.

Working first from Montfaucon's illustration of the vase, and then from the original itself, Wedgwood attempted to render the blue-black glass body and the translucent white reliefs in the medium of clay. After years of effort, the first successful copy was completed in 1790, and Sir Joshua Reynolds, president of the Royal Academy, testified that it was "a correct and faithful imitation" (Wills, 201).

In all likelihood, fewer than twenty copies of the Portland Vase were produced during Wedgwood's lifetime. Such "first-edition" vases do not bear the company trademark, but are occasionally numbered on the rim.

170, 171. Ornaments, both marked "WEDGWOOD," c. 1780-1800. *Left:* ruined column, solid-white Jasper column and base with blue slip-decorated panel, 7⅞″ high (20 cm.); *above:* ruined columns, solid-white Jasper, 7⅝″ high (19.4 cm.). The latter half of the 18th century witnessed a vogue for fanciful landscapes which included in their compositions accurately rendered illustrations of actual classical ruins. Giovanni Battista Piranesi (1720-78) was one of the most famous artists who worked in this style, and one of his etchings perhaps served as the design source for these Wedgwood ornaments. The modeling of these designs has sometimes been attributed to William Keeling, but this cannot be documented. While the fashion lasted, it was not uncommon for gentlemen to build new ruined temples and similar edifices on the grounds of their country estates.

172. *Left:* Bulb pot, "Apollo and the Muses," solid-blue Jasper with white bas-relief decoration and "orange peel" finish, 9½″ high (24.1 cm.), mark: "WEDGWOOD, WEDGWOOD," 1780-1800. The bas-relief figures on the bulb pot are variations of a common Wedgwood subject, the Muses. In comparison to the earlier Wedwood & Bentley plaque (*see* fig. 138), several of the figures on the bulb pot are quite different. Of those seen here, only Euterpe (*far left*) is identical to her counterpart on the plaque. In addition, the bulb pot decoration includes the figure of Apollo (not illustrated) who does not appear at all on the plaque.

The shape of the bulb pot is unusual; Wedgwood generally preferred a more horizontal form for pots of this kind. Also somewhat unusual is the dimpled or "orange peel" effect seen on the main body of the pot. This finish is considered desirable because it indicates 18th-century production.

173, 174. Flower holders, solid-blue Jasper with white relief, both marked "WEDGWOOD," c. 1780-1800. *Top:* "Cupid," 5½" high (14 cm.), 8⅜" wide (21.3 cm.); *above:* "Psyche," 5½" high (14 cm.), 8½" wide (21.6 cm.). During the 18th century the cultivation of exotic plants and bulbs became very fashionable, and Wedgwood attempted to meet the need for attractive, suitable containers that would allow proper arrangement and display. As was his usual practice, Wedgwood turned to classical art for inspiration and adapted the shapes of altars and other artifacts to his purpose. The flower holders shown here derive their basic form from ancient tombs or sarcophagi. The depiction of Cupid and Psyche as young adults was uncommon, but not unknown. The relief decoration—consisting of acanthus and laurel leaves, floral swags, and paterae—is carefully handled and restrained.

175. *Above:* Jug, solid-blue Jasper with white bas-relief decoration, 8½" high (21.6 cm.), mark: "WEDGWOOD," c. 1780-1800. Among Wedgwood's late 18th-century production are many objects that are heavily decorated—almost over decorated—as though Wedgwood were "showing off" the beauty and versatility of his invention. The upside-down helmet shape of the Wedgwood jug is derived from common silver shapes; Wedgwood, however, added many different elements from other objects to create a minor "tour de force." The sentimental domestic scene is attributed to Lady Elizabeth Templeton and is a common Wedgwood motif. More unusual is the feathered wheat border draped with floral swags. The graceful handle splits at the bottom to form two leaves, while a sea shell—another widely-used motif—adorns the top of the handle. Four additional borders and hand-rolled beads complete the elaborate ornamentation.

The introduction of "diced ware" gave Wedgwood a line of products that fully exploited the beautiful coloring and fine texture of the Jasper body. The execution of the intricate designs was expedited through a technological innovation—the invention of the engine-turning lathe—with which the turner could pare away discrete sections of material, mechanically rather than manually. Unlike traditional lathes, which had been in use in the pottery industry for generations, the engine-turning lathe operated with a system of weights and pulleys that regularly brought the cutting tool in contact with the surface of the object, thus cutting a checkered or "diced" pattern.

Though Basalt and the other dry bodies were suitable for engine-turning lathe decoration, it was only in the Jasper body that Wedgwood was able to achieve a fusion of design and color that resulted in rich, elegant effects displayed by objects such as those shown in plates XIV (p. 99) and XVII (p. 101). By dipping a solid-white Jasper object in colored slip before cutting the design, the resulting pattern was enhanced by the interplay of contrasting colors. After the turning was completed, bas-relief ornaments in white Jasper or in a third color were applied. It was this potential for using two, three, or more colors on a single object that made the Jasper body particularly well-suited to this type of decoration.

176. *Below (left):* Marriage vase, blue Jasper dip over white with white and green applied bas-reliefs, 7¼″ high (18.4 cm.), mark: "WEDGWOOD," c. 1780-1800. Here the diced design was varied by adjusting the lathe so that it would cut an unusual wavy pattern, rather than the more common straight checkered design. The top rim is adorned with a lily design; the foot is enriched with ribbon and acanthus bas-reliefs. Laurel leaves, quatrefoils, and paterae complete the decoration. This example has lost the perforated lid topped with two doves that gives the piece its name.

177. *Below:* Box, green Jasper dip over white with blue bas-relief decoration, 1¹⁄₁₆″ high (2.7 cm.), 3″ in diameter (7.6 cm.), unmarked, c. 1780-1800. Although unmarked, this small round box bears all the characteristics one would expect to see in a Wedgwood object. The diced pattern is cleanly handled. In making such patterns, great care had to be taken to insure that the machinery was precisely calibrated. The smallest discrepancy could produce ragged edges that would detract from the crispness of the design. The checkered pattern punctuated with quatrefoils is a common Wedgwood design, and the central motif of a female charioteer is identical to the bas-relief of Aurora found on a Jasper telescope attributed to Wedgwood (*see* fig. 153). The specific purpose for which the box was intended is open to speculation. It may have been meant to hold snuff, beauty patches, or valued trinkets.

Writing in the mid-19th century, Eliza Meteyard gave short shrift to Wedgwood's Jasper tea and dessert services, claiming: "Articles in useful forms, even for dessert, cannot come under the term 'fine art'" (Handbook, 227). Meteyard was surely overly harsh in her criticism, for in many cases Wedgwood lavished as much attention on his tea wares and dessert services in Jasper as on his purely ornamental wares. In his 1787 sales catalogue he described such items as "polished within [,] ornamented with bas-reliefs, and very highly finished." In addition to applied bas-reliefs, pierced lattice patterns (see plate XVIII) and engine-turning lathe decoration also were used.

In describing his teawares as "polished within," Wedgwood specified that they were not glazed. The lapidary polish that he was able to achieve in hollow items such as slop bowls and teacups was made possible by the extreme hardness of the Jasper body. The polishing resulted in a smooth, non-glassy, lustrous finish that William Gladstone described in the mid-19th century as "a surface soft as an infant's flesh to the touch" (Meteyard, Handbook, 313). The body was also somewhat translucent. Accompanying the description of "Tea and Coffee Equipages, &c." in the 1788 French catalogue was a carefully drawn illustration of a Jasper teacup "where the transparency of the jasper is endeavoured to be represented."

In his 1787 catalogue, Wedgwood reported that he made "tea pots, coffee pots, chocolates, sugar dishes, cream ewers . . . cabinet cups and saucers, and all articles of the tea table and dejeuner." Today these objects, together with the dessert wares, are considered to be some of the finest ever produced by Wedgwood, their utility enhancing rather than diminishing their appeal.

178. Teapot and saucer, solid-white Jasper, c. 1780-1800. Teapot— 4¼" high (10.8 cm.), mark: "WEDGWOOD"; saucer—4⅝" in diameter (11.7 cm.), mark: "Wedgwood." Similar in design to the pineapple, cauliflower, and other vegetable shapes commonly produced in creamware during the 18th century, this teapot is distinguished by its crisp modeling and its fine-grained Jasper body. The body is translucent when examined by transmitted light and exhibits a slight greenish tinge. This shape is known to have been produced by Wedgwood in the early 19th century in coarse, glazed stoneware and in Rosso Antico, but the object appears to be of 18th-century origin. The "lotus-shape" saucer is known in both grey-green and solid-white Jasper. The upper and lower case Wedgwood trademark on the example shown here is indisputable evidence of 18th-century production.

179. *Top:* Teaware, lilac Jasper dip on white with white relief, all marked "WEDGWOOD," c. 1780-1800. Teapot—5" high (12.7 cm.), can—2¹³/₁₆" high (7.1 cm.), saucer—4⅝" in diameter (11.7 cm.), cream jug—2½" high (6.4 cm.). Lilac, together with blue, green and buff, was commonly found in the pastel color schemes of Robert Adam and other prominent 18th-century architects; but though it would seem that there would have been a market for ceramics of that color, it is very uncommon in Wedgwood's production. Thomas Bentley mentioned lilac, or as he spelled it "laylock," in a letter to Wedgwood regarding a chimney piece (Jewitt, 272), but most lilac examples appear to have been made after Bentley's death in 1780. From the small number of pieces that survive, it is apparent that Wedgwood had difficulty controlling the color. It is particularly uneven in the Jasper dip pieces—thin in some spots and puddled in others—looking more like a watercolor wash than slip. The objects illustrated here were not originally sold together. The apparent differences in ornamentation indicate that the silver-shape teapot was not a mate to the arabesque-decorated cream jug and matching coffee can and saucer.

180. *Above:* Teapot—4⅜" high (11.1 cm.); saucer—5⅛" in diameter (13 cm.); handleless cup—3⅛" in diameter (7.9 cm.); cream jug—2⅝" (6.7 cm.); saucer—5⅛" in diameter (13 cm.); cup—2⅜" high (6 cm.), all marked: "WEDGWOOD," 1780-1800. As he gradually relinquished his reliance on the books of classical antiquities that had been his inspiration, Wedgwood was forced to seek out fresh sources of designs. A favorite new artist was Lady Elizabeth Templeton (1748-1800), a member of the royal household whose playful babes and gentle domestic scenes admirably suited Wedgwood's purposes. One of the designs from Lady Templeton's "Domestic Employment" series is seen here on a teapot. On the cup at left is her figure of Poor Maria, a character from Laurence Sterne's popular book *A Sentimental Journey.* The scene on the other cup (*right*) is known as "Cupid Shaving His Bow." Taken from a painting by Parmigianino (mistakenly attributed to Correggio in the 18th century), the design may have been adapted by Lady Templeton for Wedgwood's use. A tiny butterfly appears in each bas-relief scene, a simple device which serves to unify what would otherwise be a somewhat arbitrary choice of subjects.

181. Cup, solid light-blue Jasper with white bas-relief decoration and polished interior, 2½″ high (6.4 cm.), mark: "WEDG-WOOD," c. 1780-1800. A "salver with jellies" illustrated in the 1802 shape book shows this waisted, footed cup in a set of seven jelly cups on a circular, footed salver. Such cups were meant to hold colorful gelatin desserts. Complete sets of salvers with "top glasses" were advertised in Boston in 1761, and the fashion continued for many years. A cookbook published in 1762 (and reissued in 1772) recommended making a pyramid-shaped centerpiece of footed salvers of decreasing sizes placed one on top of the other. A similar centerpiece is recorded by diarist James Woodforde, who describes an elegant dinner in 1774 as including "a Pyramid of Syllabubs and Jellies."

182. Basket, solid buff-colored Jasper with white bas-relief decoration, 4½″ long (11.4 cm.), 1⅜″ high (3.5 cm.), mark: "WEDGWOOD," c. 1780-1800. The basket was probably intended as a container for sweetmeats and other confections and was most likely part of a larger dessert service. Though the shape and general "wicker work" design of the basket were molded, each perforation was punched out by hand. This very delicate example of the potter's art, embellished with white Jasper ropes and acanthus leaves, weighs less than one ounce.

*y years, Wedgwood's scientific apparatus
. a neglected aspect of the company's pro-
Not until 1978, with the opening of a ma-
ibition of Wedgwood's scientific ware and
.d correspondence at the Science Museum,
.don, have Wedgwood's achievements in this
.a received the attention they deserve.*

*Carefully controlled experiments, which were
.corded in a secret code, were an important part
of the work conducted at Wedgwood's factory, and
the knowledge gained through such experimentation contributed to the high quality of Wedgwood
products. Wedgwood's interest in scientific meth-
odology brought him in contact with Joseph Priestley, Matthew Boulton, Erasmus Darwin and
other eminent scientists and inspired him to attempt making wares suitable to the laboratory.
Wedgwood's business eventually included an
extensive line of scientific apparatus including
retorts, distilling pots, evaporating pans, crucibles,
filters, syphons, mortars and pestles. Although certain items could be made in the Queen's Ware
body, other items—particularly mortars for grind-
ing various chemical mixtures—demanded a total-
ly new composition. After considerable experimentation, Wedgwood succeeded in making a hard
stoneware body, similar but not identical to
Jasper, which fulfilled his requirements. By the
early 19th century, Wedgwood mortars were so
popular that the company's name came to be used
as a generic term—one needed only to request "a
Wedgwood" to be provided with a mortar.*

*Wedgwood was recognized as a scientist by his
peers, who elected him to the Royal Society in
1783 for his work on the pyrometer, a device for
measuring extremely high temperatures. His paper
on the device was read before the Society at its
meeting of May 9, 1782. It was no mean attain-
ment for a man whose formal schooling had been
limited to a brief span from ages six to nine.*

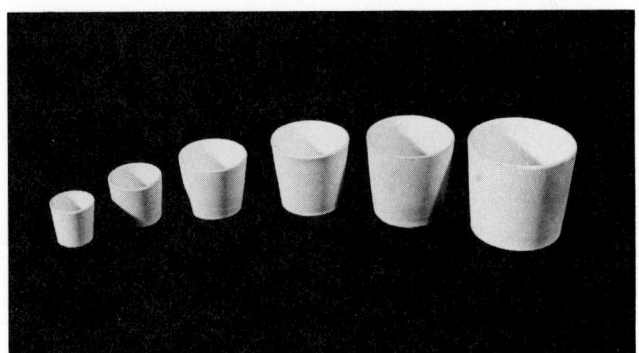

183, 184. Mortar and measuring cups, variations of the Jasper body.
Mortar—1″ high (2.5 cm.), 2$^{13}/_{16}$″ wide (7.1 cm.), mark: "Wedgwood
& Bentley," c. 1779-80; measuring cups—ranging from 2″ high (5.1
cm.) to ⅞″ high (2.2 cm.), mark: "WEDGWOOD," c. 1780-1800. In
order to be useful, mortars and similar vessels had to be made of a
material that would not flake, deteriorate, or absorb any chemicals
that would interfere with chemical reactions. Marble, which was
widely used, tended to absorb oils, while metal mortars often con-
taminated the substances that were ground in them. In 1779, after
many trials to determine the best composition and the best shape for
mortars, Wedgwood introduced his improved version at
Apothecaries' Hall and received the approval of chemists and other
scientists. Wedgwood listed mortars among the items for sale in his
1779 catalogue, saying: "The Mortars will be of great Use to *Chymists,
Experimental Philosophers* and *Apothecaries*, as well as for culinary Purposes; not being liable, like Metals or Marble, to be corroded by
Acids or any other chemical Menstruum."

Measuring cups were also part of the laboratory equipment that
Wedgwood produced. The six nesting measuring cups hold 7, 12, 22,
40, 62, and 100 milliliters respectively, or, in culinary terms, 1, 2¼, 5,
8, 12, and 20 teaspoons.

speckled appearance if examined with attention. ᴀᴇ ᴇᴇ
apt to stain, I have not yet been able to give it a porceᴇ
preserve its colour, but if I live I hope to compass it.

Josiah Wedgwood
July 28, 1779

Cane Ware, like Black Basalt and Rosso Antico, was one of the "dry body" wares made mostly from the clays of Staffordshire. It is buff to tan in color. The term "Bamboo Ware" is also used in reference to the body, an allusion not only to color but to a series of bamboo-inspired designs produced by Wedgwood. In fact, although "cane-coloured" was the factory term for the body, "bamboo" seems to have been the brand name (as Queen's Ware was the brand name for cream-colour), for the 1787 catalogue, in which Cane Ware was introduced, announces "BAMBOO, or cane-coloured *bisqué* [sic] porcelain. . . ." (The term "porcelain" was loosely interchanged with "stoneware" in the 18th century.) Wedgwood likened the Cane Ware body to the Black Basalt body except in color, and he contrasted it to the Jasper body in that the latter was "of exquisite beauty and delicacy" and capable of being evenly stained throughout its body. He contrasted it also to "A porcelain *bisqué* of extreme HARDNESS" which was acid resistant and was used for mortars and other scientific equipment.

As with Queen's Ware and Black Basalt, Wedgwood was not originating but refining a body, in this case, an ordinary iron-bearing buff body made of local clays. A letter from Josiah, Jr. (then 16 years old), written to his father from Etruria and dated March 13, 1783, gives insight into the ingredients, the experimental methods used, and the qualities sought for the body. Josiah, Jr., sent the "cane trials" to his father, and describes four recipes. The first consisted of "3 of 84 brown [a local clay], 2 of ball clay, 1 of ground flint." These evidently failed on two counts; 100 were bibulous and too "pale colored." The other three trials also had brown and ball clays, two with the addition of red clay and whiting, and one with whiting but without red clay. Unfortunately for us, Josiah, Jr., did not evaluate these combinations. Soon thereafter, in any event, Wedgwood did achieve success with the body, and by introducing it in attractive and inventive forms, he made the ware exceedingly popular. He, of course, was imitated by other Staffordshire potters.

One of the featured colors used in neoclassical interiors of the period was yellow in various shades, and the need to supply ware in these hues must have impelled Wedgwood and Bentley early in their partnership. As Wedgwood wrote to Bentley (September 9, 1771): "I am very happy to know the Fawn colour'd articles are agreeable to your wishes. I believe they will sell, for all who have seen them here have fall'n in love with them" (Farrer, II, 42).

It is not clear what these pieces were, but it is improbable that any of them still exist because, as Wedgwood explained, his early enthusiasm was prematurely expressed: "The Fawn colour body must be made upon another principle to [make] it stand for which purpose I am now making some tryals. The present has lead in its composition (though that must not be mentioned) I must

---

185. *Opposite page:* Jug, applied and molded relief with brown enamel crest, 6⅞" high (17.5 cm.), mark: "Wedgwood," c. 1783-1800.

make it without. Thickness or Thinness has nothing to do with its flying. I have tryed several pieces at home & they all fly so you had better sell no more of them" (Farrer, II, 49).

There are some pieces that still exist from the late 1770s when Wedgwood again attempted Cane-colored pieces. When Wedgwood wrote to Bentley in October of 1779, it was a statue of Voltaire (impressed "Wedgwood & Bentley" and now in the British Museum) that he used as an example of the problems he was facing with the body: "We send you two small statues of Voltaire and Rousseau made of cane-colour clay, but you will find them both so much discoloured in burning as to stand in need of a wash of paint. We covered them close in burning, knowing how apt this body is to turn brown, but in vain . . . I hope to overcome this evil, but it must be in a new body; the present is incorrigible" (Meteyard, *Handbook*, 216). Among other pieces from the period are bamboo-style square-shaped teapots in several sizes that are marked "Wedgwood & Bentley." As is true in the Black Basalt teapots of the same shape (*see* fig. 122), no matching pieces of tea equipage are known to have been made. Sharp detail, hand finishing, and a pale color characterize these teapots. The pale shade must have displeased Wedgwood as much as the firing difficulties he described above, to judge from Josiah, Jr.'s experimental analysis, but ultimately he produced a fine new body in richer hues that he called "new cane."

In addition to the desire to harmonize with the interiors of the period, Cane Ware was ideally suited to the interpretation of the bamboo motif—a new design introduced by Wedgwood to satisfy the continuing attraction of Westerners to Orientalia. Although not all Cane Ware useful wares were in the bamboo shape, the word "bamboo" was featured in the tea and coffee equipages section of the 1787 catalogue which stated that they "are made in the *bamboo* and *basaltes*, both plain, and enriched with Grecian and Etruscan ornaments." It is to be noted that "bamboo" (referring to color and/or shape) precedes "basaltes," which may indicate that the new fashion was edging out the earlier one. In addition to "useful" cane-colored wares, some purely ornamental wares were made as well.

By the mid-1780s the Jasper that Wedgwood had introduced eight or so years earlier was now so perfected that all types of pieces were capable of successful fabrication; everything from the smallest intaglio to large vases was produced. Why didn't Wedgwood give up the pursuit of the cane body made from local yellow clays in favor of the tinted Jasper such as seen in the "Apotheosis of Homer" plaque (fig. 188)? Of course using local clays was cheaper than importing the clays necessary to produce the more refined Jasper body, but evidently what Wedgwood wanted to do was to produce that color in a body that could be decorated with enamel colors such as the mat or "encaustic" colors used on Black Basalt. Although in 1775 Bentley had evidently informed Wedgwood that Jasper could be enameled: "I am glad to hear our Jasper bears enameling as I much fear'd it would not" (Farrer, II, 249), this report may have been as prematurely delivered as the earlier one concerning Cane Ware, for there is no further reference to enameled Jasper in the correspondence, nor are any pieces known to exist today. Enameled Cane Ware was made in great quantity during the 1783 to 1800 period. It is among the most valued and appreciated of the products of Josiah Wedgwood.

and included vibrant blues, yellows and greens, black, purple, and many others. Both mat, or "encaustic," and glossy enamels were employed. Both methods of bas-relief decoration—molded with the piece, or molded and applied separately—continued in use. Plate IV (p. 67), with its crisp details, appears to have been subject to extensive hand finishing after it came from the mold. The ground color appears to be slightly more buff than cane; the vivid enamel colors lend an air of elegance to the piece.

In an inventory listing made at the end of the 18th century, there are many entries under various headings of Cane Ware. The vast majority represents shapes available in other bodies as well. Under a large entry headed "fluted," however, there is an item entitled "cow handled cream bucket." The use of a recumbent cow as a cover finial is by no means uncommon for such a utilitarian piece, cow finial punch pots (for milk punch?) being listed as well. The "bucket" or "tureen" (plate XIX, p. 103), however, is not glazed in the interior, nor is there a notch to hold a spoon. This may have been an experimental form in Cane Ware only.

186. Plaque, "Apotheosis of Homer," applied relief decoration, 12" long (30.5 cm.), mark: "Wedgwood & Bentley," c. 1779-80. Although the plaque appears at first glance to be Cane Ware, it is probably an example of yellow-stained Jasper, and is included here to illustrate the contrast in crisp definition between Jasper and Cane relief decoration. It also underlines the speculation that Wedgwood produced Cane Ware partly because he found that he could not enamel Jasper Ware effectively. The Jasper body is denser in appearance and smoother to the touch than the Cane. Why more self-colored relief plaques in yellow Jasper were not produced during the 18th century is not known. Instead, the Cane body was used to produce yellow-colored items.

187. *Above (left)*: Flower holder, decorated in molded relief and enamel colors, 13¼"
high (34.9 cm.), mark: "WEDGWOOD," c. 1783-1800. Imitation of bamboo dates
from the Wedgwood & Bentley period, but this extremely large and impressive piece
is from the later period. The columns are painted in buff and green enamels to imitate bamboo leaves, and the base is many shades of brown and green. The interior
of the columns are covered with a clear glaze.

The same shape was also made in blue Jasper on which the decoration was done in
contrasting white relief rather than enamel colors. Since none of the Jasper pieces
were enameled, it would appear that the method of painting on the piece could not
be achieved in that body.

188. *Above (right)*: Bough pot, engine-turned and mat ("encaustic") enamel decoration, 8½" high (21.6 cm.), mark: "Wedgwood," c. 1783-1800. The body of this piece
was wheel thrown, and the foot and handles were added separately. The lid was
molded. The border, representing the convolvulus vine, is in colors of blue and
white over a blue background, and the rims are gilded.

189. *Left*: Tankard, molded and applied relief decoration, slip- and lead-glazed on
the rim and interior, painted with enamel, 5⅝" high (14.3 cm.), mark: "Wedgwood,"
c. 1783-1800. While the rims of Black Basalt tankards were sometimes protected
from wear with applied silver rims, a glaze was sometimes applied to the rims of Cane
Ware tankards to protect from stain as well as wear. The slip and glaze can be seen on
the concave top. From journals which discuss his methods, kept by the grandsons of
Wedgwood during the early 19th century, it is known that this white band was made
from a "Pearl Ware" slip applied to the green ware. After the initial firing, a clear
"Pearl Ware" glaze was applied. It was then fired and decorated. In this case the flow-
ing anthemion border is in a rich green. The relief decoration, "Bringing Home the
Game," was a popular subject for tankards and rum kettles (*see* figs. 107 and 110).

190. *Above:* Tea set; molded and applied relief decoration, slip- and lead-glazed on the rim of the sugar bowl and cream jug, glazed inside, painted enamel; teapot, cream jug, and sugar bowl each 5″ high (12.7 cm.); all marked "Wedgwood;" c. 1783-1800. The relief decoration on the three pieces represents the Bacchanalian children adapted from the "Feast of Bacchus," a set of six ivories that were sculpted by François Duquesnoy (1594-1646), known as Il Fiammingo (Chellis, "Sources," 131). The pieces are trimmed in blue, while the borders on the sugar and creamer have a band of white Pearl Ware slip with a rich blue anthemion design on it.

191. *Left:* Water ewer, molded and applied relief and painted enamel decoration, 10″ high (25.4 cm.), mark: "Wedgwood," c. 1783-1800. There are five separate scenes in relief around the middle of the piece. These are drawn from the same Duquesnoy ivory plaques used as a source for the tea set in the previous illustration. The groups were referred to in the catalogues as the "Fiammingo Boys." An anthemion border is painted in the rich red and black found also on Black Basalt and Queen's Ware "Greek painted" pieces.

Although ceramic conceits such as the sweetmeat dish illustrated in fig. 62 were standard in Wedgwood's production, such objects in unglazed Cane Ware that were quite capable of fooling the eye assumed a somewhat more somber purpose during the wheat famines that gripped England periodically in the late 18th and early 19th centuries. As William Jesse wrote in The Life of Brummel: "The scarcity [of 1802] was so great that the consumption of flour for pastry was prohibited in the royal household, rice being used instead . . . and Wedgewood [sic] made dishes to represent pie-crust." In a 1796 diary entry in which he described his dinner of the day, Parson Woodforde also alluded to the shortage, adding: "N.B. No kind of Pastrey, no Wheat Flour made use of and even the melted Butter thickened with Wheat-Meal . . ." (Beresford, IV, 273).

These historic references to the contrary, it is possible, however, that Wedgwood started to produce the Cane pastries still earlier, following a suggestion from Richard Lovell Edgeworth in 1786: "I think oval baking dishes from meat pies in the shape of raised paste pies . . . made of cane-coloured ware, not glazed, but nearly as possible the colour of baked paste, would be saleable articles. If any should be made, be so good as to send me half a dozen. They should have covers" (Meteyard, Handbook, 316). They do not appear in Wedgwood's invoices, however, until 1795.

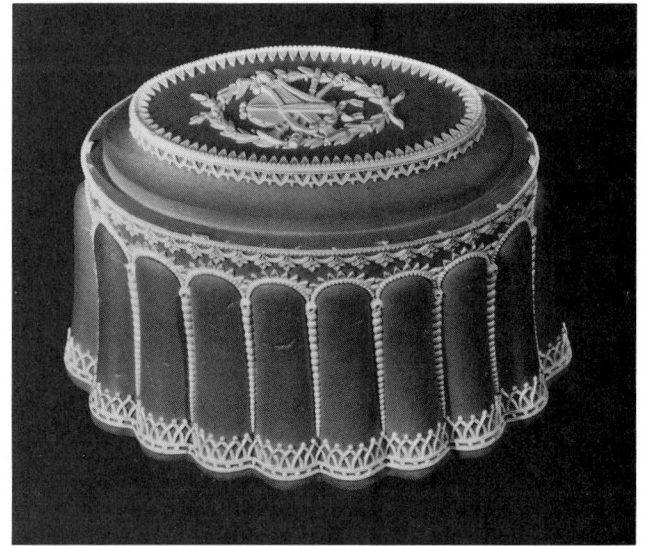

192. Cake form, molded and applied relief decoration, 5½" high (14 cm.), mark: "WEDGWOOD," c. 1795-1800. This piece was meant to give the illusion of a grand pastry dessert having been placed on the table. The sides represent lady fingers and the white decoration, which is meant to be icing, is laid on the Cane base as if it were squeezed through a pastry bag. Even drops of "icing" appear on the top. The clay body used for the decoration is probably the "WHITE PORCELAIN *bisqué*" described in the 1787 catalogue as having the same properties as the cane-colored body.

193. Pie form in three pieces, molded and applied relief decoration, glazed on the inside of the bottom piece, 13½" wide (34.3 cm.), c. 1795-1800. "No Pudding of Pye whatever . . . ," Parson Woodforde complained in his diary on June 2, 1796 (Beresford, IV, 283). To offset this sort of deprivation, pottery pie crusts filled with stewed fruit or the like were substituted for the real thing during times of wheat shortage. Most of the Wedgwood Cane Ware "pies" were made in two parts. This example, with bottom, separate "edge," and a top which fits into the edge, is an unusual form.

7. Rosso Antico

We shall never be able to make the Rosso Antico, otherwise than to put you in mind of a red Pot Teapot.

Josiah Wedgwood to Thomas Bentley
March 3, 1776

This conclusion was drawn by Wedgwood after months of experimentation undertaken to develop a stoneware body of a rich russet hue that would answer Bentley's repeated requests for a variation on the local red Staffordshire clay resembling the color of ancient gems then seen in England. As early as 1775 Bentley had suggested selling cameos and medallions in the popular red shade known as "Antico Rosso," but Wedgwood had responded negatively, saying: "My objection to it is the extreme vulgarity of red wares. If it had never been made in Tpots & the commonest wares, my objection w^d not have existed. But as it will be necessary they sh^d be sold cheap, and we sh^d give some obvious reasons for that cheapness, this alone may render it proper to make them of the red clay. I will send you a few to look at soon" (Meteyard, *Life*, II, 406).

The red wares that Wedgwood was now describing as vulgar and cheap had been one of his best-selling products when he first went into business for himself. Large orders, such as one dated October 9, 1764, from a dealer named Hardy for a "crate of your red wrought ware," attest to the popularity of the body at that time (MS 4924-6). Also, Wedgwood's own orders for redware from other potters—such as one to a local potter named Sarah Meir dated April, 1763, for "19½ dozen red china teapots"—indicate that he had more requests for redware than he could accommodate at his own factory (MS 4877-6). Bentley seems not to have shared Wedgwood's dislike of redware. Perhaps he remembered how important such ware had been to the firm only a few years earlier, when Wedgwood had set his workmen at Etruria to making redware at a time when orders for the more expensive Wedgwood & Bentley products had been slow in coming. On November 23, 1772, Wedgwood wrote to Bentley: "I do not know what we shall do with these People at the Ornamental works—we have been making a qu^{ty} of *common* red China Teapots to sell quite cheap & now we have begun upon 70 or 80 doz of the other sorts, after examining your stock acc^t to see what you had the fewest of. I have a mind to try at some plain Tiles, but our people cannot make them cheap enough to sell in any qu^{tys}" (Farrer, II, 114).

Redware had been raised from a very crude local ware in the Staffordshire area to a very impressive level of quality by two Dutch brothers, John Philip and David Elers, originally silversmiths, who made ceramic ware in England at the end of the 17th century. Wedgwood wrote to Bentley in appreciation of the work of John Philip, his brother David having served as the London representative of the firm: "The next improvement introduced by Mr. Elers was the refining of our common red clay, by sifting, and making it into Tea & Coffee Ware in imitation of the Chinese Red Porcelaine, by casting it in plaister moulds, & turning it on the outside upon Lathes, & ornamenting it with the Tea branch in relief, in imitation of the Chinese manner of ornamenting this ware."

Although the Elerses abandoned the trade by 1700, they had provided the new techniques

194. *Opposite page:* Teapot, redware with molded and applied relief, pseudo-Chinese mark, 9″ high (22.9 cm.), c. 1760-76.

necessary for potters to follow them in the production of good quality redware. Perhaps because the Elerses were bankrupt, as the *London Gazette* reported on December 12th, 1700, potters were slow to follow in the production of redware. By 1740 significant production was underway, reaching the height of popularity about the time Wedgwood went into business for himself. To meet the demand, Wedgwood was producing redware in the early 1760s, most likely using techniques that were known to him from his time as partner of Thomas Whieldon.

It is not clear from Wedgwood's correspondence what characteristics indicate a Wedgwood redware piece. The range of styles that he produced was probably wide, as suggested by an order placed with him by Robinson and Rhodes of Leeds on March 11, 1763, for "12 dry red teapotts some of them Crab tree sprouts" (Towner, *Cream-Coloured Earthenware*, 35). From this we can assume that Wedgwood was using both plain handles and spouts and those with "bumps" on them which were molded to look like limbs of a tree. It would seem that he was using molds that were common to many of the potteries.

In the *English Ceramic Circle Transactions* (1959) Robin Price presents another interesting speculation on how to identify some of Wedgwood's redware pieces. He centers his attention on the pseudo-Chinese impressed mark on redware pieces. In an attempt to suggest that their pieces were or resembled red stoneware of Yi-hsing in China, potters in England, beginning with the Elers brothers, devised a mark that was generally square and divided into small squares that enclosed Chinese characters. In addition to the Chinese characters, some of these marks have included in them the letter "W." Price suggests that the "W" is so obvious that it must have been intended. Experts at the Victoria and Albert Museum have compared a redware cup and saucer marked in this fashion with a shard found at the site of Wedgwood's early factory of Brick House in Burslem and have found a similarity suggesting that the "W" marked piece was produced at the Brick House by Josiah Wedgwood.

Although Wedgwood produced redware, or Rosso Antico as it became known, in fits and starts through the rest of his life, he saw that the potential was not good as early as February, 1765, when he wrote to his brother John: "Till I hear from Tom [Wedgwood] about the red china I am quite at a loss how to act or what to write to my chaps about these *falling stars* . . . I am determined if necessary to drop them to 12s. rather than lose my business . . ." (Price, 6).

So few examples exist today of Rosso Antico pieces made by Wedgwood during his lifetime that it would appear that he was never able to lose his prejudice against producing the ware. His philosophy regarding redware is best summed up in a letter to Bentley written on July 5, 1776: "I am afraid of the Antico Rossica made up into the subjects you mention. Everybody can make that color, & composition, but nobody, besides W. & B., can make *Jasper*. The boast of my Neighbour, that he had found it out, is idle—I would as soon believe he had discovered the Philosophers Stone.—Besides—If I was to give him the rec^t, it would half ruin him, & quite tire him out before he could make anything of it—but the R—Ant^o is made at the first essay. You will know my fears by what I have said, & I do not care to say any more than is necessary on this subject" (Farrer, 295).

Slip-decorated Rosso Antico pieces were both molded and thrown on the wheel. Wedgwood devised a method of decorating the objects that was a significant departure at the time. He coated the pieces with black slip, and this was scraped away in various areas to reveal the rich-red body that was characteristic of his redware. Wedgwood was taking advantage of the iron oxide that was present in both red and black bodies, making his Basalt and Rosso Antico bodies compatible and enabling him to fire the two together. As G. W. Elliott points out, the Wedgwood-Whieldon partnership, as well as other Staffordshire potters, was producing black pieces with a major ingredient of local red Bradwell clay mixed with ochre. When Wedgwood perfected his black body, he dropped the use of the red clay in favor of a mixture of black iron oxide, manganese oxide, and Purbeck clay. Deleting the local red clay enabled him to produce a darker and richer black than those potters who used the local red Bradwell clay. Wedgwood more than likely achieved the rich color of his Rosso Antico body by adding the red clay to his perfected Basalt body.

The red teapot pictured in plate XX (p. 104) is typical of such pieces, although it is surprisingly light for a stoneware object of such size. The uneven scraping away of the black slip is unfortunately typical. This is somewhat less obvious on the bulb pot illustrated in the same plate. The interior of this piece is covered with a clear lead glaze while the exterior is unglazed and has a very mat appearance. Regarding the glazing of teapots, Wedgwood wrote: "Any kind of Teapots with the inside Glazed, & the outside unglazed will, I fear, be apt to fly [shatter] now & then with hot water. The common red China ones do the same. We can send you some unglazed ones & your customers may then have their choice" (Farrer, II, 68).

195. Bulb pot, Rosso Antico with black slip decoration, 5" wide (12.7 cm.), mark: "WEDGWOOD," c. 1780-1800. There is no known classical model for this bulb pot. Wedgwood does not appear to have produced it in other bodies as he did with most other Rosso Antico forms. A single container, it makes handsome use of a simple and appropriate floral design. Not elegant, perhaps, in the way Wedgwood would have preferred it, it is nonetheless a charming piece.

196. Bulb pot, molded Rosso Antico body with applied relief, 9¼" wide (23.5 cm.),
mark: "Wedgwood & Bentley," c. 1769-80. The combination of an engaging cupid
relief design and a very pleasing shape make this a very popular Wedgwood piece.
The Rosso Antico color is as dark a red as Wedgwood ever produced. Copies also exist in a brown-black color, an unusual Wedgwood shade. Putti, or cupids carrying
garlands, were a classical Roman motif that was revived during the Renaissance and
can be seen, for example, on the tomb of Ilaria del Carretto by the early 15th-
century Siennese sculptor Jacabo della Quercia. Wedgwood used the motif on both
ornamental and useful wares.

Wedgwood frequently reproduced his best-selling Black Basalt in other bodies, including Rosso Antico, not only to produce the forms in a wider variety of colors, but also to refresh the appearance of his showrooms by changing the displays without the additional expense of an entirely new design. Wedgwood expressed his awareness of the necessity of employing this sales technique in a 1767 letter to Bentley in which he said: "We must have an Elegant, extensive & Conven[ien]t shewroom . . . I need not tell you the many good effects this must produce, when business, & amusement can be made to go hand in hand. Every new show, Exhibition or rarity soon grows stale in London, & is no longer regarded, after the first sight, unless utility, or some such variety . . . continues to recommend it . . ." (McKendrick, "Wedgwood: Salesman," 173).

197. *Top:* Figure, molded Rosso Antico, 4⅝" long (11.7 cm.), mark: "WEDGWOOD," c. 1780-1800. The sleeping boy, Somnus, was an extremely popular design, both in this version and in four others usually produced in Black Basalt. The figure appears to be an exact duplicate of an ivory by Arnoldus Quellien the Elder, a master of the baroque school of Antwerp. The original, dated 1641, is now in the collection of Walters Art Gallery, Baltimore. An earlier ceramic copy, inscribed "1746" and produced by the Chelsea factory in London, is now in the British Museum. In the 18th century, Sévres also produced the figure in porcelain.

198. *Above:* Bust of John Locke, 8½" high (21.6 cm.), marked "WEDGWOOD" on socle, "LOCKE" on back, c. 1780-1800. The bust of John Locke was most often molded in Black Basalt and first appeared in the Wedgwood & Bentley catalogue of 1779 in three sizes. The mold was purchased from Hoskins & Grant. The original source is a bronze that was sculpted early in the 18th century by Michael Rijsbrack (Rysbrack), who settled in London in 1720 and soon became the most popular sculptor in England except for Roubiliac. Because of Locke's fame as a champion of liberty, the bust was exceptionally popular in the newly independent American colonies. Large numbers of these busts were sent to America and may have served as models for woodcarvers; several carved replicas are extant in the United States today.

Bibliography

Citations in the text coded MS followed by a number (e.g., MS 9873-11) refer to unpublished Wedgwood correspondence and factory records housed at the University of Keele, Staffordshire.

The Queen's Ware catalogue of 1774 is reprinted in Gorely, no. 9 (1942). The Queen's Ware catalogue of 1790-95 is reprinted in Mankowitz, but is incorrectly identified as the 1774 catalogue.

The 1802 shape book is a Wedgwood factory record book of shapes and shape numbers. The water mark on the paper used for the index is datable to 1802; it is presumed, therefore, that the book illustrates forms in use up to that time. It includes pieces that were also illustrated in the earlier Queen's Ware catalogues. The book is housed at Josiah Wedgwood & Sons, Barlaston.

Barnard, Harry. *Chats on Wedgwood Ware*. New York: Frederick P. Stokes Co., 1924.

Bennion, Elizabeth. *Antique Medical Instruments*. Berkeley: University of California Press, 1979.

Bentley, Thomas and Wedgwood, Josiah. *Catalogue of Ornamental Ware*. Etruria, 1773, 1775.

_____. *Catalogue of Ornamental Ware*. 1779. Reprint. New York: The Wedgwood Society of New York, 1965.

Bindman, David, ed. *John Flaxman, R.A.* London: Royal Academy of Arts, 1979.

Birmingham Museum of Art. *The Dwight and Lucille Beeson Collection of Wedgwood*. Birmingham, Alabama: Birmingham Museum of Art, 1978.

Born, Byron A. "The Wexford Volunteers." *The Ninth Wedgwood International Seminar*. New York: The Metropolitan Museum of Art, 1964.

Boyd, Julian P., ed. *The Papers of Thomas Jefferson*. Vol. 18. November 1790-March 1791. Princeton: Princeton University Press, 1971.

Burton, Anthony. *Josiah Wedgwood*. London: André Deutsch, 1976.

Burton, William. *Josiah Wedgwood and His Pottery*. London: Cassell and Co., 1922.

Buten, Harry M. *Wedgwood and Artists*. Merion, Pennsylvania: Buten Museum of Wedgwood, 1960.

Chellis, Elizabeth. "Wedgwood Cameos and Buttons." *Antiques Journal*, October 1951, pp. 15-17; November 1951, pp. 19-21; December 1951, pp. 22-23; January 1952, p. 24.

_____. "Sources of Wedgwood's Child Motifs." *The Magazine Antiques* 46 (September, 1944): 128-31.

Clifford, Timothy. "Some English Ceramic Vases and Their Sources." *Transactions of the English Ceramic Circle*, vol. 10, part 3. Chatham: W. & J. Mackay, 1978.

Crellin, J. K. "Medical Ceramics: Their Scope and Significance." *Transactions of the English Ceramic Circle*, vol. 7, part 3. Chatham: W. & J. Mackay, 1970.

Delhom, M. Mellanay. *Documentary Ceramics and Related Materials*. Charlotte: The Mint Museum of Art, 1968.

_____. "Two Trial Plates for the Catherine Service." *The Ninth Wedgwood International Seminar*. New York: The Metropolitan Museum of Art, 1964.

des Fontaines, Una. "The Darwin Service and the First Printed Floral Patterns at Etruria." *Proceedings of the Wedgwood Society*, no. 6. London: B. T. Batsford, 1968.

_____. "The Wedgwood Collection of Sir Dalton Hooker, M.D., F.R.S. (1817-1911)." *Proceedings of the Wedgwood Society*, no. 7. London: The Wedgwood Society, 1968.

Dripps, Diana R. "Chinese Ceramics, Part 2, 'Yuan, Ming and Ch'ing." Paper read at Guide Education Workshop, April 4, 1973, at the Philadelphia Museum of Art. Mimeographed.

Duff-Dunbar, G. "Wedgwood Jelly Moulds." *Proceedings of the Wedgwood Society*, no. 1. London: B. T. Batsford, 1956.

Falkner, Frank. *The Wood Family of Burslem*. London: Chapman & Hall Ltd., 1912.

Farrer, Katherine Eufemia, ed. *Correspondence of Josiah Wedgwood, 1762-1795*. 3 vols., 1903-1906. Reprint. Didsbury, Manchester: E. J. Morten, 1973.

Finer, Ann, and Savage, George, eds. *The Selected Letters of Josiah Wedgwood*. New York: The Born & Hawes Publishing Co., 1965.

France, Peter, ed. *Thomas Bentley: Journal of a Visit to Paris 1776*. Falmer, Brighton: University of Sussex Library, 1977.

Godden, Geoffrey A. *Encyclopedia of British Pottery and Porcelain*. New York: Crown Publishers, 1966.

Gorely, Jean, ed. *Old Wedgwood*. Nos. 1-14. Wellesley: The Boston Wedgwood Society, 1934-47.

Grant, Captain M.H. *The Makers of Black Basaltes*. Edinburgh: William Blackwood and Sons, 1910.

Greenwald, Stanley H. "The Serendipity of Collecting." *The American Wedgwoodian* 1 (February, 1964): 41.

Grey, John M. *James and William Tassie*. Edinburgh, 1894.

Hall, John. *Staffordshire Portrait Figures*. New York: The World Publishing Co., 1972.

Hawes, Lloyd E. "Herculaneum Wall Paintings." *The American Wedgwoodian* 2 (December, 1965): 17-27.

Honey, W. B. *English Pottery and Porcelain*. London: Adam & Charles Black, 1962.

_____. *Wedgwood Ware*. London: Faber and Faber, 1948.

Jewitt, Llewellyn. *The Ceramic Art of Great Britain from Pre-Historic Times down to the Present Day*. 2 vols. London, 1878.

_____. *The Wedgwoods: Being a Life of Josiah Wedgwood. . . .* London, 1865.

Kelly, Alison. *Decorative Wedgwood in Architecture and Furniture*. New York: Born-Hawes Publishing Limited, 1965.

_____. "Josiah Wedgwood's London Banking Account." *Proceedings of The Wedgwood Society*, no. 9. London: The Wedgwood Society, 1975.

_____. *The Story of Wedgwood*. London: Faber & Faber, 1975.

Liverpool Art Club. *Catalogue of a Loan Collection of the Works of Josiah Wedgwood*. Compiled by Charles T. Gatty. Liverpool, 1879.

Macht, Carol. *Classical Wedgwood Designs*. New York: M. Barrows and Co., 1957.

Mallet, J. V. G. "Hogarth's Pug in Porcelain." Reprinted from the *Victoria and Albert Museum Bulletin*, vol. 3, no. 2, April 1967, pp. 45-54, with revisions and the addition of fig. 6a.

_____. "John Baddeley of Shelton, and Early Staffordshire Maker of Pottery and Porcelain." *Transactions of the English Ceramic Circle*, vol. 6, part 3. Chatham: W. & J. Mackay, 1967.

_____. "Wedgwood and the Rococo." *Proceedings of the Wedgwood Society*, no. 9. London: The Wedgwood Society, 1975.

Mankowitz, Wolf. *Wedgwood*. New York: E. P. Dutton and Co., 1953.

McCauley, Robert H. "Wedgwood Creamware with American Historical Designs." *The Magazine Antiques* 45 (January, 1944): 33-34.

McKendrick, Neil. "Josiah Wedgwood and Factory Discipline." *The Historical Journal* 4 (1961): 30-55.

_____. "Josiah Wedgwood: An Eighteenth-Century Entrepreneur in Salesmanship and Marketing Techniques." *The Economic History Review* 12 (April, 1960): 408-33.

McNab, Jessie. "Essentials of British Heraldry." *The Ninth Wedgwood International Seminar*. New York: The Metropolitan Museum of Art, 1964.

Meteyard, Eliza. *The Life of Josiah Wedgwood*. 2 vols. London, 1865-66.

_____. *The Wedgwood Handbook*. London, 1875. Reprint. Peekskill, New York: Timothy Trace, 1963.

_____. *Wedgwood Trio by Meteyard*. Reprint of *Wedgwood and His Works* (1873), *Memorials of Wedgwood* (1874), and *Choice Examples of Wedgwood's Art* (1879). Edited by Harry M. Buten. Merion, Pennsylvania: Buten Museum of Wedgwood, 1967.

Morris, Joan. "Molds and Their History." *The Ninth Wedgwood International Seminar*. New York: The Metropolitan Museum of Art, 1964.

Mountford, Arnold R. *Staffordshire Salt-glazed Stoneware*. New York: Praeger Publishers, 1971.

National Portrait Gallery. *Wedgwood Portraits and the American Revolution*. Washington: The Smithsonian Institution, 1976.

Noel Hume, Ivor. "Creamware to Pearlware: A Williamsburg Perspective." In Ian Quimby, ed. *Ceramics in America*. Charlottesville: The University Press of Virginia, 1972.

_____. "Mugs, Jugs, and Chamber Pots." *The Magazine Antiques* 90 (October, 1966): 520-22.

_____. "Pearlware: Forgotten Milestone of English Ceramic History." *The Magazine Antiques* 95 (March, 1969): 390-97.

_____. "The What, Who, and When of English Creamware Plate Design." *The Magazine Antiques* 101 (February, 1972): 350-55.

Pelehach, Patricia. "Wedgwood Dairy Ware." *The B[uten] M[useum] of W[edgwood] Bulletin* 3 (January, 1979): 2-4.

Price, E. Stanley. *John Sadler: A Liverpool Pottery Printer*. West Kirby, Cheshire: Price, 1948.

Pucci, Lawrence. "Anthony and Cleopatra." *The American Wedgwoodian* 1 (May, 1965): 88-89.

Raspe, R.E., ed. *A Descriptive Catalogue of a General Collection of Ancient and Modern Engraved Gems, Cameos, as Well as Intaglios*. London, 1791.

Rathbone, Frederick. *Old Wedgwood*. 1898. Reprint. Merion, Pennsylvania: Buten Museum of Wedgwood, 1968.

Reilly, Robin and George Savage. *Wedgwood: The Portrait Medallions*. London: Barrie and Jenkins Ltd., 1973.

Sayer, Robert. *The Ladies Amusement: Or Whole Art of Japanning Made Easy*. 1760. Facsimile ed. Newport, Monmouthshire: The Ceramic Book Company, 1966.

Science Museum. *Josiah Wedgwood: "The Arts and Sciences United."* London: Josiah Wedgwood & Sons, Ltd., 1978.

Shaw, Simeon. *History of the Staffordshire Potteries*. 1829. Reprint. New York: Praeger Publishers, 1970.

Smiles, Samuel. *Josiah Wedgwood F.R.S.: His Personal History*. London, 1897.

Smith, Alan. "John Wyke of Liverpool, and the Staffordshire Pottery Export Trade." *Northern Ceramic Society Journal* 3 (1979): 79-88.

Tait, Hugh. "The Wedgwood Collection in the British Museum, Part 1: Creamware and Redware." *Proceedings of the Wedgwood Society*, no. 4. London: B. T. Batsford, 1961.

_____. "The Wedgwood Collection in the British Museum, Part 2: Basalt and Jasper-wares." *Proceedings of the Wedgwood Society*, no. 5. London: The Wedgwood Society, 1963.

Tattersall, Bruce. *Stubbs & Wedgwood*. London: The Tate Gallery, 1974.

Thirion, H. *Les Adam et Clodion*. Paris, 1885.

Towner, Donald. *Creamware*. London: Faber and Faber, 1978.

_____. "David Rhodes – Enameller." *Transactions of the English Ceramics Circle*, vol. 4, part 4. London: Harrison and Sons, 1959.

_____. "William Greatbatch and the Early Wares." *Transactions of the English Ceramics Circle*, vol. 5. Chatham: Cory, Adams & Mackay, 1963.

Turberville, A. S., ed. *Johnson's England: An Account of the Life & Manners of His Age*. 2 vols. Oxford: The Clarendon Press, 1933.

Wedgwood, Josiah. *Catalogue of Ornamental Ware*. 1787. Reprint. Edited by Eliza Meteyard. London, 1873.

Wedgwood, Josiah, and Ormsbee, Thomas H. *Staffordshire Pottery*. New York: Robert M. McBride, 1947.

Wheildon, Colin. "Who on Earth is Salomon Gessner?" *Wedgwood News* [The Wedgwood Society of Australia] 7 (June, 1979): 6-7.

Williamson, George C. *The Imperial Russian Dinner Service*. London: George Bell and Sons, 1909.

Wills, Geoffrey. "Sir William Hamilton and the Portland Vase." *Apollo* (September, 1979): 195-201.

Windle, Mrs. John T. "Creamware Epergnes." *The Ninth Wedgwood International Seminar*. New York: The Metropolitan Museum of Art, 1964.

Woodforde, James. *The Diary of a Country Parson*. Edited by John Beresford. 5 vols. London: The Oxford University Press, 1924-31.

Credits

1. Wedgwood Museum, Barlaston. 2. Mr. and Mrs. David E. Zeitlin. 3. Mrs. Robert D. Chellis. 4. Ibid. 5. Dr. and Mrs. Alvin M. Kanter. 6. Mr. and Mrs. Samuel Laver. 7. Buten Museum of Wedgwood. 8. Bernard and Lydia Starr. 9. Theodore Lunn Miller. 10. Dr. and Mrs. Alvin M. Kanter. 11. Mr. and Mrs. Samuel Laver. 12. Dr. and Mrs. Alvin M. Kanter. 13. Smithsonian Institution, Robert H. McCauley Collection. 14. Mrs. Arthur Goldsmith. 15. Mr. and Mrs. Byron A. Born. 16. Buten Museum of Wedgwood. 17. Ibid. 18. Dr. and Mrs. Alvin M. Kanter. 19. Mr. and Mrs. Samuel Laver. 20. Buten Museum of Wedgwood. 21. Mr. and Mrs. David E. Zeitlin. 22. Ibid. 23. Dean and Mary Rockwell. 24. Mr. and Mrs. Henry P. Bridges, Jr. 25. Mr. and Mrs. Byron A. Born. 26. Mr. and Mrs. Samuel Laver. 27. *Left:* Mr. and Mrs. Byron A. Born; *center:* Dr. and Mrs. Victor H. Polikoff; *right:* Mr. and Mrs. Samuel Laver. 28. Mr. and Mrs. Byron A. Born. 29. Delhom Gallery, Mint Museum. 30. Buten Museum of Wedgwood. 31. Mr. and Mrs. Byron A. Born. 32. Dr. and Mrs. Alvin M. Kanter. 33. Mr. and Mrs. Samuel Laver. 34. Buten Museum of Wedgwood. 35. Private collection. 36. Dr. and Mrs. Alvin M. Kanter. 37. Smithsonian Institution, gift of Mr. and Mrs. Jack Leon. 38. Art Institute of Chicago. 39. Mr. and Mrs. Byron A. Born. 40. Private collection. 41. Mrs. Charles Reisse. 42. Buten Museum of Wedgwood. 43. Mr. and Mrs. Byron A. Born. 44. Buten Museum of Wedgwood. 45. Mr. and Mrs. Byron A. Born. 46. Private collection. 47. Smithsonian Institution, gift of Dr. Lloyd E. Hawes.

48. Private collection. 49. Mrs. Louis Henkels. 50. Ibid. 51. Mr. and Mrs. David E. Zeitlin. 52. Miles Collection, Brooklyn Museum. 53. Private collection.

54. Mr. and Mrs. Byron A. Born. 55. Mrs. Robert D. Chellis. 56. Buten Museum of Wedgwood. 57. Mr. and Mrs. Byron A. Born. 58. Buten Museum of Wedgwood. 59. Mr. and Mrs. Byron A. Born. 60. Private collection. 61. Dr. and Mrs. Alvin M. Kanter. 62. Mr. and Mrs. William C. Whitlow. 63. Dr. and Mrs. Alvin M. Kanter. 64. Ibid. 65. Mrs. Louis Henkels. 66. Buten Museum of Wedgwood. 67. Mr. and Mrs. Samuel Laver. 68. Mr. and Mrs. David E. Zeitlin. 69. Mr. and Mrs. Byron A. Born.

70. Bernard and Lydia Starr. 71. Wedgwood Museum, Barlaston. 72. Private collection. 73. Lawrence Marshall Pucci. 74. Delhom Gallery, Mint Museum. 75. Mr. and Mrs. Byron A. Born. 76. Private collection. 77. Ibid. 78. Dr. and Mrs. Stanley H. Greenwald. 79. Mrs. Stewart W. McClelland. 80. Mr. and Mrs. John K. Olsen. 81. Stanley Nager. 82. Buten Museum of Wedgwood. 83. Private collection. 84. Lawrence Marshall Pucci. 85. Mrs. Louis Henkels. 86. Ibid. 87. Dr. and Mrs. Victor H. Polikoff. 88. Dr. and Mrs. Alvin M. Kanter. 89. Ibid. 90. Mr. and Mrs. Stuart Caine. 91. Mr. and Mrs. Samuel Laver. 92. Smithsonian Institution, gift of Eugene D. Buchanan. 93. Dr. and Mrs. Alvin M. Kanter. 94. Private collection. 95. Mr. and Mrs. Arnold Barsky. 96. Mr. and Mrs. Samuel Laver. 97. Buten Museum of Wedgwood. 98. Salmagundi Club. 99. Mr. and Mrs. David E. Zeitlin. 100. Ibid. 101. Private collection. 102. Metropolitan Museum of Art. 103. Mr. and Mrs. Roy Adams. 104. Mrs. Louis Henkels. 105. Art Institute of Chicago. 106. Ibid. 107. Dr. and Mrs. Alvin M. Kanter. 108. Mr. and Mrs. Samuel Laver. 109. Cooper-Hewitt Museum, the Smithsonian Institution's National Museum of Design. 110. Mr. and Mrs. Stuart Caine. 111. Dr. and Mrs. E. Heisel. 112. Metropolitan Museum of Art. 113. Ibid. 114. Mr. and Mrs. Samuel Laver. 115. Mr. and Mrs. David E. Zeitlin. 116. Mr. and Mrs. William M. Schaefer. 117. Private collection. 118. Bernard and Lydia Starr. 119. Mr. and Mrs. Byron A. Born. 120. William Rockhill Nelson Gallery. 121. Miles Collection, Brooklyn Museum. 122. Mr. and Mrs. Stuart Caine. 123. Dr. and Mrs. Alvin M. Kanter. 124. Mr. and Mrs. Byron A. Born. 125. Mr. and Mrs. R. H. Worstall. 126. Buten Museum of Wedgwood. 127. Museum of Fine Arts, Boston. 128. Buten Museum of Wedgwood.

129. Bernard and Lydia Starr. 130. Buten Museum of Wedgwood. 131. Smithsonian Institution, gift of Eugene D. Buchanan. 132. Dr. and Mrs. Alvin M. Kanter. 133. Mr. and Mrs. Francis Slivinski. 134. Dr. and Mrs. Alvin M. Kanter. 135. *Left:* Mrs. Louis Henkels; *right* and *center:* Buten Museum of Wedgwood. 136. John and Catherine Holdstock Collins. 137. Mr. and Mrs. David E. Zeitlin. 138. Miles Collection, Brooklyn Museum. 139. Arthur R. Luedders. 140. Art Institute of Chicago. 141. Mr. and Mrs. Byron A. Born. 142. Mrs. Louis Henkels. 143. Art Institute of Chicago. 144. Mrs. Arthur Goldsmith. 145. Dr. and Mrs. Alvin M. Kanter. 146.

Ibid. 147. Ibid. 148. Philadelphia Museum of Art. 149. Mr. and Mrs. Byron A. Born. 150. Mr. and Mrs. Melvin J. Schwartz. 151. *Above:* Dr. and Mrs. Paul Collins; *below:* Rosenbach Museum and Library. 152. Willis B. Snell. 153. Ibid. 154. Mr. and Mrs. Howard M. Lewis. 155. Buten Museum of Wedgwood. 156. Museum of Fine Arts, Boston. 157. Private collection. 158. Art Institute of Chicago. 159. Mr. and Mrs. Byron A. Born. 160. Stanley Nager. 161. Dr. and Mrs. Jerome Mones. 162. Miles Collection, Brooklyn Museum. 163. Wedgwood Museum, Barlaston. 164. Art Institute of Chicago. 165. Bernard and Lydia Starr. 166. Metropolitan Museum of Art. 167. Victoria and Albert Museum. 168. Ruth and Stanley Wax. 169. Dr. and Mrs. Leonard Rakow. 170. Private collection. 171. Mr. and Mrs. David E. Zeitlin. 172. Art Institute of Chicago. 173. Buten Museum of Wedgwood. 174. Private collection. 175. Nottingham Castle Museum. 176. Mr. and Mrs. David E. Zeitlin. 177. Metropolitan Museum of Art. 178. Private collection. 179. Philadelphia Museum of Art. 180. Mr. K. M. Deutscher. 181. Mr. and Mrs. Byron A. Born. 182. Mr. and Mrs. Stuart Caine. 183. Buten Museum of Wedgwood. 184. Ibid.

185. Private collection. 186. Ibid. 187. Mr. and Mrs. Byron A. Born. 188. Mr. and Mrs. Samuel Laver. 189. Buten Museum of Wedgwood. 190. Dr. and Mrs. Victor H. Polikoff. 191. Dr. and Mrs. Leonard Rakow. 192. Buten Museum of Wedgwood. 193. Dr. and Mrs. Alvin M. Kanter.

194. Private collection. 195. Mrs. Louis Henkels. 196. Miles Collection, Brooklyn Museum. 197. Jacobs Collection. 198. Ibid.

I. John and Catherine Holdstock Collins. II. *Bottom row, left to right:* Mr. and Mrs. David E. Zeitlin, Private collection, John and Catherine Holdstock Collins; *top row:* Mr. and Mrs. David E. Zeitlin. III. Bernard and Lydia Starr. IV. Mr. and Mrs. Byron A. Born. V. Buten Museum of Wedgwood. VI. Private collection. VII. Ibid. VIII. Buten Museum of Wedgwood. IX. Mr. and Mrs. Samuel Laver. X. Mr. and Mrs. Arnold Barsky. XI. John and Catherine Holdstock Collins. XII. Private collection. XIII. Ibid. XIV. Ibid. XV. Buten Museum of Wedgwood. XVI. Private collection. XVII. Bernard and Lydia Starr. XVIII. *Clockwise from top:* Mr. Willis B. Snell, Mr. and Mrs. Byron A. Born, Private collection, Ibid. XIX. Buten Museum of Wedgwood. XX. Ibid.

Index